FILM REVIEW 1971-72

FILM REVIEW
1971-72

edited by F. Maurice Speed

W. H. Allen
London
1971

Printed in Great Britain by
Fletcher & Son Ltd, Norwich
for the publishers
W. H. Allen & Co. Ltd.,
Essex Street, London WC2.
Bound by
Webb, Son & Co. Ltd.,
London.
ISBN 0 491 00258 0

Book design by Ken Reilly and Associates Ltd.

CONTENTS

Introduction   *page* 7

In Memoriam   13

Where are they Now?   21

Waiting in the Wings   28

Posters and Credits   30

Dutch Cinema   35

The Day of the Cassette is Nigh   39

Shakespeare on the Screen   41

Movies and Music   51

Openings and Closings   54

Film Magazines   59

The Neglected Ones   63

The Making of an Epic   68

World Round-Up   73

Releases of the Year in Pictures   83

The Continental Film   160

Awards and Festivals   192

The In-betweens   196

Film Future   201

Releases of the Year in Detail   215

Index   241

INTRODUCTION

The big topic of discussion in the cinema this year, as last, has been the erosion of pornography not only films designed deliberately as such, but also as an ingredient of major features of serious intent. And the reason for this has been that in a period when the cinema generally is going through a time of crisis – at least in America and this country – there has been a desperate effort to please the box-office. In this connection it is salutory I think to remember sometimes that in the cinema, as in the theatre and all other forms of entertainment, you in the long run get what you want. I don't mean you, Sir, or you, Madam, or anyone else in particular, but you, the public generally. It is the patrons which dictate what kind of film – or play, or whatever – will be seen in the future. For though on occasions even the wisest supplier of public entertainment can be, and often is, wildly wrong, the great majority who live by entertaining the public strive, naturally, to please that public, to make the kind of film they think you want. They have to. One or two major errors in judgement that bring disaster at the box-office and they're out of business. On the other hand, the right, lucky assessment of climate, mood and taste, and the Rolls and the country mansion will be permanently theirs.

This means, then, that the recent flood of pornographic and near-pornographic movies that has been occupying too much for too long of our cinema screens is a straightforward reflection of public taste? To an extent yes, this is indeed so. What has happened in fact is that perhaps envious of the small and grimy smut purveyors flourishing in the new, relaxed moral climate, acutely aware of the possibilities of

the situation left by a retreating if not actually dissembled censorship, the bigger boys have in many cases decided that they didn't see why they should be left behind in the permissive race and have accordingly edged in part if not in whole towards, if not actual pornography then certainly something very akin to it.

But, as always in the cinema (fortunately in this case!) the whole thing has been overdone. As each producer has attempted to leap-frog his fellow and offer something more sexily sensational, more daring, blacker and bluer and sicker, the inevitable reaction has set in, first from the critics and other writers on cinema and then from the public. The turn-about, the swing back prophesied by many writers (including, I may add with all due modesty, this one) has become discernible. The crudity, the coarseness, the leering, the lip-smacking titillation reached a point where it became just too much for even a permissive period audience to take. And in any case once the novelty impact had worn off the boredom began to set in. Nothing is more boring than crude pornography. I know we are in for a lot more cinematic mud yet, but I like to think that with the profits on this kind of film tailing off and the box-office chinking more merrily for less sensational films even the fast-buck moviemakers will be forced to look in other directions for material.

An important piece of evidence in support of this contention is *Love Story*, an inexpensive, openly sentimental story of young love which had tremendous impact in America (to everyone's surprise, I am told) and then won the distinction of being selected as Britain's Royal Performance Film for 1971 and is going on to make a British "bomb"

in terms of cash return.

Knowing the almost complete lack of balance which has always afflicted the film industry one wonders, with certain misgivings, what this success will do. Will corn follow porn? Shall we within a year or so be facing a succession of drippingly pathetic movies as we are rushed back to the worst kind of romantic rubbish? As it is usual for producers to dash for the gravy train, and as such cycles produce films of a pattern which get increasingly shoddy and awful, one can only fear the worst while hoping for the best – that the new wave will stem the old and produce some sort of sane and happy compromise.

    *   *   *

From trends to facts and figures. Less films being made, less people going to the cinemas. That's the story, unfortunately by now the old story. I haven't seen production figures for other countries but 1970 saw the curve certainly sweeping down in this one. Whereas in 1968 we made 93 films, and turned out 76 in 1969, the total was only 67 for the whole of 1970. There was certainly a reverse trend discernible during the earlier parts of 1971 but whether this improvement will be sustained is at this point anyone's guess.

Certainly the American dollars which financed a great part of British production in the sixties are no longer available. Now the British producers must get their backing in this country and this has never been exactly easy. New set-ups for sharing of risks, and profits, appear inevitable and schemes are now being worked out to achieve this. But whatever happens the next few years are going to be difficult for the British moviemakers. One hopes they will learn from

8 the dangers, profit from the crisis and emerge finally stronger and more able than before.

*   *   *

In the British production scene one of the most exciting initially (and saddest eventually) events was the appointment of Bryan Forbes, the brilliant young writer–director–producer–actor, as ABPC head of production. Forbes, given the job of filling the vast Elstree studios, giving continuity of work and making some films pretty quickly, achieved the object. The several films he made may not have been either critically or commercially memorable but as I see it they were never intended as more than what they were; extremely competently produced run-of-the-mill movies which offered good entertainment value. They culminated in Forbes's own quite outstanding personal production of *The Raging Moon* – which his own circuit, ABC, didn't even give a circuit release! Why and exactly what happened we shall probably know at some future date, but in March Forbes announced his resignation, a year earlier than his contract was due to expire.

It was a great pity, for Forbes had stoutly maintained his own high moral and business standards throughout. His films did not compromise: they contained no sexual titillation or deviation, they were all technically first-rate. If he was in fact sacked – and some newspapers did use the word – though Forbes himself maintains that it was he who resigned, and on good terms with his boss Delfont – it was a tragedy for the British film industry, for Forbes is a brilliant maker of films and an outstanding executive as well as artist and technician.

Another sad studio milestone was the closing down at the end of 1970 of the fine MGM studios at Borehamwood, with its ten stages and considerable grounds. Bought by a property developer, it will be pulled down and some 1,000 houses will be erected in its place.

In contrast it was cheering to read only a few weeks later that the old Bray studios had been taken over and a big re-organisation and development was planned for them.

*   *   *

There have been less customers as I said above. In fact the cinema continues to lose its audience in spite of the fact that we had all hoped this decrease might have levelled off by now. According to the Board of Trade figures one can make the calculation that over the year 1970 as a whole something between six and seven million less people were going to the cinema in this country than in previous years; but, by the way, were paying rather more in total cash figure to do so.

It is, incidentally, a most interesting exercise to read through the list of most financially successful films released in America during 1970. It includes such obvious titles as *Butch Cassidy, Love Story, M*A*S*H, Patton, Tora! Tora! Tora!* and *Easy Rider* – also *Anne of the Thousand Days, The Out-of-Towners* (a grand comedy which never even had a general release here and in fact is one of the films in my "Neglected Ones" feature), *Joe* and *Z*. All these are among the forty-seven greatest money-spinners of the year, those films which earned four or more million dollars within the twelve-month period, and it is salutary to note that of all these films only two or three are sexily suspect, with one or two getting there by the publicity achieved by their very terribleness!

*   *   *

An event of some importance announced in the early part of 1971 was the retirement from the post of cinematic censor-in-chief John Trevelyan, the most loquacious and forthright man ever to hold the post; retiring, he is reported to have said, because he had become tired of the sex and violence with which he has been increasingly beset. Taking over the post is forty-nine-year-old Stephen Murphy, until now senior programme officer with ITV and for some twenty years concerned with radio and TV. He is likely, one feels, to carry on the new tradition brought to the job by Trevelyan, who has always believed in constructive criticism rather than repression but has become increasingly concerned with the way that the film generally has of late been becoming pornographically out of hand. Mr. Murphy will face a situation in which more and more X certificates are being handed out every year, less and less U. To quote a most useful chart compiled on this subject by the lively trade newspaper *Today's Cinema* the number of "X" films has risen from under 100 in 1965 to well over double that number in 1969 and 1970, while "U" films in that period have dropped from 150 to 105 and "A"s from 145 to 85.* This drop in the family film is a major cause of concern for it will in the long run drive from the habit of cinemagoing those very people who have always formed the backbone of the regular audience. In the same periodical, by the way, star Britt Ekland pinpointed the matter in a letter to the editor:

"Being a mum in London on Saturdays and Sundays is very difficult. 'What shall we do today, Mummy?' is a question often asked. "What does one do on a weekend, when the

museums, the zoos, the safari parks and the fun-fairs have all been exhausted?

"Let's go to a movie?

"Well, you search in vain for a film even vaguely suitable for the four–eight-year-olds. "We, my daughter Victoria and myself, ended up seeing *Paint Your Wagon* on a Saturday matinée. Surely that film was not made specifically with young children in mind, but it was the only movie in the London area suitable. As I could see from the audience, other mums and dads had also been searching in vain for something to take their children to see."

       ★   ★   ★

In this country, incidentally, a Gallup Poll sponsored by the *Daily Telegraph* came up with *Battle of Britain* as the most popular film of 1970 (especially with the males), a list which featured *Anne of the Thousand Days* in second place and *The Sound of Music* third (dropping the first place it had occupied for the previous five years of the poll!) Astonishingly in next place came *Gone With The Wind*.

The constant row about the release patterns of the big two circuits kept simmering throughout the year, with an occasional outburst occurring. Certainly there is room for criticism when a little gem like *Kes* can't get a wider showing than it had, while another movie of dubious intent gets a "blanket" booking. However, with the patterns already in process of change, with a double-release occurring a number of times (which means four films released the same week; various cinemas shuffling the programmes available), the whole matter reached governmental level by way of the report of film releasing made by the Monopolies Commission.

* Since writing (opposite) *Today's Cinema* has published the following story: "American film-makers have decided to take the X out of Sex. They are cutting back – in some cases banning further production of X-type movies . . . The decision is the result of a storm of complaints by exhibitors, combined with declining box-office receipts . . ."
And MGM's President James Aubrey has been quoted as saying that permissive films which might have been successful six months ago aren't that now: "The whole country has undergone a remarkable reversal in taste."
In this country the film industry, licensing authorities and Home Office officials are getting together to discuss the position of the film clubs and their showing of "blue" uncensored films with a view to legislate that *all* films publicly shown should be liable to censorship.

One of the more interesting stories of the year was the appointment of Bryan Forbes (right; shown talking with *Eyewitness* director John Hough) as production chief for Associated British at Elstree, a post he subsequently relinquished after completing one of the two years originally planned: his resignation making the headlines in all the national newspapers – and leaving, among all the inspired guesses, a lot of questions so far unanswered!

10

Likely to be one of the more controversial productions of late 1971 or early 1972 is the Roman Polanski directed, with-it version of Shakespeare's *Macbeth*, notable among other things for the fact that the famous sleepwalking scene is to be played in the nude.

Already a young director of considerable note, Peter Yates, with films like *Bullitt* and *John and Mary* to his credit, this year added *Murphy's War* to his list.

One of the films produced within the Forbes programme was the highly successful *The Railway Children*, a screen adaptation of the delightful old children's classic by actor Lionel Jeffries, whom Forbes gave a chance as the director of his own script. In this scene Jeffries explains in advance to his cast (Sally Thomsett, Jenny Agutter and Gary Warren) how he wants a sequence to be set up.

Incidentally, another, admittedly small circuit of cinemas was born this year when in March (1971) Leslie Grade announced his intention of opening about a dozen new cinemas by the end of 1972, starting with the 350-seater The Galaxy at Shepherd's Bush. It will be a small circuit of small cinemas, all between the 350–500-seater mark, offering what it is hoped will be family entertainment.

* * *

Turning to technical matters now, it appears that the 3-D film isn't as dead as we thought it might be. In Russia, where cinema attendance figures are still rising happily, they have been experimenting for some time with a system not necessitating the wearing of glasses and now apparently are well advanced. In America, too, they are showing renewed interest in the stereoscopic film, made now by a hologram process which incorporates a laser beam in both the projection and production of such a film. At the moment the maximum for an audience for this kind of film is limited by technical reasons to about 100 (at the outside) but almost certainly the reasons for this limitation will in due course be overcome. Other technical advances are likely to be less revolutionary and largely designed to reduce cost and increase ease of projection and production, while at the same time improving the quality. For instance, few people appreciate the vast strides that have been made even during the past two or three years in the quality of colour cinematography. The fact that the improvements have been gradual has veiled the actual degree of excellence.

The pattern for the future cinemas is emerging ever more clearly as one after

II

The year saw the birth of what is likely to be a new and considerable British comedy series of films in *Up Pompeii!*, a cinema adaptation of the already highly popular television series starring Frankie Howerd. Second "Up" film was soon being made with the allusive title *Up the Chastity Belt*. Taken on the set of "Pompeii", this picture shows star Julie Ege with producer Ned Sherrin (left) and new director Bob Kellett (right).

The cinematic shape of things to come? This is the artist's impression of the New Bloomsbury Cinema, an integral part of the Bloomsbury Centre Development project which is due to open in the autumn of 1971. It will seat 500 people, be underground – with a direct link with an adjacent underground car park – and be fully air-conditioned.

12 another of the big cinemas are "twinned" or converted into three or even more smaller ones under the one old roof. In London's West End this has brought its own particular problem, for within two years the number of cinemas has grown from forty to fifty (with at least four more planned as I write) and with the shortage of new products which we hear so much about one wonders from where the large numbers of showcase cinemas will get all their new films. (You will find further details of all these changes in cinemas on a later page.)

* * *

In America the boardroom battles of yesteryear seem to have eased off a little. After trying to bite its own tail very noisily for a long period, the MGM Lion is roaring and apparently raring to go again. Towards the end of 1970 the board announced their intentions of carrying through a large production programme. Their Revolt of the Campus cycle has ended; their rush to please Youth has finished too, they announced. In future they would be making films of general appeal with major stars like William Holden, George C. Scott, Mae West – yes, and Twiggy!

After this broadside Leo roared into the new year with an attempt to merge with Fox, a foray which turned into the really big boardroom struggle of the year. Darryl F. Zanuck, after sacking his own son Richard from his job of production chief, set about repelling boarders and after a great battle was able to announce victory by the end of January: there would be no merger. Fox, strongly settled in the black, would continue to go it – successfully – alone.

Meanwhile the release company pattern was changing in this country. Paramount and Universal merged their distribution in America and started to plan to extend this scene to this country. Warner's, absent for some while from the distribution scene, have opened new offices in London and announce their intention of distributing their movies again. And the distribution scene has been enlivened recently by a number of new companies emerging, small but obviously ambitious.

Looking back now for a moment of assessment, I don't feel that the period covered by this volume has been a particularly good one. While there have been some rewarding and exciting hours in the cinemas, there have been too many boring ones.

I never commit myself, as you may have noticed – or haven't done so for years – to listing the "best" films of the year. That always strikes me as ludicrous: opinions, critical as well as others, differ greatly. So I will only say that of all the movies I have seen in this period only a few I recall with real warmth or admiration: and they are very much a mixed bag; *Borsalino, Tora! Tora! Tora!, Take the Money and Run, The Raging Moon, Aristocrats, L'Enfant Sauvage, Ryan's Daughter, The Circus* (re-issue), *The Railway Children,* the John Wayne Westerns, *There's a Girl in My Soup, Say Hello to Yesterday, Murphy's War, Start the Revolution Without Me, riverrun, Wanda, Private Life of Sherlock Holmes, Le Grand Amour, The Things of Life, Scrooge, Waterloo, L'Aveu* and *Erotissimo, Pookie, The Out-of-Towners* and *Butch Cassidy*: oh, yes, and *Two Mules for Sister Sara.* That's not a complete list, not by any means, just those films which spring to my mind as the ones I have personally enjoyed. I accept that your personal list would, I'm pretty sure, be a very different compilation!

Federico Fellini at work – directing his *Satyricon*. A scene from the documentary film about the making of the film – *Ciao, Federico!*

IN MEMORIAM

ED BEGLEY, who collapsed and died at a Los Angeles party on April 29 (1970) at the age of 69, was a well-known character actor on the stage and television as well as in films; the last including *Tulsa*; *Sorry, Wrong Number*; *Twelve Angry Men*; *The Great Gatsby*; *Street With No Name*; *Sweet Bird of Youth* – the role which won him the 1963 Best Supporting Actor "Oscar". Born in Hartford, Conn., Begley, giving up school at the age of 13, drifted from job to job until he managed to get a position as a radio announcer in 1931; having thus got his foot into Show Business, he never afterwards moved it anywhere but further in!

INGER STEVENS, found dead from acute barbiturate poisoning on the floor of her flat on April 30 (1970), was only 35 when she died. Daughter of a Swedish professor, born in Stockholm (real name Stensland), she originally appeared in local amateur shows. When the family went to America she ran away from home to appear in vaudeville. Her first film, *Man on Fire* (with Bing Crosby) was made in 1956 and she then went on to make 13 films during the next 13 years, as well as appearing regularly on TV and on the stage. Some of her best-known films include *The Buccaneer, Madigan, House of Cards* and *Five Card Stud*. Her last movie was *A Dream of Kings*.

GYPSY ROSE LEE, who died in a Los Angeles hospital of cancer on April 26 (1970), will almost certainly go down in history as the shapely gal who made Strip-Tease into an acceptable art. She shed her garments with discretion, polish and complete lack of vulgarity! At the same time as she was "stripping" she was in her spare time

becoming a successful writer, not only of articles in such august publications as "The New Yorker", but also of a number of novels, one of which, "The G-String Murders", was later filmed as *Lady of Burlesque* (last film); among her other films were *Belle of the Yukon, The Stripper* and *The Trouble With Angels*.

ANITA LOUISE was 53 when she died of a stroke in April (1970). Born in New York, Miss Louise started her acting career at the age of 5. Her first husband was film producer

Buddy Adler; her second, Henry Burger, an importer. Her numerous film credits include *Anthony Adverse, Madame Du Barry, The Green Light* and more recently *Retreat, Hell!* For the past few years she had not made any movies, or indeed really worked at all, devoting most of her time and energy to the social whirl and to good causes.

Most vintage moviegoers will recall lovely little CATHY O'DONNELL as the war-torn soldier's girl-friend in *The Best Years of Our Lives*, in which she made her screen debut. Later she appeared in *The Miniver Story, Detective Story, They Live By Night, The Man from Laramie* and *Ben Hur*. Born in Alabama in 1925, she died after a long illness in April (1970), aged 45.

SONNY TUFTS was the rich man's son (his father was a Boston banker) who couldn't keep away from Show Business. From singing in a church choir he won an audition for the New York Metropolitan Opera, but he never sang there: he turned to the pop world of the period and was soon a popular cabaret act, and at one time he was leading his own dance band. His looks gained him an audition and a contract in films, which included *Duffy's Tavern, The Virginian, Easy Living, Seven Year Itch* and many more. He had not been seen on the screen for some time prior to his death in a Santa Monica hospital (where he had been taken with pneumonia) on June 4 (1970), at the age of 59.

CHESTER MORRIS, that tough-looking, handsome character with the firm chin, was recruited to the films in 1928 by D. W. Griffith, who gave him the lead in his *Alibi*.

14 His subsequent 85 films included the memorable *The Big House*, *Unchained* and no less than 36 "Boston Blackie" films on which his public reputation will safely rest. His last screen appearance was in this year's release, *The Great White Hope*. He was still working when he died, at the age of 69, from an overdose of barbiturates.

Taken ill during the shooting of Marcel Camus' *The Atlantic Wall*, that great French comic actor BOURVIL struggled on to the end of his part and then died, at the age of 57, in Paris on September 23 (1970). Farm-born André Rainbourg (his real Normandy name) gained a foothold in Show Business via the vaudeville stage. But from the time he made his first film his cinematic reputation rapidly grew to heroic proportions; thanks to his superb performances in films like *La Traversée de Paris*, *The Green Mare* and many others in which his astonished expression in the midst of chaos, his self-satisfied smile and his delighted leer were exploited to the fullest advantage. His last films were *The Christmas Tree* (he was the best thing in the film, an American

production) and *The Brain*, and *Monte Carlo or Bust*.

One of the real veterans of the drawing-room movie comedies, EDWARD EVERETT HORTON died in California on September 30 (1970) at the age of 83. For many years prominent in the theatre, he made a great number of films and could justifiably be termed one of the screen's major comedy players. Starting out in the theatre in 1908, he made his first movie in 1916 and was thereafter seldom long absent

from the screen, making a vast number of appearances and often emerging as the best thing in the film! Some of his better known movies include *The Front Page*, *Alice in Wonderland* (he played The Mad Hatter), *Arsenic and Old Lace* and those classic musicals *The Gay Divorcee* and *Top Hat*. Born in Brooklyn, E. E. Horton's career really began when he landed a role with the Gilbert and Sullivan company at the age of 20.

Though primarily a stage player, cockney

character actor WALLY PATCH made a number of films during his long career which started out on the old Variety Halls way back in 1912. Seven years later he made his first film. Some of his better known performances were in *The Great Companions*, *Bank Holiday*, *Quiet Wedding*, *The Guinea Pig*, *I'm All Right Jack* and *Sparrows Can't Sing*. He was 82 when he died on November 18 (1970) at Denville Hall, the Variety Artists Benevolent Home.

Though she will be remembered for her serene beauty, FRANCES FARMER had anything but a serene life. She was for a time known to drink too heavily and, indeed, between 1942 and 1949 spent quite a bit of time in mental institutions. It was her success in the Broadway production of *Golden Boy* which took her to Hollywood and her first film, *Come And Get It* in 1936. Subsequently she appeared in a number of movies including *Ebb Tide*, *Toast of New Orleans* and *Son of Fury*. Released from hospital in 1950 she returned to Seattle, her birth place, and actually worked in a hotel under an assumed name for a while. She made one further movie, *The Party Crashers*, in 1958 before she died on August 1 (1970) from cancer, on the Indianapolis farm where she had lived for the past several years.

CLAUD ALLISTER, sporting a monocle and a vapid smile, was famous for his "silly ass" roles. Born 1891, he made his film debut in 1929 in *The Private Life of Henry VIII* in 1932 and thereafter made a number of movies among which his role as "Algy" in The Bulldog Drummond series may be more easily recalled. He was 76 when he died on

July 26 (1970) in Santa Barbara after a long illness.

Not many moviegoers knew that tough man PRESTON FOSTER, who died (July 1970) after a lengthy illness aged 69, had actually started out in life as a shipping clerk and was an operatic star long before he made his first film. He was also a quite noted composer and was writing songs more or less until his death. Having moved over from opera to straight drama and become a Broadway stage star, he made his screen debut (in *Nothing But the Truth*) in 1930,

subsequently making in excess of a hundred movies until his last, *Chubasco* in 1967, when he was semi-retired. Some of his more noteworthy pictures include *The Informer*, *Annie Oakley*, *Geronimo*, *News Is Made At Night* and *Last Days of Pompeii*.

For more than 60 years old-timer MARJORIE RAMBEAU was star of stage and screen and after a bad accident in 1945 (from which she never fully recovered) she went on acting in a wheelchair or on crutches! She was preparing to celebrate her 81st birthday, for which she had come out of hospital, when she died on July 7 (1970) at her Palm Springs home. Cast in the title role in a stage production of "Camille" at the age of 13, Miss Rambeau was never afterwards idle and graced a vast number of movies from the '30's including *The Rains Came*, *Tugboat Annie Sails Again*, and *Tobacco Road*.

Refusing to allow an amputated leg (in 1965) to interfere with his career, 71-year-old JAY C. FLIPPEN, a former Al Jolson understudy, passed 56 years in one or another branch of Show Business. When he died on February 3 (1971) he had, only a week or so before, completed his last movie, Fox's *Seven Minutes*. His career started in a minstrel show at the age of 15 and later he became a headline variety act. On Broadway he appeared in many great successes such as *Artists and Models* and *Hellzapoppin*. His first film was *Brute Force* in 1947, thereafter he made comedies and drama with equal success including *Strategic Air Command*, *Flying Leathernecks*, *The Wild One*, *ThunderBay*, *Hellfighters* and *Cat Ballou*.

Nobody who had seen him will ever forget CHARLIE RUGGLES, with his delightful vocal mannerism and dimpled chuckle. He started his stage career in small parts in 1905, later going into a number of straight and musical Broadway productions. He first went into films in 1915, returning to the studios in 1929 in *Gentlemen of the Press*. A few of his many films include *Ruggles of Red Gap*, *If I Had a Million*, *Charley's Aunt* and *Alice in Wonderland*. Latterly he had been largely concentrating on TV, though for the last few years (he was 84 when he

died on December 23, 1970) he had been living in semi-retirement.

Though he appeared to be international, FERNAND GRAVET, who died in Paris on November 2 (1970) aged 65, was actually Belgian by birth. His stage success in France led to him being offered Hollywood stardom in Warners' *The King and the Chorus Girl*. Some of his other American films included *The Great Waltz*, *Fools for Scandal* and, one of his last, the sadly neglected Bryan Forbes film *The Madwoman*

16 *of Chaillot*. One of his best-known later films was Max Ophuls' *La Ronde*. His American films were only the tip of the iceberg – he had more than 100 continental performances in films to his credit.

HAROLD LLOYD, who died last year at the age of 77 on his palatial Hollywood estate, was one of the greatest stars of the golden era of screen comedy; an individual and inventive comedian who in a period when comedy was king was brought to the top by public acclaim of his scrupulously

clean, wholesome sense of truly cinematic fun. Emerging from his Hal Roach and Mack Sennett schooling, he was starred as "Lonesome Luke" and as such made a series of short films. It wasn't until 1917 that the sudden inspiration of the addition to his make-up of a pair of horn-rimmed spectacles gave him a new image and finally established as a public favourite the serious, studious-looking simpleton – struggling against an unscrupulous world of go-getters and crooks – who always wins out *and* wins the girl.

Lloyd eventually ventured from shorts to features and the success of *Grandma's Boy* led to the long line of uproarious long films such as *Safety Last, Doctor's Orders, Speedy, Girl Shy* and *Welcome Danger*. So to those great films of the 30's, *The Milky Way* and *Professor Beware*. Hollywood honoured Lloyd in 1952 with an Academy Award for a Master Comedian and Good Citizen.

BEBE DANIELS for the last few years of her life had been a semi-invalid, after suffering a serious stroke. Born in Dallas, Texas, of a theatrical family (her father, incidentally was born in Scotland, her mother in Spain) she was just 10 weeks old when she made her first appearance on stage. At 7 she made her first movie and by 14 was playing adult roles for Hal Roach: for 4 years she was with Harold Lloyd in his "Lonesome Luke" series. Under Cecil B. De Mille's tutorage she made a number of movies. Her first talkie was *Rio Rita* in 1929, the first of a number of musicals she made. She married Ben Lyon in 1930 and the family moved to Britain during the war to make their permanent home here and to appear right through the blitz in the gay radio family

series "Hi Gang" and "Life with the Lyons". She died on March 16 (1971) from a final stroke at the age of 71.

FERNANDEL, who died in Paris, aged 67, on February 26 (1971) after a long illness, was one of the best-loved, internationally acclaimed and most talented French comedians ever to become a star of the movies. Born in Marseilles (real name, Fernand Contandin) on May 8, 1903, he was already organising theatricals when he was at school. But it was as a touring singer that he

began his professional career and he was 25 when he made his Paris debut, two years later getting his first film role in Guitry's *Le Blanc et le Noir*. His series of superb, witty, Don Camillo comedies brought him international fame. His 120 film credits include very few outside France or Italy (the exceptions being *Paris Honeymoon* and *Around the World in 80 Days*). Fernandel, though famed as a comedian, could play straight and even tragic roles and in fact did so on a few occasions. His trade-mark was his perfect, rubbery face, with its toothy grin or lugubrious expressions.

The screen's first cowboy star, BRONCO BILLY ANDERSON had reached the age of 90 when he died – long retired – this year (Jan. 20, 1971) in a Hollywood hospital. It was he who played, in 1903, in Edwin Porter's history-making *The Great Train Robbery*, the first film to have a plot and for which Little Rock-born Anderson learnt to ride and shoot. Soon promoted to director-star, Anderson with Ben Turpin and George K. Spoor formed the famous film firm of Essanay, and in the small studio they built in

Los Angeles, made their first Bronco Billy film in 1908. Anderson wrote, directed and starred in 375 of the series during the next seven years. In 1915 his company put Chaplin under contract and Anderson had by then come a long way from his first salary cheque of 50 cents an hour! After he sold out his Essanay interest Anderson never managed to recover his earlier success and in 1920 he retired to live on a small income from his investments.

Another old Western veteran player who

"passed on" this year – January 16 (1971) – was 73-year-old KERMIT MAYNARD, former world rodeo champ, and star of many Westerns of the 30's period, including *Wild Bill Hickock*, *Sandy of the Mounted*, *The Fighting Texan*, and *The Panhanton Patrol*. Kermit is survived by his even more famous older brother, cowboy actor Ken.

JOHN PADDY CARSTAIRS, son of famous stage comedian Nelson "Bunch" Keyes, who died this year from a sudden heart attack, made his first film while he was still at Repton School. He went on to direct

a long line of British comedies and comedy-thrillers including *The Chiltern Hundreds*, *Up to His Neck* and, of course, several Norman Wisdom films. Never for a moment idle, he painted a great number of pictures – having regular West End one-man shows of his works – and wrote (as well as some screenplays), a long line of Show Business novels (*Vinegar and Brown Paper*, etc.) and lively detection thrillers. Small, dapper, effervescent, he was a wonderful companion and his knowledge of Show Business in general, and films in particular, was vast.

JOHN BOLES, who died in the spring of 1971, will always be remembered by vintage moviegoers for his performance in that Paul Whiteman 1930's musical *The King of Jazz*, but he had in fact made his first film, *This is Marriage*, some five years before that. Other films for which he will be remembered are *Back Street* (made in 1932), *Stella Dallas*, *Only Yesterday*, *Imitation of Life*, *Craig's Wife* and a couple of Shirley Temple films. In the middle forties he began to develop oil interests and after that he made only one film, *Babes in Baghdad* (in 1952). He died where he had lived since 1952, in San Angelo, Texas. He was 73.

BASIL DEARDEN, killed when his car crashed on the M4 Motorway early in the spring of 1971, was a director of polish and great technical expertise. A graduate of the old Ealing Studios in their greatest days under Sir Michael Balcon, his directing or writing credits include several of the Will Hay comedies and George Formby films. His first solo direction was of *The Bells Go Down* in 1943; later he made a classic thriller called *Dead of Night*, *Frieda* (which

brought Mai Zetterling to the British cinema), *Saraband for Dead Lovers*, *The Blue Lamp*, and *The Smallest Show On Earth*. He formed a successful director–producer partnership with another Ealing old boy, Michael Relph, with whom he made a number of successes: the two were in fact preparing their next film together when Dearden was killed, at the age of 60.

One of Britain's leading comedy actors, CECIL PARKER, who died this spring

(1971), aged 73, had been on the stage since 1922 and screen from '33 (when he made *The Silver Spoon*). His screen successes include *Caesar and Cleopatra*, *Cuckoo In The Nest*, *The Citadel*, *The Lady Vanishes* and many, many others. One of his last films was Attenborough's *Oh! What A Lovely War*. Urbane, brilliantly professional with a superb sense of timing, his range was wide; and even though he was usually cast in comedy roles he could on occasion produce a performance of quiet, chilling menace.

SETH HOLT was something of a back-room boy in British cinema in that though he had a long and varied career in films, from actor to documentary editor, from feature film editor to director – of *Nowhere To Go* in 1958 – his name was virtually unknown to the moviegoing public. Though he carried on with other jobs in between (including a return to editing) he continued to produce a slim stream of very professionally directed films: among them, *Taste of Fear*, *Station Six Sahara* and *The Nanny*. He was only 47 when he died suddenly early this spring (1971).

A cheerful, gay personality and a hard-working actress, HY HAZEL, who collapsed at her home and died on the way to hospital in May 1970, at the age of 47, started her theatrical career at the age of seven (in 1929) in a production of *The Winter's Tale*. After work as mannequin and model she started a career in stage musicals and although her work was principally done on the stage she did appear in a number of films, including *The Body Said No*, *The Franchise Affair* and *The Yellow Balloon*.

PATRICK WYMARK, who died very suddenly in Sydney, Australia, last October (1970) at the early age of 44, two nights before he was due to open in a stage production there, was mainly famed for his many television appearances, but he did appear with success in a number of films including *Repulsion*, *The Psychopath*, *Where Eagles Dare*, *Cromwell*. His, by the way, was the voice of Churchill in the documentary *The Finest Hours*.

BILLIE BURKE was the glamorous girl who knew how to age gracefully, slipping

easily into the unique character actress she became. Daughter of the singing Irish clown, Billy Burke, Billie was educated in England and France and began her theatrical career when she was 14 in "The Schoolgirl". It was in 1907 in "My Wife" that she became established as a comedienne and gradually developed that fluttery, dithery style which became so delightfully her own. Signed up for *Peggy*, by Thomas Ince, Billie made several silent films before meeting Ziegfeld in 1913 and marrying him the following year. Her great number of film appearances include *Dinner at Eight, Topper, The Young in Heart* and *Sergeant Rutledge* – made in 1960 and her last. She was 84 when she died on May 14 (1970), in Los Angeles.

MARY CLARE, who died in August (1970), at the age of 76, was primarily a stage actress of considerable range who made a series of films intermittently from around the mid-20's. She could play a comedy role or a chillingly macabre one with equal facility and among her movies are *Hindle Wakes, The Lady Vanishes, Mrs. Pym of Scotland Yard* (she played Mrs. Pym), *The Night Has Eyes*

and the 1948 film of *Oliver Twist*. She had been retired for some years prior to her decease.

ALBERT LAMORISSE, died June (1970), will always be recalled for his wonderful direction of *The Red Balloon*. Some of his other French films, most of them below feature length but several of them small masterpieces, include *Crin Blanc, Fifi La Plume* and *Stowaway in the Sky*. He was 48.

FRITZ KORTNER, died July (1970), was an Austrian actor of some international reputation, though largely confined to broken-accent roles in Hollywood. His best-known films include *Pandora's Box, Dreyfus*, and *The Hitler Gang*. He was 78.

FOLCO LULLI, the Italian actor who died in May (1970), will be recalled by most moviegoers for his quite memorable performance in *The Wages of Fear*.

BARNEY BALABAN, who died in March (1971), was the longtime president of Paramount Pictures and during his long reign (1936–1964) brought the company to the peak of its success. He had retained an honorary chairmanship at his death, at the age of 83. A former exhibitor, he knew what the public wanted and tried to give it to them at a reasonable cost.

NAUNTON WAYNE died in November (1970). His earlier successes included compering the first West End non-stop variety shows at the London Pavilion. A great raconteur, he conveyed perfectly the image of the comic Englishman. His stories were witty, often long, mostly dry. The son

of a Welsh solicitor, born in 1901, his success in the musical *1066 And All That* finally established his stage reputation. On the screen he developed a remarkably successful partnership with the late Basil Radford which was beautifully developed in *The Lady Vanishes* and *Dead of Night*. He had a unique personality which came across equally well in the intimacy of cabaret, the larger demands of the stage or the different techniques of the radio and film.

EDMUND LOWE, who died after a long illness on April 21 (1971) in California at the age of 81, was originally destined for the Church. He then decided on a career with the Law, but eventually settled for the stage! Reputed to be one of the best dressed actors in the business, Lowe started his acting career in 1911, not making his screen debut until 1923, in *The Silent Command* and *Vive La France*. His greatest screen success came as the rough Sergeant in *What Price Glory?* which made so much money that two sequels were made with Lowe playing the same character. Included in the 70-plus films in which he appeared are *Dinner at Eight, In*

20 *Old Arizona*, *Seven Sinners*, *Good Sam* and *Heller in Pink Tights*. A gradual decline in health over the last 20 years of his life had largely limited his working.

GLENDA FARRELL, who died at the age of 67 at her New York home on May 1 (1971) was one of the screen's greatest deliverers of the wisecrack: and with her unique mouth shape could literally whip them out like lashes! Though she appeared in many films in the 30's and 40's including *Little Caesar* (her screen debut), *I Am a Fugitive from a Chain Gang*, *Gold Diggers of 1935* and the "Torchy Blane" series of movies, she always preferred the stage and, latterly, television. She was a real professional – starting at the age of 7 by playing Little Eva in *Uncle Tom's Cabin*. She was still acting, in a play called *40 Carats*, in 1969, when she became ill and had to withdraw from the cast, thereafter never fully recovering.

TERENCE DE MARNEY, who was killed by a tube train at High Street, Kensington Station on May 25 (1971), was far better known for his stage work than his films. London born (March 1, 1909), he first appeared on the stage in 1923 in a sketch at the Coliseum. Subsequently he was always busy acting, directing or, of recent years, setting up shows. His range was very wide though he quite obviously loved playing the kind of role he did so well when they revived Grand Guignol some years back: the role of the menace. De Marney's films included *I Killed the Count*, *Uneasy Terms* (in which he played with obvious relish Peter Cheyney's character Slim Callaghan), *Death is a Woman* and *All Neat in Black Stockings*, one of his last film appearances in 1969.

CHIPS RAFFERTY, who died at the end of May (1971), was the first big Australian international film star. With a wide experience before he entered the movies Chips – whose real name, incidentally, was John Goffage – was a tall, rangy character with an easy-going personality which came over well on the screen. His first film was *Dad Rudd* in 1939 but it was in *40,000 Horsemen* his next the following year that he made his biggest hit. Later movies included *The Loves of Joanna Godden*, *The Overlanders*, *The Sundowners*, *Mutiny on the Bounty* and *They're a Weird Mob*.

AUDIE MURPHY, who died in a plane crash at the end of May (1971) was starred in films as a result of his World War Two reputation. The most decorated American soldier (his 24 medals included America's highest honour) killer of a considerable number of the enemy, he was gently eased into his screen career by way of parts in a number of low-budget Westerns. His debut was in *Beyond Glory* in 1948. He subsequently appeared in first feature films like *The Red Badge of Courage*, *Destry* and *The Quiet American*. Latterly his large business interest (it was while taking care of a new one that the private plane in which he was travelling to the meeting crashed into a mountain) had led to a decline in the number of his film appearances but he was actually negotiating a new contract at the time of his death. Born in Kingston, Texas, in 1924, his extraordinarily youthful appearance remained with him to the last.

WHERE ARE THEY NOW?

by Anthony Slide

Alma Taylor and Shayle Gardner in *Comin' Thro' the Rye*.

More than forty years have passed since *The Times*, in the spring of 1929, published a study of Britain's leading "film artists". There was Alma Taylor, "a gracious young lady", Betty Balfour, "the most popular British girl on the screen today", Estelle Brody, "a fascinating Canadian brunette", Mabel Poulton, "a cockney and an ex-typist and proud of it", John Stuart, "the hero of many British pictures", and Chili Bouchier, "a promising youngster", not to mention Lillian Hall Davis, Mary Odette, Joan Morgan and Chrissie White. Even as that *Times* article was written, the silent cinema was dying – not with a whimper, but in a burst of glory, which the sound film was to be hard put to equal. Times were to change and films with them; some of Britain's silent stars managed to make the transition into sound, some fell by the wayside, while others were happy to retire when still young and relatively famous. Alma Taylor can probably claim to be Britain's first film star, although Mae Clarke, who appeared as the nursemaid in *Rescued by Rover*, might dispute this (she's still alive and living in Acton). Miss Taylor made her name appearing in productions for Cecil Hepworth; she was the heroine of both the 1916 and 1923 versions of *Comin' Thro' the Rye*. She made her last screen appearance in Frank Launder's 1957 *Blue Murder at St. Trinian's*. Last heard of, Miss Taylor was living in the London suburb of Balham, but too shy to speak to anyone. Alma Taylor's partner in Hepworth's *Tilly the Tomboy* series, Chrissie White, is not so reticent, and often comes up to London from her Surrey cottage to reminisce about the silent era on radio and television. However, she has not graced the cinema screens since 1933, when she starred in husband Henry Edwards's *General John Regan* – Edwards passed away in 1952. If you were to ask me when I last saw Betty Balfour prior to writing this piece, I would say last Tuesday when we had tea together at the Dorchester. She still looks as beautiful as ever, and it is hardly possible that it is now more than fifty years since she made her screen début in *Nothing Else Matters*. Betty was born in London on March 27, 1903, and had made her first public appearance in a children's pantomime in Kensington in 1913. She was already an established stage actress when T. A. Welsh saw her in *Medora* at the Alhambra Theatre, and introduced her to his partner, George Pearson (the two had formed the Welsh–Pearson Company in 1918, their first film being *The Better 'Ole*). So it was that early in 1920, Betty made her first trip to the Company's tiny studios in Harlesden, to appear – in a relatively small role as a slavey – in *Nothing Else Matters*. Hugh E. Wright took the leading role of the comedian, who after falling on hard times, realises that "the riddle of life is love . . . and that nothing else matters". The comedian's wife was played by Moyna MacGill, who was later to follow her daughter, Angela Lansbury, to Hollywood, and appear in a number of films there from 1945 to 1951. Betty's guardian was her Aunt, and Betty recalls an amusing incident during the shooting of one scene in the film, in which she enters a newsagent's to purchase a romantic novel: "Well, I had to say 'Have you *The Bleeding Heart*?' and the newsagent said, 'No, but I've got the bloody hump.' And George asked me to register an expression to the camera, so he

22

Alma Taylor talks to David Knight and Margo Lorenz on the set of Basil Dearden's *Out of the Clouds* (1955).

Chrissie White.

Chrissie White and Henry Edwards in *General John Regan*.

Betty Balfour in *Love, Life and Laughter*.

said, 'Look at Aunt Sally over there!' My God – there was my aunt."

Mary Finds the Gold gave Betty her first starring role, and then in April 1921, George Pearson began shooting his most famous film, *Squibs*, from which a whole series developed, *Squibs Wins the Calcutta Sweep*, *Squibs Honeymoon*, etc. Betty became "Britain's Queen of Happiness", brightening the dim days of the post-war depression, a period so movingly and accurately portrayed by George Pearson in his 1924 *Reveille*. Betty considers her best work to have been in Pearson's *Love, Life and Laughter*, produced in the winter of 1922/23. "It was the finest," she recently remarked, when we were discussing the film with George Pearson. Edward Craig, who was later as "Edward Carrick" to become Britain's leading art director, told me that he and Thorold Dickinson saw it together in the summer of 1923, and the film was undoubtedly responsible for their both adopting a career in films.

The coming of sound did not diminish Betty Balfour's popularity; she was active in films until the mid-Thirties when she retired from the screen in order to concentrate upon bringing up her son, David. She returned to the screen briefly in 1945 to star in Columbia's *29 Acacia Avenue*, and was seen on the London stage in 1952 as the mother in *The Golden Grain* at the Embassy Theatre, Swiss Cottage, but the death of King George VI brought the play to an abrupt end. Now Betty lives quietly in West London; she keeps very much to herself and has no contact with any of her former silent screen colleagues apart from George Pearson, whom she has visited on the odd occasion with me.

Mabel Poulton also made her screen début in *Nothing Else Matters*. She recalled for me how this came about: "I was a typist at the London Alhambra many years ago, and they were doing a film of *Broken Blossoms* with Lillian Gish, and the pressman said, 'Well, you're the absolute double of Lillian Gish, would you like to go on the stage and do the prologue, you have to lie on a bier and pretend you're dead, and you mustn't sneeze or move or anything like that.' Well, of course, it was extra money and I was very young, and I was delighted to do the little prologue. Well from that, somebody saw me from Welsh–Pearson, and offered me a year's contract because they liked the look of me."

After *Nothing Else Matters*, this delightful, petite blonde appeared with Betty Balfour again in *Mary Finds the Gold*, and was then given the lead in Welsh–Pearson's *The Old Curiosity Shop*, under the direction of Thomas Bentley. Mabel was then called to Paris to play the role of Violine Fleuri in Abel Gance's *Napoleon*, but although Gance was very much in favour of her playing the part, his financial backers were not, but Mabel's trip was not a complete waste of time for she was invited by Germaine Dulac to star in *L'Ame d'Artiste*. A series of comedy dramas for Archibald Nettlefold Productions followed, with titles such as *Wild Cat Hetty* and *Not Quite a Lady*. Then came Mabel's greatest triumph. "One day I saw in the paper that Dorothy Gish was going to play in a wonderful book that I'd read by Margaret Kennedy called *The Constant Nymph* in the part of Tessa. And I had read this book, and thought if I could only play that part. Suddenly I read that she was ill, so without saying anything to

Betty Balfour with George Pearson in 1957 at a party to launch Pearson's autobiography.

Mabel Poulton and Moyna MacGill in *Nothing Else Matters*.

Mabel Poulton as Tessa in *The Constant Nymph*.

Joan Morgan.

24

Chili Bouchier in *You Know What Sailors Are.*

Chili Bouchier chats with Mr. and Mrs. Sandy Powell at a reception given by *The Silent Picture* at the National Film Theatre in 1969. (Photo by Raymond Julian-Huxley.)

Lillian Hall Davis.

Lillian Hall Davis with John Stuart on one of the sets at the Victorine Studios, Nice, for *Roses of Picardy*. Director, Maurice Elvey, is stood on the camera platform.

anybody, I went along to Michael Balcon in Leicester Square, walked round the houses about ten times with nerves; went in, and said 'Would you please give me a test for Tessa?' Well after many arguments, I at last got the part, and went with Ivor Novello to the Austrian Tyrol to play in it. It was a wonderful experience. He was marvellous, so kind, so sweet. One of the nicest people that you could possibly meet."

Mabel's cockney accent unhappily prevented her having a successful career in talkies, despite an early triumph in Basil Dean's *Escape*. In the mid-Thirties, her fiancé was offered a post with an oil company in Persia, and so he took Mabel with him as his wife, and the screen lost her for ever. They returned to this country some years ago, and now live in a block of flats, which they own in Chelsea. Mabel is still available should the right part turn up, but her only appearance in recent years has been in an episode of the *No Hiding Place* television series.

Mabel Poulton may have facially resembled Lillian Gish, but the British actress whose acting was most often favourably compared to that of Miss Gish was Joan Morgan. The daughter of British producer and director, Sidney Morgan, Joan made her first screen appearances, from 1914 onwards, in her father's productions at his Shoreham studios. Then in 1920, as she recalled for me: "When I was just fifteen I made a film of Dickens's *Little Dorrit*. Now Dickens said she was twenty-two and looked half that age, so I was about the half-way mark. I was very young-looking for my age; I was a small and rather childish type. At this time Bryant Washburn, the great American star, came over to make a film in London, called *The*

 id="2"

John Stuart and Virginia Valli in *The Pleasure Garden* (frame enlargement).

Studio publicity for *Not for Sale* showing Mary Odette and that popular British character actress, Mary Brough.

John Stuart meets his one-time director, Alfred Hitchcock, at a Stockholm party in 1969.

Road to London, and was looking for a leading lady. It just never occurred to me to think of myself in this context. Anyway, Washburn came to the trade show of *Little Dorrit*, and asked to see me afterwards. Of course, when he saw how young I looked he said, 'Is this the girl?' But he engaged me, and I think that was the peak of my career. This was a great feather in my cap. He later offered me a five-year contract, which father refused. That was the unhappiest moment of my career!''

With a speaking voice as beautiful as her features (Miss Morgan was always considered Britain's prettiest silent star), her career lasted well into the sound era. At the same time she was making a reputation as a playwright and novelist. One of her novels, *Camera*, is a fascinating fictionalised account of life in the early British studios. Joan Morgan now lives and works in Henley-on-Thames.

If Joan Morgan was the British Lillian Gish, the honour – if such it was – of being the British Clara Bow belonged to Chili Bouchier. Hammersmith-born Miss Bouchier is really a star of the talkies, as she appeared in only a few late silents; she first attracted the public's attention as a bathing belle, basking on the sands at Cromer, in A. V. Bramble and Anthony Asquith's *Shooting Stars*. Her first starring role came in 1928, when Bramble directed *Chick*, based on the novel by Edgar Wallace, and this was followed by *Palais de Danse*, directed by Maurice Elvey. As Chili recalled in a recent article in *Films and Filming*, "Now the press were beginning to notice that I had 'It'. When authoress Elinor Glyn came to London and announced that, in her opinion, there were only two English actresses who

26 John Stuart and Estelle Brody in *Hindle Wakes*.

John Stuart (far left) and Estelle Brody examine the Visitors' Book at the Gaumont Cinema, Chelsea, 1952.

possessed this quality, myself and Elissa Landi, I then became England's 'It' Girl." Chili Bouchier was at the peak of her screen fame in the early Thirties, starring in such memorable films as *Carnival* and *The Blue Danube*. Herbert Wilcox, the producer of many of her talkie successes, changed her screen name to Dorothy, as he considered Chili a difficult name to pronounce; there are many who would have considered it more intelligent to alter her surname. In recent years, Chili Bouchier has made few screen appearances, but she appears regularly on the stage (she made her début as Bella Winberg in Cochran's *Magnolia Street* at the Adelphi Theatre), and has published an autobiography extolling the spiritualist religion. She now lives in fashionable Dolphin Square, where her neighbours include Ben Lyon.

The British silent cinema's most tragic star was undoubtedly the beautiful, if hard-faced, Lillian Hall Davis. Miss Davis had entered films in 1918, playing a supporting role in George Pearson's *The Better 'Ole*. However, it was with the release of Graham Cutts's *The Wonderful Story* in 1922 that she achieved stardom. Throughout the Twenties she was seldom away from the studios; she was Hitchcock's leading lady in *The Ring* and *The Farmer's Wife*, and gives a memorable performance in Walter Summers's *Maisie's Marriage* (based on *Married Love* by Dr. Marie Stopes). At the same time she was making a name for herself on the Continent: in Italy playing opposite Emil Jannings in *Quo Vadis?*, in Germany in films for Joe May and Lothar Mendes, and in France in René Clair's *La Proie du Vent* and Jacques de Baroncelli's *Nitchévo*. Then came sound. She appeared in only two features, and retired from the screen supposedly because her voice was unsuited to talkies, a suggestion disclaimed by those who worked with her in the Twenties and say that she had a pleasing speaking voice. Whatever the reason, her disappointment was without a doubt the cause of her death by her own hand at her Golders Green home on October 24, 1933. She was thirty-four. There are, of course, always mysteries surrounding the whereabouts of many silent stars. Stars such as Mary Odette, always to be seen around the British studios in the Twenties in the company of her mother. Born Odette Goimbault in Dieppe on August 10, 1901, she made her first British film in 1916. In 1919, the popular film magazine, *Pictures and the Picturegoer*, ran a competition to choose a new name for her, and finally Mary Odette was chosen from ten thousand other suggestions. She was an active campaigner against vivisection until 1928, when she starred in her last film, an atrocious picture titled *Emerald of the East*, and seemed to lose interest in both the Anti-Vivisection League and the cinema. On June 1, 1932, at St. Pancras Town Hall, she married a journalist, John Hardacre, and was never heard of again. Should she by any chance read this piece, I assure her she still has at least one admirer left.

Sooner or later every British leading lady of the silent cinema – indeed most leading ladies of the British cinema until the Forties – would play opposite John Stuart. Edinburgh-born John Stuart, now in his 73rd year, has starred in 150 British productions, beginning in 1920 with *Her Son*, playing the title role with Violet Hopson as his mother. (Yes – Violet Hopson is still alive and living in Essex.) Forty-two

further silent films followed, including Hitchcock's first feature, *The Pleasure Garden* and John's favourite silent film, Maurice Elvey's *Roses of Picardy*. John now lives in Knightsbridge, still available for film, theatre and television work; his last feature film was the 1966 Children's Film Foundation production, *Son of the Sahara*. It was a great pity there was no part for him in *The Railway Children*, as I'm sure many people must remember with affection his appearances in the various serialised versions of that marvellous book on television. And how many remember him in that forerunner of the *Dr. Who* series, *The Lost Planet*?

In 1926 John signed a three-year contract with the Gaumont Company (at a salary of £20 a week when filming and £10 a week otherwise!), and appeared for the first time opposite Estelle Brody in *Mademoiselle from Armentiéres*. Estelle had already appeared in one previous film, *White Heat*, but this was her first starring role. She told me that although born in the USA, Gaumont decided that it would be best if she claimed to be Canadian, as the British public might object to an American appearing in native productions! The Gaumont Company need have had little fear for she soon had a tremendous following with her appearances opposite Stuart in *Hindle Wakes* (John also appeared in the talkie version), *The Glad Eye*, *The Flight Commander*, *The Sailor Takes a Wife* and *Kitty*. What a shock contemporary audiences must have got when they saw *Kitty*, which begins silent and then becomes a talkie, and heard Estelle as a cockney girl talking with a transatlantic accent.

With the coming of sound, Estelle returned to the States "to learn all about talkies",

and appeared in a number of short films. However, it was to be a very long time before she was able to put her knowledge of talkies to any use in England, for she was not seen again in a film until 1950, when she played a small part in *They Were Not Divided*. A number of further parts followed, including that of Mademoiselle from Armentières in *Lilli Marlene*. She decided to retire from the screen, she told me, when she was asked to play the wife of that fine character actor, Dermot Kelly ("I couldn't sink any lower than playing the wife of an Irish labourer. When they asked me to do this, I decided it was time to quit."). She had lived only a block away from John Stuart until 1969, when she and her husband, a former literary agent, set up home in Malta.

Estelle and John last appeared together in 1952 on the stage of the Gaumont, Chelsea, to celebrate the 25th anniversary of Gaumont–British Pictures. They sang "Mademoiselle from Armentières" and "Roses of Picardy" together, and recalled an exciting – if not a great – age of British film-making.

MAMOUN HASSAN
– one of the directors of tomorrow
by Oswell Blakeston

Production still: The director of *The Meeting* fixing a paper dial over the station clock so that it will show "the correct time" in the film.
A production still from Mamoun Hassan's prize-winning film *The Meeting*.

WAITING IN THE WINGS

He has lived for twenty years in England, where he has taken a degree in engineering; but even in his student days he felt that he was wasting time when he was not thinking about films. As soon as he had passed his exams at the university, he became a film-cutter against all the odds of a closed-shop profession. His name is Mamoun Hassan, and you may have seen it on credits, for he has directed five films, three documentaries and two short-story works, one of which, *The Meeting* (1964), won The Oberhausen Prize, and the other, *Living On The Box* (1968), had the distinction of being written by Penelope Gilliat. But he is still waiting for the first big breakthrough with a full-length feature.

He can expect, at this stage of his career, to be encouraged to work for months on a script, and then to find that the project has been dropped for one of those mysterious reasons which inspire producers to break the hearts of new talent. Yet, strangely enough, Hassan, having suffered the brinkmanship of three "set-ups" which dematerialised only at the last moment before going on the floor, is optimistic.

"There are now," he says, "so many variables. Yesterday it was five thousand to one that a young director could get a story into production; but today – one never knows."

But his optimism is not really based on the hazards of "marketing" but on the new revolution which has brought about the new "could-be's". The great thing, he says, is that people are learning that there is no such thing as "a film subject" as cinema itself isn't committed to a subject. Today, a director is not completely mad if he tries to interest the gentlemen of high finance in something which yesterday would have been instantly labelled a "non-subject". Today, a director can work to promote a story that is "his" story and not simply a commodity, and . . . he just might be lucky.

Z, a film which would have been an impossible project yesterday, has made fantastic money at the box-office; while a recent Hollywood musical, with all the trusted glamour formulae, flopped. The financiers have had to rethink, to learn, as film audiences have learnt, *that genre does not define quality*.

It has taken a long time for the top brass to make this discovery; but now it does bring hope, hope for quality, the plus of the spirit, as the next phase of film history when the present interlude of gimmickry has phased itself out.

It is priority for quality which we can expect from a young director like Mamoun Hassan who has grown up with this revolution in film thinking.

"Audiences," he says, "have not used up all their feelings. That is not why they are drifting away from the cinema. But they have become blasé about films which substitute excitement for feeling."

And then he may surprise you by saying that he likes to think of himself as an educator; but he does not mean that he wants to instruct, but to *share* with others what he knows. The new commitment, he says, is for a director to deal with what he knows.

For instance, he himself feels a great poignancy in the situation of the citizen who has to choose whether or not to become involved in the issues of our time. Most of us feel indignation when we hear of injustice, but dare we go further and accept some responsibility of being our brother's defender? It is something Hassan knows; and he also knows that for him *poetry means being involved*.

His new films, then, will be about questions of sincerity. A man has a change of heart; but how genuine is it? how long will it last? Such problems are of deep concern to all of us, and are inexhaustible in dramatic presentation; and they could be adult films now that we no longer rule out any area of life as a "non-subject".

Yes, the new films must be made by directors who would stand to lose in spiritual terms if the film failed.

One of the first marks of such films, Mamoun Hassan suggests, will be the recovery of the image disciplined by narrative sense. Tomorrow's directors should no longer have to fret about some proof that film is an art form; they will be able to take this for granted, and they will be free to get on with making films *in order to share something valuable*. They will tell us that if we fall in love on the last day of this threatened world, it will still be the best day of our lives.

If Hassan is typical of the new generation of directors waiting to take over – and I believe he is – then indeed we can all be optimistic. My one hope is that by the time this appears in print, Hassan will have started on his first feature film, one to show us that films could become the sun-lamps of the soul, and that commitment in sincerity is the magic for holding audiences who have found that "entertainment" does not necessarily mean being trivial.

The poster advertising Warner Brothers' film *The Jazz Singer*.

POSTERS AND CREDITS
by Ralph Stephenson

"Good wine needs no bush", but at the same time "It pays to advertise". In a nutshell we have the case for and against the publicity salesman, the ad-man, the hard, the soft, the medium sell. In the past in many artistic fields, the salesman has been regarded as a necessary evil, or, going further, a sort of "hard-to-get" or "hard-to-understand" publicity has been operated, sometimes enabling the artist to sell to a minute public at astronomical prices. But not with the cinema – here it has always been the big drum, the showman, the crescendo of adjectives – the best, the most, the greatest. Stunts, leaflets, personal appearances, scandals, sob-stories, gala premières, diamond necklaces, fabulous salaries, X-certificates – anything that might hit the headlines, catch the public imagination, and sell the picture, has been the order of the day. The publicity budget, often running into many figures, has been a feature of pretty well every motion picture that has set the cameras rolling, from the days of *Intolerance* onwards. So publicity is important, and here we look at two elements in the publicity set-up – film credits and film posters.

In the very early days, the people who worked on motion pictures – actors and actresses, directors, cameramen, film editors, musicians, make-up men (and women), set designers, costumiers and the rest – were anonymous. Nameless folk artists, as unknown as the decorators of early porcelain or the composers of border ballads. The producers of motion pictures, the production companies, the film studios, were quite content to have it that way. The company's name headed the picture, often its only identification mark, the company sold it, or showed it themselves to the public, and the less the public cared about the individual film-makers, the less their reputation, then the weaker their bargaining position vis-à-vis their employers. For this reason many studios at first opposed the star-system as it was called, though they came to accept it and exploit it to the limit in their own interest, when they saw that, as well as costing them more in salaries, it would bring vastly increased box-office revenues.

In the nature of things, it was the actors and actresses who broke through to public acclaim, and perhaps the early stars are still the most famous, since they are known to young and old alike, they are remote enough to have become legendary, yet there has not been time for their memory to fade – Lillian Gish, Mary Pickford, Rudolph Valentino, Greta Garbo, Charlie Chaplin, Buster Keaton. Faced with a love-affair between the public and popular film-stars which they could turn to advantage, the studios readily accepted the situation. However, other film-makers failed to obtain the same recognition, and to this day the film-going public will bother about only a handful of directors – Hitchcock, Bergman, Fellini, René Clair and a few others – and hardly knows more about cameramen, art directors, or sound engineers than it does about the parts of a computer.

It is not surprising then that the credits of a picture, the long list of names which appear at the beginning or end of every film, are simply a boring interruption to ninety per cent of the audience. Nevertheless they represent (especially in these days of contracts, agents, trade-unions and attempted fairness to all) what leading skilled film-makers justifiably expect as a return for the labour and expertise they put into making a picture. Just as much as a fee or salary or percentage, they want "their name on the picture", and it may be important for their career to have it included. The fact of getting their names on the screen, the order in which they appear, the length of time they are shown, the size of the letters – all may be the subject of written agreement, to be observed as carefully as precedence among VIPs on a ceremonial occasion.

The line has to be drawn somewhere, and extras, assistant technicians, lab men and the like do not expect to get their names on the screen. But the tendency seems to be for lists to get longer and longer, no doubt because more people are involved as film-making becomes more complex, and also because union or contractual requirements increase. In the case of minor figures sometimes so many names appear on the screen at once, it would be beyond the fastest reader's capacity to take them all in. One suspects that one purpose of including them is (like the "cast of thousands") to impress the audience with the scale of the picture. In *The Parade's Gone By* Kevin Brownlow wrote ". . . there are too many people connected with film production. The confusions surrounding credits are endless and even . . . the people who work on a picture may twist history to their own advantage." For many years film credits were a bare list of names, perhaps backed or trimmed with drawings or decorations, but in the last twenty years the presentation of credits has been transformed. Prior to the fifties the most notable credits seem to have been those of John P. Fulton (*Frankenstein*

THE CINEMA News and Property Gazette, Wednesday, March 4, 1936

2 PHENOMENAL
WEEKS AT RADIO
CITY MUSIC HALL

Braving the blizzards of the worst winter New York has known for decades, crowds packed the world's largest theatre and compelled a hold-over of "The Petrified Forest"

Read these reviews of the Hit which critics hailed as "seven times better than the average melodrama"

"Seven times better than the average melodrama. An excellent film, filled with excitement, humor and romance. Beautifully written, superbly acted, robust melodrama. There is an atmosphere of brilliant writing as well as excellent acting about every moment of it. Indeed the whole thing is played so richly, so rightly that the film emerges as a work of distinction."
—World-Telegram

"A production of most distinguished calibre. Tense, swift, hot melodrama and blazing action. This is perhaps, Mr. Howard's finest role."
—American

"Animate and vital. The Warners continue to display their skill at transcribing plays into film. With this excellent version of 'Ceiling Zero' scarcely out of the first running they now have wrought an entirely satisfactory screen edition of 'The Petrified Forest' one of the graces of the theatre last season."
—Times

"Returned from the Hollywood studios even more effective than when it left Broadway as a stage play."
—Sun

"Absorbing, brilliantly written, splendidly directed, handsomely produced."
—Mirror

For the fifth time this week

WARNER BROS
will prove their Leadership

PICCADILLY THEATRE
FRIDAY, MARCH 6 . . . . 8.45 p.m.

Cert. "A" • Released September 21

LESLIE
HOWARD • • DAVIS
BETTE
"The Petrified Forest"

With GENEVIEVE TOBIN • DICK FORAN • HUMPHREY BOGART • JOSEPH SAWYER • EDDIE ACUFF • CHARLEY GRAPEWIN   Directed by ARCHIE L. MAYO

Meets the Wolfman, 1943) and the spoken credits of Sacha Guitry who gave amusing comments on his co-workers, but they were like an oasis in the desert. Nowadays credits are shown combined with an original, mobile, graphic design which suits the style or mood of the picture, or else they appear against a film background, a scene which serves as a prelude to the story proper. Sometimes the director moves straight into the story, then when the audience is involved and interested, the credits follow. An attempt to introduce better credits was made in the early fifties by Paul Julian of UPA, but he failed to make an immediate breakthrough (though he later designed credits for Corman's films and Vadim's *Barbarella*), and the first artist to transform this aspect of cinema was Saul Bass. Bass was born in 1920, was an art student at Brooklyn College and a freelance graphic designer from 1952. His first credits were for *Carmen Jones*, director Otto Preminger. Bass was always inventive, had a splendid eye for design, and his credits were something new in film history. Through the fifties and sixties he led the way and a list of *his* credits reads like a roll-call of the most successful movies – *The Man With the Golden Arm*,

The poster advertising *The Petrified Forest*.

The Big Knife, The Seven Year Itch, Storm Centre, Saint Joan, Bonjour Tristesse, The Pride and the Passion, Around the World in 80 Days, The Big Country, Vertigo, Anatomy of a Murder, North by North-West, Spartacus, Exodus, Psycho, West-Side Story, Advise and Consent, Walk on the Wild Side, The Victors, Bunny Lake is Missing, Seconds, Grand Prix. Others followed, and other artists who have designed fine credits, to name the most important only, are Irving Reis (*The Bedspread*), Richard Fleischer (*The Vikings*), Depatie-Freleng (*The Pink Panther, Sex and the Single Girl*), Robert Brownjohn (*From Russia With Love, Goldfinger*), Ronald Searle (*Those Magnificent Men in their Flying Machines*), Saul Steinberg (*The Trouble with Harry*), Robert Freeman (*A Hard Day's Night, The Knack, Help!* all directed by Richard Lester), Maurice Binder (*Doctor No, Repulsion, Two for the Road, The Billion Dollar Brain*), Jean Fouchet (*Topkapi, The Longest Day*), Richard Kuhn (*Love with the Proper Stranger, Tokyo Olympiad, Our Man Flint, Quick Before it Melts*). The style of credits has varied enormously and Saul Bass and other artists have used graphic design, animation and photography. Special mention should be made of animation which lends itself to this work, and may range from Alexandre Alexeieff's austere credits for Orson Welles's *The Trial* from Kafka's novel, to Dick Williams's period drawings for *The Charge of the Light Brigade* which, with their images of Britannia, Turkey and the Russian Bear, brilliantly guyed the political cartoons of the time. Some of the artists mentioned in the previous paragraph are also animators, but none has been more fertile

than Dick Williams whose feature credits include *What's New Pussycat?, A Funny Thing Happened on the Way to the Forum, The Liquidator* and *Every Home Should Have One*.

The last word on credits must go to a neat little Yugoslav cartoon by Borivoj Dovnikovic called *Bes Naslova (Without Credits)*. An important little man comes on screen to make an announcement, introduce an act, sing, recite, play – exactly what we never know because he never gets started. Before he can open his mouth he is interrupted by rows of credits which sail in from the side of the screen, drop from the ceiling, spring up from the floor. He dodges them, pushes at them, tries to hold them back, growing all the time crosser and crosser. But they come crowding in, endless names, more and more unlikely jobs – deputy continuity assistant, wig research adviser – until at last, fed up, disgusted, defeated, the little man stamps off and *The End* comes up on the screen. Film posters are another feature of motion picture publicity which has undergone a transformation in recent years. Poster art is one of this century's achievements, the pioneers being Toulouse-Lautrec, Aubrey Beardsley, and Lorca, one of the exponents of *art nouveau*. The recruiting posters of the First World War were famous, as also were Bubbles, He-won't-be-happy-till-he-gets-it, and His-Master's-Voice. *Art deco* poster artists of the twenties were Gesmar, Kiffer, Carlu and Cassandre using aggressive Bauhaus lettering and modified cubist influence, and in this country there were McKnight Kauffer and Ashley Havinden. At about the same time Russian posters were celebrated for their bold, imaginative composition and forceful impact. Later

34 London Transport produced a series of delightful, light-hearted posters by leading artists, and many industrial firms (Guinness, Shell, etc.) became known for the humour or quality of their poster advertising.

Where did the cinema stand in this field? It seems extraordinary that for many years cinema posters made a comparatively poor showing. Not only were motion pictures considered one of the visual arts, but one would have thought it important to display artistic, well-designed posters to attract larger audiences. However, the fact remains that for many years the average film poster was unexciting and unoriginal, and nowadays it is an unrewarding experience to thumb through a glossy volume reproducing Hollywood's poster image of the thirties. One can find reasons why cinema posters were slow to develop as an art form in their own right. The cinema sprang from the theatre and, as with the theatre bill, the important thing was to get the star's name and image across to the public in the biggest print and largest image possible; how crudely or finely this was done was a secondary consideration. To head the bill was as important for an actor in a film as in a play, and, as in the case of credits, the order of names and size of letters was often a matter of contractual obligation. The cinema had an additional problem in the number of names which had to be displayed, and which interfered with, or distracted from or blemished, the graphic composition of the poster as a whole. Also in the palmy days of the movies, audiences flocked to the picture-palaces, and there was no pressing need to study new or better means of attracting them. Then too, top cinema executives were go-getting types, lacking the most refined taste, and the mixed-up architectural styles of the picture-palaces matched the stereotyped, muddled style of the film posters. Early film posters in fact compare favourably with those of the cinema's most prosperous era.

Another factor affecting film posters was the attempt to use photography or an imitation of photography, in an art medium which was not suited to it. It was natural perhaps to think of the poster as an extension of the film itself, but it is in fact an entirely different medium and requires a different approach and different treatment. The luminosity, the subtle chiaroscuro, the natural depth and relief of the photograph, are unobtainable by lithography and printing. Instead, bold composition; strong colouring or powerful black-and-white; freedom in modifying natural shapes and proportions in imaginative ways so as to reinforce the impact; flat figures and landscapes, or even distortion, or exaggeration of natural perspective – these are the qualities that make effective poster work, as early poster artists instinctively realised.

In the cinema there were a few outstanding individual posters, as for instance the striking black-and-white design (with strong distortion of perspective) for the first sound feature, *The Jazz Singer* starring Al Jolson. But for many years the average poster for advertising motion pictures carried poor likenesses of the leading players taken from photographs which lost all their quality in the printing process and were given in monochrome or muddy half-tints, garnished with a tasteless sauce of badly-designed lettering.

After the Second World War there came a fresh impetus from Eastern Europe. Notably in Poland from 1946, three eminent graphic artists, Tadeusz Trepkowski, Henryk Tomaszewski and Eryk Lipinski, gave a new look to film advertising, their work flourished and was carried on by a new generation – which included the animators Jan Lenica and Walerian Borowczyk. In the fifties and sixties Polish film posters have achieved a world reputation and are sought by collectors everywhere. They expressed, according to one writer, "a new poetry of the film poster". In Germany at a later date, artists followed with bold, striking designs, and in other countries standards have gradually improved. Here we have had film posters by Felix Topolski, Osbert Lancaster and Edmund Bawden, and the general level now stands comparison with work in other fields. No single individual has achieved the same outstanding reputation as Saul Bass in the field of credits, but a number of talented graphic artists have contributed, and the policy of distribution companies and exhibitors is more liberal and aware.

In the end we come back to our original two quotations – "It pays to advertise" and "Good wine needs no bush", and the fact that the two are complementary as well as contradictory. It is all very well to say that the important thing is the body of the picture on the screen, and that other matters – posters, credits, press advertising, cinema buildings – are of relatively little import. It is equally true to say that one aspect will have an influence on the other, and an improvement in the external image of motion pictures reflects, and can help to sustain, an improvement in the quality of the films themselves. To some extent the cinema will have the publicity it deserves.

DUTCH CINEMA

A Survey of Holland's Film Industry
by Peter Cowie

A scene from Frans Zwartjes's film *Home Sweet Home*.

Scenes from Hattum Hoving's film *Sailing*.

Scenes from Bert Haanstra's *The Voice of the Water – De Stem van het Water*.

In an age of specialists, the Dutch cinema shares supremacy with Canada in the short film field. International awards are won by the dozen every year (Bert Haanstra alone has over sixty), and few countries enjoy such a broad-minded and generous system of sponsorship as far as films are concerned. But of course shorts tend, like aperitifs, to be forgotten after the main fare in art cinema and film society programmes, and so to the casual moviegoer this Dutch industry is relatively unknown. It has no Bergman or Buñuel to make it fashionable, no "New Wave", and no world-renowned film school like FAMU in Czechoslovakia. Yet within these limitations, the achievement of the Netherlands has been extraordinary.

Even in Holland itself a home-grown film is often viewed with derision. The Dutch laugh when they hear their own throaty language coming from the screen. They believe that films, like cars and watches, are best imported from abroad. The population of the Netherlands is too widely dispersed. There are too many cities and too much ancient prejudice among them. Calvinism still colours national life and attitudes more than dikes or tulips do, and experiment in the arts is looked on with suspicion by the bulk of Dutchmen. Young directors in recent years have tried with might and main to elevate Dutch cinema into a feature film industry. But their efforts have failed. The reason? Partly a lack of good script-writers. Partly a lack of experience at producer level. But primarily the absence of a long film tradition, for Holland (unlike Sweden, for example) has never been cut off from the flow of foreign product, never forced, cinematically, to subsist on her own. Only the short films have been able to

leapfrog such problems. The classics among them – Bert Haanstra's *Glass*, Hattum Hoving's *Sailing*, John Ferno's *Sky over Holland* – have dispensed with commentary, relying instead on an infinitely subtle blend of sound and image that can be appreciated in any country and at any time. Not surprisingly, Dutch directors are probably the finest film editors in the world.

The man who really began this search for perfection was Joris Ivens. Like Robert Flaherty and Pare Lorentz (with both of whom he collaborated), Ivens was a visionary, fascinated by man's ability continually to adapt himself to nature's capricious demands. He was the chronicler *par excellence* (in *New Earth* and *Zuiderzee*) of the Dutch campaign against the sea, and this involvement in man's struggles led him in later years to become a tireless challenger of Fascism, whether in Spain (*Spanish Earth*) or China (*400 Millions*). Ivens, unlike most Dutch film-makers, has been a nomad by instinct, and has completed documentaries in over a dozen lands. His style has a rigour that has distinguished the best Dutch films ever since. The structure that he used in *Rain* (1929) – situation, incident, return to *status quo ante* – has been followed frequently in recent years in such Dutch shorts as *Sunday Sun* (Jan van der Hoeven) and *Aqua di Roma* (by Boud Smit).

Bert Haanstra remains a father figure for even the angriest and most frustrated of the young directors in Holland. While obviously a documentarist at heart, and a skilful exponent of the "hidden camera" technique, Haanstra has brought to his work a distinctive combination of warmth, candour, and amusement. He has a profound

and vigorous respect for man's capacity for sadness, gaiety, individuality, and self-sufficiency. Early successes like *Mirror of Holland* (1950) and *Panta rhei* (1951) revealed a natural rhythm in his style. The succession of self-portraits blending into each other in *Rembrandt* (1956) and the symphony of processes described in *Glass* (1958) are among the purest sequences in all documentary. *Glass* won an Academy Award for Haanstra and has been released in over 1,500 prints throughout the world. During the Sixties he completed two full-length studies of life in the Netherlands: *The Human Dutch* and *The Voice of the Water*, both composed of variegated impressions and sentiments by no means limited to the Netherlands.

Herman van der Horst, the other portal figure of postwar Dutch cinema, lacks the smiling approach to life that makes Haanstra's work so appealing, but his best films – *Steady!*, *Pan*, and *Amsterdam* – have adroitly integrated people into a landscape and a way of life and, especially in his North Sea fishing documentaries, into a dynamic communion with the water that recalls Grierson's *Drifters*.

The Ministry of Culture and Recreation in The Hague has been an enormous bulwark for these men and for scores of other talented directors since the war. Each year, on the basis of recommendations from the Arts Council Film Committee, it grants up to £1 million solely to finance films to be shot by independent directors. Even the much-maligned feature films are aided similarly, by a Production Fund to which both the government and the Netherlands Cinema League contribute handsomely. The Films Division of the Netherlands Government

38 and Information Service concerns itself with the sale and promotion of the shorts, and literally thousands of prints are currently in circulation among commercial distributors and educational establishments outside Holland.

Even if a film-maker cannot convince the Arts Council of the worthiness of his project, he can often turn to one of the country's enlightened sponsors – KLM, for example, or Shell, or Philips – or try to pre-empt an international audience by shooting in English (as Pim de la Parra and Wim Verstappen have done with their "Scorpio" films). Nearly all the principal directors have their own production facilities, whether they be in discreet

Bert Haanstra directing one of his films.

terraced houses overlooking the canals of Amsterdam, or in a secluded garden like Haanstra's, far from the main cities. Although the early seventies have not produced a new "school" of directional talents, there are some film-makers of considerable interest. Among these individualists, Frans Zwartjes is the most unusual. Shooting his black-and-white pictures for as little as £50, handling every detail of the production himself, and using his wife and friends as actresses, he has established an instantly recognisable world of guilt and desire, frustration and claustrophobia, leavened with a Bunuelian wit. There is no dialogue in his short films, but music (composed by Zwartjes) plays a vital role, controlling the rhythm and even the visual patterns of each film. In his latest short, *Through the Garden*, he seems to break free of his interior fantasies, to conclude on a note of liberation as he scampers around his orchard in speeded-up motion, as if, like Méliès, he were discovering the cinema for the first time, and communicates his joy in vivid filmic terms. Hattum Hoving, known the world over for *Sailing*, has released another extraordinary short, *Light*, in 1971. Taking its cue from Haydn's *Creation* music, it celebrates Man's absorption in and by light. Hoving catches in a montage of brilliant colour visuals the elusive, yet all-pervasive function of light in life, light natural and light artificial.

Paul Verhoeven's *The Wrestler* is that rarity, a successful short-story film. Shot in colour in the town of Gouda, it tells of a father who finds out that his son is relating, so to say, with the wife of a massive wrestler. A "fixed" match takes place, with ironic results. This film is neat and unpretentious, and is scripted by Kees Holierhoek, potentially one of the few genuine "film writers" in Dutch cinema.

Jan Oonk's *The Marble* uses a fish-eye lens to achieve comic effects as a small boy pursues his favourite marble on a scooter through town and country. Fluent and amusing, it has that dimension of wish-dreaming that children appreciate so much. And another recent film about a little boy, *Five Candles*, is just as imaginative, sidestepping coyness and sentimentality as it describes a lonely old lady's encounter with a boy who has just flung a ball through her drawing-room window. She is charmed by his candour, he by her eagerness to believe in him. The barriers between youth and age merge with deceptive ease in this first film by two men from outside the cinema field, Walt Verwey and Leighton D. Gage.

For all the cries of woe, then, the Dutch cinema persists. Bert Haanstra, credited with some of the best early scenes in Jacques Tati's *Trafic*, is immersed in a complex film about the resemblances between animal and human behaviour. He has already been on location in Tanzania, and is presently visiting Antarctica, Panama, and even the Galapagos. The result, he promises, will not be just another nature film, but a profound, entertaining inquiry into the theories of Lorenz, Morris and other ethologists. Then Fons Rademakers's feature-length drama, *Mira*, was selected for Cannes in 1971, and Han van Gelder's *Adventures in Perception*, a vivid guide to the graphic world of the artist Escher, is busily touring the festivals. When all is said and done, the Dutch cinema has yielded much more than its modest talents care to admit.

THE DAY OF THE CASSETTE IS NIGH

by David Heisler,
Audio Visual Editor,
Central Press Features.

Ever since the advent of television it has been realised that this medium of entertainment and information suffers one severe disability; it cannot provide a full personal choice of viewing.

When you switch on you can only watch programmes chosen by the network you are tuned in to. Specialist programmes about your favourite hobbies like angling, watching great movies or tinkering about with your car are usually broadcast at inconvenient times or are not made at all.

But the situation is to be completely changed.

By this time next year the era of the videocassette (a cartridge containing a film programme with a soundtrack) and the videodisc (a record with sound and pictures) will be upon us.

Development of this new medium has been taking place over the past ten years in the laboratories of some of the world's leading electrical concerns.

And the principle is simple. A player about the size of a tape recorder is connected to any domestic television set by a thin cable which is plugged into the TV aerial socket.

A cassette or disc on any subject is easily fitted on to or into the player and when it is switched on the very programme you have chosen appears on the TV screen.

Variety

By the end of this year there will be three major systems available in this country. The first will be the EVR player, which will cost £360 and is being made by the Rank Bush Murphy organisation.

The actual cassettes are being supplied by a plant built at a cost of £3,000,000 at Basildon, Essex, which can produce 1,000,000 a year.

The American Ampex company is introducing its £400 Instavideo system soon after and a camera to record programmes will be sold as an extra.

Then, during winter Philips of Holland, will be selling their machines, which will cost about £250 and will have a recording capability.

Next year the Decca radar and record group will be introducing its Teldec videodisc. This it has developed jointly with Telefunken, the West German electrical giant.

All the cassettes can play for 60 minutes and initially will be expensive. Depending on whether they carry programmes or are virgin – ready to be recorded on to – they each will cost from £5 to £35.

But the videodisc, which can only play for up to 15 minutes, is not expected to cost more than an ordinary LP record, and its player, which can take up to two hours of programme, will only cost about £100.

And in 1973, the American RCA Corporation say, they will have a £170 machine for sale. It will use a vinyl tape cassette (made of the material used to wrap meat in supermarkets) and the programmes will be very cheap.

Preparation

Throughout the world libraries of old and original programmes are being built up to meet the expected demands of the new product.

David Frost is a director of the international Optronics library organisation, which has acquired the cassette and videodisc rights to more than 7,000 programmes.

The Avco Embassy concern, which is

40 limiting the sales of its Cartrivision system (a television set with a built in cassette unit) to North America, is building up a library which eventually will allow its customers to have a choice of more than 1,000 feature film titles on cassettes.

Entertainers like the Rolling Stones and Judy Collins have been asked to make special programmes for this system.

The major film companies including MGM, Twentieth Century-Fox and Columbia, are estimated to have between them 30,000 to 40,000 old films with a cassette value; and have been approached by the makers of various systems to let them be used by the new medium.

At the same time there are many sceptics who predict demand will mainly be for completely original programmes.

Sir Lew Grade, deputy chairman and chief executive of the independent television company, Associated Television (ATV) is one who thinks this will be the case.

He has negotiated a production agreement with one of America's big three television networks, ABC, to establish jointly a cassette programme making and marketing company and he says that ATV is willing to spend $40,000,000 (£16,640,000) on these programmes.

About a dozen production companies have sprung up to make programmes for cassette and in America some 60 organisations have committed themselves to supplying programmes to the various systems.

Singer Tony Bennett has made a pilot film for cassette featuring himself, and comedians Dick Martin and Dan Rowan have made cassette programmes which are being distributed to hospitals and hotels.

Later this year Management Agency and Music (MAM), a talent agency, which numbers among its clients Tom Jones and Engelbert Humperdinck, is expected to establish a cassette production company.

Promotion

Many big names in industry and commerce have associated themselves in the promotion of the new aid.

The Penguin Longmans book publishing group has tied up with the Crown Agents of London, a supplier of aid, finance and skills to developing countries, and a finance house to form Crown Cassette Communications. This company will make and market programmes. And W. H. Smith, the news shop chain, has established a division simply to deal with the distribution of the yet unmarketed idea. European interest is great too and Smith's is a member of a Continental cassette and disc handling consortium, made up of some of this region's leading publishing wholesalers.

The future

The United Kingdom is almost certainly going to be one of the big four world markets for the product.

But it is feared that public enthusiasm will be dampened by the following factors. There is no interchangeability in the design of the rival cassettes, unlike the situation with the audio-cassettes used in millions of portable tape recorders.

And non-industrial or business users may have to pay a purchase tax of $36\frac{2}{3}$ per cent. For these reasons the manufacturers are first supplying their players to education and industry, and already half a dozen education authorities in the North of England and the Midlands have ordered EVR versions.

Even with all these problems, market researchers show that by the end of 1975, there will be between 150,000 and 200,000 players of all types in use throughout the country.

In America, where about half a million machines are likely to be sold in 1975, the television companies are worrying that audiences will prefer to watch cassettes rather than their programmes.

Here, social changes occur more slowly and the idea of this happening is only regarded as a far-off bad dream by TV executives. What will the effect of the new medium be? An indication of things to come is the situation current in Tokyo.

There, cinema owners are complaining of unfair competition from tea parlours and hotels, who have installed professional videotape recorders (as used in television studios) which are connected to television sets.

On these are shown "pink" films; better known in Britain as blue movies.

SHAKESPEARE ON THE SCREEN

by Ivan Butler

Douglas Fairbanks and Mary Pickford in the original, silent film of *The Taming of the Shrew*.

Watching "Shakespeare" on a silent screen is like watching a silent film of an orchestra playing a Beethoven symphony – and about as much can be gained from either. Take away the text, and all that remains are the plots – which were not his anyway – and the mouthings and posturing of dumb actors (though a faint shadow of the beauty and dignity of Forbes-Robertson's *Hamlet* could be momentarily glimpsed). "Shakespeare on the Silent Screen" is therefore a contradiction in terms: if it's silent, it isn't Shakespeare. However, for the sake of completeness the following brief list of some of the more important productions is included (over 300 silent films in all were made of the plots Shakespeare himself borrowed for his plays).

1899
One of the first – probably the actual first – piece of filmed "Shakespeare" – a scene from Beerbohm Tree's stage production of *King John*.

1900
Sarah Bernhardt in the duel scene from *Hamlet*, photographed in France by Clément Maurice.

1905
"A Duel Scene" from *Macbeth*, photographed by D. W. Griffith's famous cameraman Billy Bitzer.

1908
The flood begins. *The Taming of the Shrew* (directed by D. W. Griffith with Florence Lawrence) from Biograph: *As You Like It*, from Kalem: *Romeo and Juliet* (with Florence Lawrence and Paul Panzer), *The Merchant of Venice, Antony and Cleopatra, Julius Caesar, Richard III, Macbeth, Othello*, all one-reelers directed by W. V. Ranous, from Vitagraph. "The most

42 powerful effusion of Shakespeare's genius," said a contemporary poster of *Richard III*.

1909
King Lear and *A Midsummer Night's Dream* (Maurice Costello, *Lysander*; Gladys Hulette, *Puck*) from Vitagraph. A series of tableaux from Sir Frank Benson's production of *Richard III*.

1910
Twelfth Night from Vitagraph (Charles Kent, *Malvolio*; Julia Swayne Gordon; Marin Sais).

1911
Romeo and Juliet from Thanhouser.

1912
As You Like It from Vitagraph (Maurice Costello; James Young; Robert Gaillard; Leo Delaney; Rose Coghlan, *Rosalind*; Rose Tapley; James Morrison). *The Merchant of Venice* from Thanhouser (Harry Benham; Florence La Badie).

1913
Sir Johnston Forbes-Robertson's *Hamlet* – one of the most famous silent records of a Shakespearean performance. Directed by Hay Plumb, produced by Cecil Hepworth, decor by Hawes Craven. Sir Johnston Forbes-Robertson, *Hamlet*; Walter Ringham, *Claudius*; S. A. Cookson, *Horatio*; J. H. Barnes, *Polonius*; Alexander Scott-Gatty, *Laertes*; Percy Rhodes, *Ghost*; Montague Rutherford, *Rosencrantz*; E. A. Ross, *Guildenstern*; Robert Atkins, *First Player*; Gertrude Elliott, *Ophelia*; Adeline Bourne, *Gertrude*. The film cost £10,000, and ran about 80 minutes. *Richard III* from Sterling, with Frederick Warde.

1914
Julius Caesar, an Italian spectacular, with Antony Novelli as *Marc Antony*. (This is probably the production in which Brutus turns out to be Caesar's son.)

1916
Macbeth, from Triangle, with Beerbohm Tree and Constance Collier. *King Lear* from Thanhouser, with Frederick Warde, *Lear*; Lorraine Huling, *Cordelia*; Boyd Marshall. Two rival *Romeo and Juliets*: from Metro with Francis X. Bushman, *Romeo*; Beverly Bayne, *Juliet*; Albert Cummings, *Friar Laurence*; John Davidson, *Paris*: and from Fox, with Harry Hilliard, *Romeo*; Theda Bara, *Juliet*; Alice Gale; John Webb Dillon; Edwin Holt; Helen Tracy. Several one-reel versions also appeared.

1923
Othello from Germany with Emil Jannings, *Othello*; Lya de Putti, *Desdemona*; Werner Krauss, *Iago*. Asta Nielsen's feminine *Hamlet* is included here solely because of its fame – a Danish production, silent, based not on the play but on Nordic legends, wherein Hamlet actually turns out to be a woman, can hardly be called filmed "Shakespeare", even in inverted commas.

Thereafter, the rest was silence.

1928
John Barrymore recited a few lines from *Richard III* (standing on a mound of bodies before a lurid backcloth) in, of all things, an all-star, all-singing, all-talking, all-dancing Warner Brothers revue, *The Show of Shows*. This was the first glimpse of Shakespeare, as opposed to "Shakespeare", on the screen – and also the only memorable moment in that mish-mash.

1929
The Taming of the Shrew. The first complete Shakespearean film. The unfortunate credit "Additional dialogue by Sam Taylor" has roused immoderately jeering laughter ever since – in truth it was insignificant and inoffensive. The *Observer* said at the time: "Before we make superior noises of disgust let us remember that the business of 'pepping up' Shakespeare is an old English industry." The film was on the whole a reasonable effort, and deserves a kinder memory, in spite of being an unfortunate choice, perhaps, for the only film in which Mary Pickford appeared together with her (then but not much longer) husband, Douglas Fairbanks. He was, apparently, extremely difficult during its production. The approach to the play assumed that Katherina gathered what Petruchio was up to, and fell in with it to humour him. Director, Sam Taylor. Photography, Karl Struss. With Douglas Fairbanks, *Petruchio*; Mary Pickford, *Katherina*; Edwin Maxwell, *Baptista*; Joseph Cawthorn, *Gremio*; Geoffrey Wardwell, *Hortensio*; Dorothy Jordan, *Bianca*.

1935
A Midsummer Night's Dream. Max Reinhardt's famous – or notorious – Shakespearean decoration, complete with orchestra of goblins. Directed in association with William Dieterle. Scenes were rearranged and vital passages cut – too much emphasis placed on the fairy element. The result, however, was often so beautiful to look at (e.g. the Dance of the Hands, by Bronislava Nijinska) that even the purist must forgive much. Young Mickey Rooney an engagingly impish Puck, and Victor Jory a notably imposing Oberon. Photography, Hal Mohr. With James Cagney, *Bottom*; Joe E. Brown, *Flute*; Hugh Herbert, *Snout*; Frank McHugh, *Quince*; Victor Jory,

A scene from the 1908 Vitagraph film of *Othello*.

James Cagney as Bottom in Warner's mid-thirties, Max Reinhardt version of *A Midsummer Night's Dream*.

44

A scene from Peter Hall's recent Royal Shakespearean Company's film of the same play.

Oberon; Anita Louise, *Titania*; Olivia de Havilland, *Hermia*; Ross Alexander, *Demetrius*; Grant Mitchell, *Egeus*; Verree Teesdale, *Hippolyta*; Dick Powell, *Lysander*; Jean Muir, *Helena*; Ian Hunter, *Theseus*; Mickey Rooney, *Puck*; Dewey Robinson, *Snug*; Otis Harlan, *Starveling*; Hobart Cavanagh, *Philostrate*.

1936

Romeo and Juliet. Directed by George Cukor. Text virtually untouched save for interpolations from other Shakespearean sources. Miss Shearer an extremely mature fourteen-year-old, and Leslie Howard over-age to match. Laurence Olivier is reported to have refused the part because "Shakespeare should never be filmed"! Photographer, William Daniels. Settings, Cedric Gibbons, Oliver Messel. With Leslie Howard, *Romeo*; Norma Shearer, *Juliet*; John Barrymore, *Mercutio*; Edna May Oliver, *Nurse*; Basil Rathbone, *Tybalt*; C. Aubrey Smith, *Capulet*; Reginald Denny, *Benvolio*; Ralph Forbes, *Paris*; Conway Tearle, *Prince of Verona*; Henry Kolker, *Friar Laurence*; Robert Warwick, *Montague*; Virginia Hammond, *Lady Montague*; Violet Kemble-Cooper, *Lady Capulet*.

1936

As You Like It. Directed by Paul Czinner. Performances superior (as a whole) to settings and directional innovations, to which both text and characters have been subordinated. Bergner, according to J. C. Trewin, a "coy and romping Rosalind". Photographer, Hal Rosson. Music, William Walton. With Elisabeth Bergner, *Rosalind*; Laurence Olivier, *Orlando*; Henry Ainley, *Exiled Duke*; Leon Quartermaine, *Jaques*; Felix Aylmer, *Frederick*; Austin Trevor, *Le Beau*; Stuart Robertson, *Amiens*;

Lionel Braham, *Charles*; John Laurie, *Oliver*; J. Fisher White, *Adam*; Mackenzie Ward, *Touchstone*; Aubrey Mather, *Corin*; Richard Ainley, *Sylvius*; Peter Bull, *William*; Sophie Stewart, *Celia*; Dorice Fordred, *Audrey*.

1944
Henry V. Probably the most famous of all Shakespearean films, the real breakthrough. Passes with ease from a realistic setting of the Globe Theatre (so entertaining one longed for more of it) to tapestry-inspired non-realistic scenery, to naturalism in the battle scenes, and back again. Frequently and deservedly revived. Directed by Laurence Olivier. Photographers, Robert Krasker, Jack Hildyard. Music, William Walton. With Laurence Olivier, *Henry V*; Robert Newton, *Ancient Pistol*; Leslie Banks, *Chorus*; Renee Asherson, *Princess Katherine*; Esmond Knight, *Fluellen*; Leo Genn, *Constable of France*; Felix Aylmer, *Archbishop of Canterbury*; Ralph Truman, *Mountjoy*; Nicholas Hannen, *Exeter*; Harcourt Williams, *Charles VI of France*; Robert Helpmann, *Bishop of Ely*; Freda Jackson, *Mistress Quickly*; Ivy St. Helier, *Alice*; Ernest Thesiger, *Duke of Berri*; Max Adrian, *The Dauphin*; Francis Lister, *Duke of Orleans*; Niall McGinnis, *MacMorris*; Valentine Dyall, *Burgundy*; George Robey, *Falstaff*; Russell Thorndike, *Bourbon*; Michael Warre, *Gloucester*; Janet Burnell, *Isabel of France*.

1946
Julius Caesar. Remarkable 16-mm. film made by a young North-Western University student, David Bradley (he had previously made a 16-mm. *Macbeth*) using actual Chicago locations. Notable also for the appearance of the young Charlton Heston as

Mark Antony. Music, John Becker. With David Bradley, *Brutus*; Grosvenor Glenn, *Cassius*.

1948
Hamlet. Second of Olivier's great trilogy. Done in black-and-white because, in Olivier's words, "I see *Hamlet* as an engraving rather than as a painting." Notable for massive castle setting. Rosencrantz and Guildenstern omitted, also Second Gravedigger and – unfortunately – Fortinbras, whose entrance at the end provides the vital "life goes on" close to the tragedy. Ophelia's suicide and the sea-battle visualised. Above all, a noble version. Photographer, Desmond Dickinson. Music, William Walton. With Laurence Olivier, *Hamlet*; Jean Simmons, *Ophelia*; Eileen Herlie, *Gertrude*; Basil Sydney, *Claudius*; Felix Aylmer, *Polonius*; Norman Woolland, *Horatio*; Terence Morgan, *Laertes*; Stanley Holloway, *Gravedigger*; Peter Cushing, *Osric*; Esmond Knight, *Bernardo*; Anthony Quayle, *Marcellus*; Harcourt Williams, *First Player*.

1948
Macbeth. Orson Welles's powerful, grim and brutal characterisation, non-bolstered by weak support. Bleeding Sergeant and much else cut. Macbeth's "pleasant seat" belies the description. Odd atmosphere of tribal Mongolia. Always to be remembered that Welles was disgracefully hampered by miserly budgets. Directed by Orson Welles. Photographer, John L. Russell. With Orson Welles, *Macbeth*; Jeanette Nolan, *Lady Macbeth*; Dan O'Herlihy, *Macduff*; Edgar Barrier, *Banquo*; Roddy McDowall, *Malcolm*; Erskine Sanford, *Duncan*; John Dierkes, *Ross*; Keene Curtis, *Lennox*; Peggy Webber, *Lady Macduff*; Laurence

Tuttle, Brainerd Duffield, Charles Lederer, *Witches*; Christopher Welles, *Macduff's son*; Morgan Farley, *Doctor*; George Chirello, *Seyton*.

1951
Othello. Equally powerful performance from Welles in curtailed but cinematically exciting version made partly in Morocco. Directed by Orson Welles. Photographers, Anchise Brizzi, G. R. Aldo, Georgo Fanto. With Orson Welles, *Othello*; Michéal MacLiammóir, *Iago*; Suzanne Cloutier, *Desdemona*; Robert Coote, *Roderigo*; Hilton Edwards, *Brabantio*; Michael Lawrence, *Cassio*; Fay Compton, *Emilia*; Nicholas Bruce, *Lodovico*; Jean Davis, *Montano*; Doris Dowling, *Bianca*.

1953
Julius Caesar. Memorable no-nonsense black-and-white version. Brando's performance very much a matter of personal taste – ten marks out of ten, or one, according to individual reaction. Mason, Gielgud and Calhern full marks without reserve. Directed by Joseph L. Mankiewicz. Photographer, Joseph Ruttenberg. Settings, Cedric Gibbons, Edward Carfagno. Music, Miklos Rozsa. With Marlon Brando, *Mark Antony*; James Mason, *Brutus*; John Gielgud, *Cassius*; Louis Calhern, *Caesar*; Edmond O'Brien, *Casca*; Greer Garson, *Calpurnia*; Deborah Kerr, *Portia*; George Macready, *Marullus*; Michael Pate, *Flavius*; Alan Napier, *Cicero*; John Hoyt, *Decius Brutus*; Tom Powers, *Metellus Cimber*; William Cottrell, *Cinna*; Jack Raine, *Trebonius*; Douglas Watson, *Octavius*.

1954
Romeo and Juliet. Great Britain/Italy edition, directed by Roberto Castellani. Unkindly received. Usual criticism of cuts

46 and interpolations: also, with much more reason, of dubbing of Italian players in smaller parts, even Mercutio! He was also cut to a sliver and deprived of Queen Mab speech. Juliet first seen being dried after a bath: "Now the other one," she says, putting out a foot. Visually beautiful. Photographer, Robert Krasker. Music, Roman Vlad. With Laurence Harvey, *Romeo*; Susan Shentall, *Juliet*; Flora Robson, *Nurse*; Mervyn Johns, *Friar Tuck*; Bill Travers, *Benvolio*; Sebastian Cabot, *Capulet*; Lydia Sherwood, *Lady Capulet*; Norman Woolland, *Paris*; Aldo Zollo, *Mercutio*.

1956
Richard III. The third "Olivier", and arguably the best of all. Certainly the most exciting, with superb cast, and Olivier himself a monument of evil magnificence. Only the battle scenes – save for his death – disappointing. Photographer, Otto Heller. Settings, Carmen Dillon. Music, William Walton. With Laurence Olivier, *Richard III*; John Gielgud, *Clarence*; Ralph Richardson, *Buckingham*; Cedric Hardwicke, *Edward IV*; Claire Bloom, *Lady Anne*; Mary Kerridge, *Queen Elizabeth*; Pamela Brown, *Jane Shore*; Alec Clunes, *Hastings*; Michael Gough, *Dighton*; Stanley Baker, *Henry Tudor*; Norman Woolland, *Catesby*; Helen Haye, *Duchess of York*; Patrick Troughton, *Tyrrell*; Clive Morton, *Rivers*; Andrew Cruickshank, *Brakenbury*.

1961
Macbeth. Maurice Evans and Judith Anderson in British film directed by George Schaefer. Oddly un-grim settings and atmosphere result in a strange lack of tragic stature. Described by one critic as "safe, tame, respectable" – fatal adjectives!

Final confrontation with witches turns out to be no more than a nasty dream. Photographer, Fred A. Young. Music, Richard Addinsell. With Maurice Evans, *Macbeth*; Judith Anderson, *Lady Macbeth*; Michael Hordern, *Banquo*; Ian Bannen, *Macduff*; Felix Aylmer, *Doctor*; Malcolm Keen, *Duncan*; William Hutt, *Ross*; Charles Carson, *Caithness*; Jeremy Brett, *Malcolm*; Megs Jenkins, *Gentlewoman*; Barry Warren, *Donalbain*; Trader Faulkner, *Seyton*; George Rose, *Porter*; Scot Finch, *Fleance*; Robert Brown, *Bloody Sergeant*; Valerie Taylor, Anita Sharpe Bolster, April Olrich, *Witches*; Michael Ripper, Douglas Wilmer, *Murderers*.

1965
Chimes at Midnight. Orson Welles's amalgamation of the two parts of *Henry IV* with emphasis on Falstaff, and extending to cover his death – seen as a parable of the decay of Merrie England. Poor technicalities such as the dubbing and post-synchronisation (mainly on account of lack of funds) do not materially diminish Orson Welles's fine and moving performance. Unsurpassed battle sequence. *Richard II*, *Henry V* and *The Merry Wives of Windsor* also drawn upon. Directed by Orson Welles. Photographer, Edmond Richard. Music, Angelo Lavagnino. With Orson Welles, *Falstaff*; John Gielgud, *Henry IV*, Keith Baxter, *Prince Hal*; Margaret Rutherford, *Mistress Quickly*; Jeanne Moreau, *Doll Tearsheet*; Norman Rodway, *Henry Percy*; Marina Vlady, *Kate Percy*; Alan Webb, *Justice Shallow*; Tony Beckley, *Poins*; Fernando Rey, *Worcester*; Walter Chiari, *Silence*; Michael Aldridge, *Pistol*; Beatrice Welles, *the Child*.

1966
The Taming of the Shrew. Famous Zeffirelli anti-purist knockabout. "Scriptwriters" Paul Dehn, D'Amico and Zeffirelli acknowledge debt to Shakespeare "without whom we would have been at a loss for words". Finely photographed (entirely in studio) by Oswald Morris and Luciano Trasatti. Feste's song from *Twelfth Night* shoved in. Music, Nino Rota. Settings, Giuseppe Mariani, Elvin Webb. With Richard Burton, *Petruchio*; Elizabeth Taylor, *Katherina*; Michael Hordern, *Baptista*; Cyril Cusack, *Grumio*; Michael York, *Lucentio*; Alfred Lynch, *Tranio*; Natasha Pyne, *Bianca*; Alan Webb, *Gremio*; Victor Spinetti, *Hortensio*; Mark Dignam, *Vicentio*; Giancarlo Cobelli, *Priest*; Roy Holder, *Biondello*; Alberto Bonucci, *Nathaniel*.

1966
Othello. Filmed record of Olivier's National Theatre performance. Powerful, very black Othello. Memorably good Iago from Frank Finlay. (His superb Brutus in a later televised *Julius Caesar* should be shown on a cinema screen.) Directed by Stuart Burge, from John Dexter's stage production. Photographer, Geoffrey Unsworth. With Laurence Olivier, *Othello*; Maggie Smith, *Desdemona*; Frank Finlay, *Iago*; Joyce Redman, *Emilia*; Derek Jacobi, *Cassio*; Robert Lang, *Roderigo*; Kenneth Mackintosh, *Lodovico*; Anthony Nicholls, *Brabantio*; Sheila Reid, *Bianca*; Harry Lomax, *Duke of Venice*.

1968
Romeo and Juliet. Zeffirelli's second go. Visually stunning. Two lovers for once really *young* make the whole thing credible and more than compensate for their

Yuri Jarvet playing the title-role in a USSR production of *King Lear* (1971).

Sir John Gielgud and Robert Vaughn in Peter Snell's production of *Julius Caesar*.

48 inadequacies (touching rather than ruinous, and in any case not so great as some critics declared) in speaking the verse. Not for a single instance could it be believed that Norma Shearer and Leslie Howard, for instance, or all the other mature Romeos and Juliets, would have let the family squabbling stand in their way. Photographer, Pasquale De Santis. Music, Nino Rota. With Leonard Whiting, *Romeo*; Olivia Hussey, *Juliet*; Milo O'Shea, *Friar Laurence*; Michael York, *Tybalt*; John McEnery, *Mercutio*; Pat Heywood, *Nurse*; Natasha Parry, *Lady Capulet*; Paul Hardwick, *Capulet*; Robert Stephens, *Prince of Verona*; Roberto Bisacco, *Paris*; Keith Skinner, *Balthazar*; Richard Warwick, *Gregory*; Bruce Robinson, *Benvolio*.

1968

The Winter's Tale. Filmed record of Edinburgh Festival production by Frank Dunlop. Interesting mainly as chance to see one of the less available plays. One or two good performances, but technically grade two – or even three. Photographer, Oswald Morris. Music, Jim Dale, Anthony Bowles. With Laurence Harvey, *Leontes*; Jane Asher, *Perdita*; Diana Churchill, *Paulina*; Moira Redmond, *Hermione*; Jim Dale, *Autolycus*; Esmond Knight, *Camillo*; Richard Gale, *Polixenes*; David Weston, *Florizel/Archidamas*; John Gray, *Clown*; Allan Foss, *Antigonus*; Cherry Morris, *Emilia*; Joy Ring, *Mopsa*; Joanna Wake, *Dorcas*; Terry Palmer, *Cleomines*; Frank Barry, *Mamillius*.

1969

A Midsummer Night's Dream. Peter Hall's controversial, witty and interesting production which accepts that Shakespeare actually meant what he said when he has Titania remark that her quarrel with Oberon has upset the order of the seasons. Shot, therefore, and with perfect logicality, during a period of rain. Opens with pleasantly impudent joke – façade of an eighteenth-century English mansion superimposed with the title ATHENS. Full value given, as might be expected, to the verse. Handheld camera becomes slightly trying, and post-synchronising inclined to flatten the voices: but it deserves much better treatment, critically and commercially, than it has so far received. Produced by Michael Birkett, directed by Peter Hall. Photographer, Peter Suschitzky. Music, Guy Woolfenden. With Derek Godfrey, *Theseus*; Barbara Jefford, *Hippolyta*; Hugh Sullivan, *Philostrate*; Nicholas Selby, *Egeus*; David Warner, *Lysander*; Michael Jayston, *Demetrius*; Diana Rigg, *Helena*; Helen Mirren, *Hermia*; Ian Richardson, *Oberon*; Judi Dench, *Titania*; Ian Holm, *Puck*; Paul Rogers, *Bottom*; Sebastian Shaw, *Quince*; Bill Travers, *Snout*; John Normington, *Flute*; Clive Swift, *Snug*; Donald Eccles, *Starveling*.

1969

Julius Caesar. A disappointment. Scenic pleasures do not compensate for a mangled and patchily performed text, despite Heston, Gielgud, Richard Johnson, Jill Bennett and – notably – Robert Vaughn. Biggest let-down is the Brutus of Jason Robards – a good actor looking acutely lost and unhappy. Cutting the text after the "noblest Roman of them all" is an unfortunate touch of irony. Directed by Stuart Burge. Photographer, Ken Higgins. Music, Michael Lewis. With Charlton Heston, *Mark Antony*; John Gielgud, *Julius Caesar*; Jason Robards, *Brutus*; Richard Johnson, *Cassius*; Robert Vaughn, *Casca*; Richard Chamberlain, *Octavius*; Jill Bennett, *Calpurnia*; Diana Rigg, *Portia*; Christopher Lee, *Artemidorus*; Andrew Crawford, *Volumnius*; David Dodimead, *Lepidus*; Alan Browning, *Marullus*; Peter Eyre, *Cinna the Poet*; André Morell, *Cicero*; Derek Godfrey, *Decius Brutus*; Edwin Finn, *Publius*; Norman Bowler, *Titinius*; Preston Lockwood, *Trebonius*; John Moffatt, *Popilius Lena*.

1969

Hamlet. Tony Richardson's film of his stage production, shot entirely in the ex-railway Round House, with general atmosphere of a smoke-grimed, red-brick Elsinore – mostly in the dark and with much close-up, a Queen who looks younger than her son and an invisible – but rather effective – Ghost. Anthony Hopkins a notable Claudius. Williamson's Hamlet powerful and often moving, but blighted at times by seemingly wilful vowel distortions with almost risible results. ("The point envenom'd TEW!") Ending again – unhappily – cut. Photographer, Gerry Fisher. With Nicol Williamson, *Hamlet*; Anthony Hopkins, *Claudius*; Judy Parfitt, *Gertrude*; Marianne Faithfull, *Ophelia*; Mark Dignam, *Polonius*; Michael Pennington, *Laertes*; Gordon Jackson, *Horatio*; Ben Aris, *Rosencrantz*; Clive Graham, *Guildenstern*; Peter Gale, *Osric*; Roger Livesey, *Gravedigger/Lucianus*; John Carney, *Marcellus/Player King*.

1970/1

King Lear. Paul Scofield's unforgettable Lear secured for posterity and for a wider audience than the theatre permits. Shot entirely on location in North Jutland, and photographed in black-and-white. The latter – an adventurous step in 1970 – was chosen by Peter Brook, the director, because he felt that in this instance colour would merely have provided unnecessary distraction, whereas black-and-white reduces what is on the screen to its essentials – particularly for powerful close-ups of the human face. Remembering, for instance, Dreyer's *Passion of Joan of Arc* and *Day of Wrath*, this seems incontestable. Director, Peter Brook. Photographer, Henning Kristiansen. Settings, Georges Wakhevitch. With Paul Scofield, *Lear*; Irene Worth, *Goneril*; Alan Webb, *Gloucester*; Tom Fleming, *Kent*; Patrick McGee, *Cornwall*; Cyril Cusack, *Albany*; Jack MacGowran, *Fool*; Susan Engel, *Regan*; Anne-Lise Gabold, *Cordelia*; Ian Hogg, *Edmund*; Robert Lloyd, *Edgar*; Barry Stanton, *Oswald*.

1971

Macbeth. Roman Polanski's eagerly awaited version, still in production at the time of writing. Adapted for the screen by the

on Finch in the title-role in Roman Polanski's new screen version of *Macbeth*.

50 director and Kenneth Tynan, with a younger Macbeth than usual. Location work in Wales and Northumberland. Photographer, Gilbert Taylor. Settings, Wilfrid Shingleton. With Jon Finch, *Macbeth*; Francesca Annis, *Lady Macbeth*; Martin Shaw, *Banquo*; Nicholas Selby, *Duncan*; John Stride, *Ross*; Stephan Chase, *Malcolm*; Paul Shelley, *Donalbain*; Terence Bayler, *Macduff*; Andrew Laurence, *Lennox*; Patricia Mason, *Gentlewoman*; Richard Pearson, *Doctor*; Sydney Bromley, *Porter*; Noelle Rimmington, Maisie MacFarquhar, Elsie Taylor, *Witches*.

Although this survey concentrates on Shakespeare filmed in the language in which he wrote, one or two foreign versions must be noted.

1955
The Taming of the Shrew. A Spanish adaptation with Carmen Sevilla and Alberto Closas.

1955
Othello. U.S.S.R. Later disastrously dubbed with an English cast doing their best against insuperable odds. Director, Sergei Yutkevich. With Sergei Bondarchuk (English – Howard Marion Crawford), *Othello*; Irina Skobtseva (Kathleen Byron), *Desdemona*; Andrei Popov (Arnold Diamond), *Iago*; Vladimir Soshalsky (Patrick Westwood), *Cassio*.

1958
A Midsummer Night's Dream. Czechoslovakian puppet film by Jiri Trnka. Visually enchanting, but English voices were – apparently not too successfully – dubbed in.

1964
Hamlet. U.S.S.R. Probably the most famous foreign-language version of any Shakespearean play. To describe Smoktunovsky as "the best of all Hamlets" (as has been done) is meaningless in an English context because it is impossible to judge his speech, but he looks and sounds good. Visually enthralling, and the best handling of the Ghost yet. Text heavily cut, and based on Pasternak's translation. Director, Grigori Kozintsev. With Innokenti Smoktunovsky, *Hamlet*; Michail Nazwanon, *Claudius*; Elza Radzin-Szolkonis, *Gertrude*; Anastasia Vertinskaya, *Ophelia*.

1965
Throne of Blood. A Japanese version of *Macbeth* which adopts the style of the Noh plays, without Shakespeare's text, transporting the story into mediaeval Japan and turning Macbeth into a samurai hardly qualifies as a "Shakespeare", let alone a Shakespeare, film, and is noted here solely because of the critical acclaim it has received. Director, Akira Kurosawa. With Toshiro Mifune as the Macbeth based character.

1971
King Lear. U.S.S.R. Not yet released. Location work at the Ivangorod fortress, built during the reign of Ivan the Terrible, with sets erected within its confines. Director, Grigori Kozintsev. Photographer, Jonas Gritsus. With Yuri Jarvet, *Lear*; Elsa Radzins, *Goneril*; Donatas Banionis, *Albany*; Regimantas Adomaitis, *Edmund*.

Excluded from the above filmography are the numerous films which include snippets of Shakespeare (e.g. Richard Burton's *Prince of Players*) and those vaguely based on "Shakespearean" plots, such as *Joe Macbeth*, *West Side Story*, *The Boys from Syracuse*, etc., etc.

A complete coverage of the subject is made in a new book by Roger Manvell, entitled *Shakespeare and Film*, to be published in the Autumn of 1971 by J. M. Dent.

For a full study of the silent period the reader is referred to Robert Hamilton Ball's *Shakespeare on Silent Film*. Edward Wagenknecht's *The Movies in the Age of Innocence* also contains interesting facts, and stills will be found in Daniel Blum's *Pictorial History of the Silent Screen*. Works on individual directors, such as Peter Cowie's *The Cinema of Orson Welles*, deal in fuller detail than is possible here with individual films, as do publications such as the British Film Institute's *Monthly Film Bulletin*. The *Journal of the Society of Film and Television Arts*, Autumn 1969, is devoted to Shakespeare on the screen, and a useful outline appears in Leslie Halliwell's *The Filmgoer's Companion*. The American magazine *Films in Review* ran two excellent and exhaustive articles in 1956 and 1969, though casting their nets, it may be thought rather wide: a story of Richard III "without Shakespearean dialogue" entitled *Tower of London* (with Boris Karloff), or *Forbidden Planet* "a superior sci-fi in which some discern parallels to *The Tempest*", hardly qualify for inclusion in "Shakespeare on the Screen".

The Way a Marriage is Arranged
Ned Sherrin, Carl Davis with
occasional interruptions by **John Mountjoy**

Composer Carl Davis.

52 I recall talking to Moira Lister about play production and, as an aside, mentioning the complete silence of the supporting cast throughout a courtroom-scene play *A Woman Named Anne* then at the Duke of York's, London. She responded by explaining a play's functioning composition and the dependence of each player upon the other. Hence the importance of these players' parts in confirming the courtroom's credibility. But not only them. There were invisible technicians. Other workmen, too. Her words came to my mind reading feature film credits and noting, as I always do, the name of the music man whose work supplied the background (in some movies it is almost the foreground) of the particular picture.

Music is very much part of a picture for me. It has often kept me in my cinema seat when I was otherwise tempted to leave. But I realised I had never wondered until then *how* the music I enjoyed got into the film I was watching.

The musicians surely could not be on the set out of sight? – their playing recorded as the actors acted. (How about a Western? They couldn't play on horseback!) In a large lorry, for instance, driven over mountain greenery or at speedtrack pace behind racing horses.

It all sounds silly when I read my conjectures on paper. But then, I am a starstruck picturegoer! Viva Raquel Welch! Which is why I asked Ned Sherrin, now producing pictures as continually as a devout Irish wife delivers babies, and Carl Davis, composer, conductor and piano player.

Mr. Sherrin, at the time we talked, had just finished his first "Up" film. He was already casting the second and producing another picture in between. I fancy the "Up" series was encouraged by the phenomenal box office success of the "Carry On" series started B.C. (or so it often seems!) by Peter Rogers. First "Up" is *Up Pompeii*; the second, *Up the Chastity Belt*. After that, you are as wise as me. I can only murmur "Up Ned Sherrin" – only because he said what I think sounds sense.

Carl Davis was knee deep in scores for a Mermaid Theatre, London, musical. He, too, had just finished *Up Pompeii* and an absolute contrast in depth for *I, Monster*, a British Lion blood-curdler with Peter Cushing and Christopher Lee. He was waiting on *Up the Chastity Belt*.

Carl comes from New York. He lives and works in a Battersea flat – fully equipped for all the mechanics of movie music making. Framed in Cranks Restaurant, London, doorway he looked like "I, Monster", which I quickly found hadn't rubbed off on him. Mr. Sherrin was correct. "You'll find him immensely witty. And you will hear some of his wit in his *Up Pompeii* music."

Mr. Sherrin says that music is an important constituent in a film's impact, in its success as a picture production – not to be confused with cinema receipts. But he also argues that it shouldn't *seem* important. The moment it seems useful to the story, it is probably being too useful. Some music must be rather frustrating for composers because although it contributes to the picture, it might (perhaps *must*) not be noticed. But it certainly audibly and undeniably performs an almost co-starring role in romantic cinema.

Movie music certainly shouldn't be wallpaper music. If there is no essential need for it, then don't have it, he says. I certainly wouldn't. When a director does he confesses, in effect, that he is unsure about his finished job.

Mr. Sherrin used a theme march by Ray Davis of The Kinks for *The Virgin Soldiers* and John Cameron's music for *Every Home Should Have One*. Cameron, a clever jazz musician, has a tremendous sense of humour and Mr. Sherrin opined that one was constantly aware that his music heightened the story joke.

Carl saw *Up Pompeii* as a comic strip with persons who played one line which rarely varied. Michael Hordern is a bumbling senator, his wife, frivolous and silly, their daughter and son, equally so, and so on. Characters follow the TV series in the main, though not the players. They are Barbara Murray, Lance Percival, Patrick Cargill, Adrienne Posta, Bill Fraser, Royce Mills, Madeline Smith, Bernard Bresslaw, Roy Hudd, Julie Ege, Laraine Humphreys, Ian Trigger, and Aubrey Woods.

Carl chose an appropriate instrument for the principal players. Every time they appear they are preceded by their instrument's sound in corresponding theme. Happy or unhappy, fearful or bold. Frankie Howerd, around whom the "Up" series revolves (or dissolves if we don't think the films are as funny as Mr. Sherrin does) is announced by a bassoon, Michael Hordern, a cello, Adrienne Posta, a French horn and Julie Ege, an alto sax supported by strings and harps. Carl's job was writing for effect rather than a melodic theme.

But what makes him choose his music and how does he put it on film? That, said I over Cranks coffee, is the question. The method must be the same for all movies.

"But of course," Carl confirmed, "although

music is an integral part of the picture the way we go about it is quite distinct operationally. I hope you didn't visualise an orchestra playing in the set's wings or anything like that. When players make passionate love they don't have the violin you might hear to help them. That comes later. They do it cold – in one sense."
When does "that comes later" find its musical way on to film? I asked.
"I don't do a thing until the film is finished. There is no point. But as soon as it is in coherent form, perhaps a rough-cut, then I see it. My brief is to enhance its effectiveness. Nothing more. Some scenes suggest music. Others don't. The next thing is the sort of music. And the instruments which best feed that music. This is when I make what I call my shopping list – combinations of instruments. I hear what they sound like through my inner ear."
Carl sees the film a second time. He is then able to accept, reject or rethink his first conclusions. He discusses his proposals with the director. Nothing is yet sacred. It is at the "I think . . ." stage.
He is getting closer to the moment he will go home and compose. But not until there is a reel-by-reel breakdown in the editing room. This is the time when there is complete and thorough examination of the cinematic moments when music fulfils a positive function.
The next stage finds him in his Battersea flat studio studying the masses of detailed notes prepared by an industrious secretary in the editing room. Like : at zero there is a close-up of Frankie Howerd's face. At three seconds he pinches Adrienne Posta's bottom, at five seconds she slaps his face, at seven, he falls over, and so on. What with

cue sheets and time sheets, the description "masses" is a near-understatement. Now comes Carl's composition. You might think he'd never get round to it. But composing is the least of his problems. He writes fast. Ten days will see him through. It is the organising, the planning and the book-keeping which take the time. There were 80 cues in this comedy. That's no laughing matter! Before Carl's music goes on to paper there must be cross-checks to avoid last-minute errors causing upset. A copyist takes the music and derives the parts. Carl books his musicians. By now everything is cut and dried. Carl knows what he intends to do and how he will do it.
The recording day arrives. The orchestra, its size dictated by the picture's budget, is assembled. Carl takes his conductor's stick. The film with its cue-marks starts. The orchestra obeys the cues. And that's that. Well, almost. Not quite. The recording took four days, incidentally.
The final stage is putting the film together. It is called the dubbing session or the dub. Only then can one fully realise what defects there are. This is the crucial period in the picture's life. The sound track must speak with a coherent voice. It needs balance, manipulation, perhaps even alteration. Now or never. And there are alterations. A ha'p'orth of cutting can be worth-while. Carl's approach to *The Bofors Gun* and *I, Monster* is basically the same although each of those is a sub-level movie whereas *Up Pompeii* and other "Up" films are completely surface. But the process is the same throughout. The finished film depends on the editor's sensitivity. Each is dependent – and at this point very dependent – upon the other. Which is where we came in.

Star of *Up Pompeii* Frankie Howerd discusses a scene in the film with laurel-wreathed producer Ned Sherrin.

Postscript by Ned Sherrin
There are a number of clever composers looking for work. I mean the comparative unknowns. The names are never short because they save someone searching. I like "unknowns" because their work proves they were worth shopping for. Enthusiasm, excitement, realism is infectious. It helps all of us. Frankie Howerd is in himself complete justification for the "Up" series.

54

The new ABC West End twin cinemas –
built within the old Saville Theatre in
Shaftesbury Avenue – ABC 1 and ABC 2.

The interior of the two cinemas,
ABC 1 (*left*) and ABC 2 (*right*).

OPENINGS AND CLOSINGS

No doubt about it, this has been the year of Gemini – with one or two triplets thrown in for good measure. It is this fact which makes the slowing-down of the closure rate (e.g. January–August 1970 showing a debit balance of 3 against a debit balance of 19 for the corresponding period the previous year), less cheering than at first appears. The rate of decline in cinema *seats* would be more significant. Even if we ignore the fact that many cinemas are now smaller than they used to be, the total we are left with is pretty depressing: 1,591 houses throughout the

whole country. (Moscow, incidentally, has 120 cinemas, and the average Muscovite visits them some 60 times a year.) Though no similar figures are available for this year (1970) the following are an indication of the trend towards smaller houses during the period 1968/9:

	1968	1969
Up to 500 seats	331	334
501–1,000	583	575
1,001–1,500	417	406
1,501–2,000	226	206
Over 2,000	74	60

It is reasonable to assume that the trend has considerably accelerated during the subsequent period.

In the same way, from the long-term view it is not the box-office takings (up) which are important so much as the admission numbers (down). The former indicates the progress of inflation, the latter shows the true state of cinema-going. A paper presented by the chief executive of EMI, John Read, on the leisure market, stated that in 1961 the average attendance at the cinema per person in the United Kingdom was 9 times a year – in 1969, 5 times a year. One per cent regarded the cinema as their major leisure pursuit.

However, let us leave the arid fields of statistics and conduct our usual, necessarily selective, tour of the actual building scene. The bracketed figures after the name of a cinema indicate the seating capacity.

The Princess Cinema, Wigan, closed in January 1970 on account of there "not being enough good films for three cinemas"! The two which are left serve a population of 78,780. In Thirsk the Ritz, closed October 1969, was reopened for Saturday (children's matinée) and Sunday performances, and in Brighton, Classic Cinemas converted the New Vogue – formerly the Ace, Lewes Road – for showing films in the old circle (336) and bingo in the stalls. Half a cinema is better than no films. Opening film was *Easy Rider*.

In February the residents of Allerton, Liverpool, saved something for themselves from the wreck of their 1,500-seater cinema. A 500-seater will be included, as a result of their demands, in a new supermarket project. In the same month the Regal, Saltcoats,

Ayrshire, underwent a £30,000 face-lift, reopening with 70-mm. equipment and new, better-spaced seating. This latter is a welcome trend to be seen in most rebuilding plans: better one hundred comfortable patrons who will come again than one hundred and twenty who will refuse to subject their cramped limbs to the torture a second time. In the same month two Cinecenta cinemas, the Scala Superama, Birmingham (650), opened by Compton in 1965, and the Superama, Derby (600), were taken over by Rank. The Cinecenta story is a somewhat sad one. The four-house complex still operates in Panton Street, London SW1, but has had to retreat from its noble aspirations "to present cinemagoers with a wide range of films they might never have had the opportunity of seeing because of the present restricted facilities. . . . Research indicates quite clearly that our cinemagoers are becoming increasingly more individual and discriminating in their tastes . . ." But alas, present programmes consist more often of popular reissues, "second runs", and productions of a more earthy (perhaps one should say fleshy) and less rarified nature.

Rank entered the picture in March with the reconstructed Shepherd's Bush Odeon – as a cine-bingo twin: a useful example of putting the devil's money to good purpose. The new auditorium (815) is sited in the circle of the old cinema and has an escalator – the second in the country, the first being in the Marble Arch Odeon. Reopening film was *Butch Cassidy and the Sundance Kid*.

The first ABC twin opened in April at Leeds, replacing the old Ritz, which seated 1,900 and was built in 1935. The conversion cost about £275,000. ABC 1

56 (670) started up with *Paint Your Wagon* and ABC 2 (867) with *Spring and Port Wine*. The following month the same company (which has now changed its name from Associated British Picture Corporation to EMI Film and Theatre Corporation, though the cinemas will still be known as ABCs) reopened its Falmouth house after extensive modernisation. The first week was taken up by a production of the Falmouth Operatic Society, but thereafter the plan was to present pre-release films, with occasional "live" shows. The Staines ABC was closed, but only for twin conversion, and it should be operating again in its new bi-form, if all goes well, long before this review appears.

In the same month Rank closed the 1,100-seater Regent, Abbeymount, Edinburgh, with no plans for redevelopment. At the other end of the scale, however, it opened its first 16-mm. cinema – the Preston Cine-Lounge (105 including 26 Pullman luxury armchairs), with *The Prime of Miss Jean Brodie*. Another Rank mini-cinema opened in Nottingham and, with other companies following suit, there may well be quite a number of these 16-mm. houses before very long. A wide range of programmes is shown, recent releases, reissues, and a larger proportion of specialised (including foreign) films than might be possible in 35-mm.

The Leicester Square Ritz started up again in May 1970 after considerable alteration and reseating (389 against 412). This comfortable little West End house – immensely popular during the war on account of its underground situation – opened in 1936. Its most famous film, *Gone With the Wind*, ran for four solid years.

Its reopening presentation, *The Strawberry Statement*, was somewhat less of a masterpiece.

ABC delivered another twin in June – this time in Bournemouth. This was the old Westover ABC converted at a cost of £260,000. Opening films were, ABC 1 (644), *Paint Your Wagon*; ABC 2 (982), *All the Way Up*. High drama was enacted in Lerwick, Shetland Isles: the North Star cinema was in danger of going over to bingo. Alarums were sounded and a campaign was launched by residents, headed magnificently by the town's schoolchildren. The Education Committee launched a formal objection with the licensing court, Shetland County Council backed them. Result – the cinema was reprieved – for the time being. At the time of writing, a similar battle is being fought for the retention of the Rex, Northwood. All very splendid, but if sufficient of the people supported their local cinemas in the first place no such campaigns would be necessary. The question any cinema owner must feel inclined to put is: "OK, but if *I* continue to *run* the place, will *you* ever *visit* it?"

Closures in July 1970 included two ABC theatres, Kentish Town, and Cheetham Hill, Manchester (the former permanently). Dufftown Picture House, Scotland, had to shut down because of the new Gaming Act Levy on occasional bingo sessions. Filling those evenings with worthwhile films might, after all, have proved less disastrous. To add insult to injury, though the St. George's Cinema, York, was knocked down, its frontage was to be preserved as a work of architectural interest! Better news this month came from the North, where the Hugh Orr independent circuit converted the old Morecambe Empire into Empire One (1,200) and a small Empire Two (250). The same town's Arcadian had previously been reseated down from 1,000 to 600 for comfort's sake. The same concern re-equipped the Alexandra, Coventry, as Theatre One (635). Nuneaton Scala returned to films from bingo because the Palace was damaged by fire.

Essoldo opened its first pair in July at Tunbridge Wells as Essoldo 1 (450), with *Anne of the Thousand Days*, and Essoldo 2 (366), with *Carry On Up the Jungle*. During the previous year and a half the company had refashioned eight cinemas. At about the same time the justly renowned little Ionic at Golders Green, London, came into the news with plans for rebuilding. The project has not developed very far as yet, but even if it falls through patrons can remain assured the cinema will stay as it is, with historical interest and unique atmosphere to compensate for some lack of the very latest in comfort, and a long-lasting policy of respecting both the intelligence of its audience and the integrity of its films: by refusing, for instance, the abhorrent dubbed versions of foreign-language films in favour of subtitles. "In fact," declares the manager, Mr. Humphreys, "when I have such a film booked I am rung up by intending patrons to make sure before they come that it *is* the subtitled version they will see." *O si sic omnes!*

The Star Group was active in August. Twins arrived in Carlisle on the site of the old Palace (756), as Studio 1 (578) and Studio 2 (351), resulting, unusually, in an increase of seats. Opening films were *Oliver!* and *Carry On Up the Jungle*. Projection is on the increasingly used periscope principle. Also from Star came a new twin in the town centre development of Burnley, Lancs. – Studio 1 (450) and 2 (230). Entrance is by pedestrian "travelator" from the precinct square.

A melancholy little note was struck in September by the closing of the Classic, Airdrie. "It will be particularly missed," notes *Today's Cinema* sadly, "by the 500 to 700 children who have been attending the special Saturday matinées." More cheerfully, the Palace, Longridge, Preston, after enduring three years of bingo, returned to life as a cinema following requests from local residents. Before its descent from grace it was a theatre.

October 1970 was notable for the launching of two triplets – neither of them, be it noted, in England. On the site of the old Paramount in Glasgow (built in 1934) Rank opened Odeon 1 (1,138) with *Cromwell*, Odeon 2 (1,243) with *Airport* and Odeon 3 (558) with *The Virgin and the Gypsy*. Odeon 3 is unusual in such complexes in having a separate circle as well as stalls. Claimed as the largest of its kind in Europe, the conversion cost £450,000. The other triple was in Dublin, built by EMI Cinemas & Leisure Ltd. where the Adelphi once stood, and now known as Adelphi 1 (614), formerly the balcony; Adelphi 2 (1,052), formerly the stalls; and Adelphi 3 (360), formerly the restaurant. Opening films were *Kelly's Heroes*, *Chisum* and *Z*, respectively. Cost – £300,000. Plans were also put under way by ABC for the first London suburban triple, at Romford. It is hoped this will open in mid-1971. The Arcadian, Bradford, was redecorated and started as a Commonwealth Film Club for the city's 30,000 Indian and Pakistani community,

the fifth cinema in the town to be so designed.

An important November event was the opening, at a fortnight's interval, of the two cinemas in the shell of the Warner Theatre, Leicester Square: the first, the West End (890), with *There Was a Crooked Man*; the second, the Rendezvous (686), with *The Rise and Rise of Michael Rimmer*. Both are startlingly modern in decor. The West End's ceiling looks as if it had been sown upside-down with lampshades which had grown into a vast – and slightly top-heavy – display of multi-sized cylinders. The screen is coyly half-hidden by two glittering segments which move away to either side. My personal preference is very much for the Rendezvous, one of the most attractive decors I have seen. The colour motif is blue-green, and the uncurtained screen is met at each side by white blocked constructions. Masking pieces move into position as the lights dim, and the total effect is attractive and impressive. An irregular cluster of lights resembling little coloured stalactites drops from the back part of the ceiling. The total effect is extremely attractive – provided the white side-pieces retain their present spotless brilliance. Both cinemas are very comfortable.

In November, also, ABCs 1 (606) and 2 (910) replaced the old Savoy at Leicester (built in 1937) with *Kelly's Heroes* and *A Man Called Horse* respectively; and Rank opened Odeons 1 (455) and 2 (1,235) at Southend. The ground floor of the Southend complex is a supermarket run by Cater Brothers. The original cinema was known as the Astoria, built in 1935, and became an Odeon in 1944. Opening films

Another example of twinning – the Warner Cinema now converted into two smaller cinemas, The Warner West End and The Warner Rendezvous.

58 for the new pair were *Anne of the Thousand Days* and *Battle of Britain*. The conversion cost £450,000.

Brian Tattersall, head of Unit Four Cinemas, reopened the York Cinema, Hulme, Manchester, as a Unit Four 16-mm. house, incorporating three 102-seaters and one 210-seater. The first Unit Four was started at Brierfield in the autumn of 1969, where each of the four mini-cinemas now has 70 seats. Opening films at Hulme were *The Virgin Soldiers*, *Funny Girl*, *Guess Who's Coming to Dinner* and *Alfred the Great*. Because of the disturbance they might cause in such small houses children are not admitted unaccompanied, even to a U programme. And not to be left out of all this flurry of openings, Kirkintilloch has plans to set up a venue where films can be shown on two days a week, following suggestions from a local residents' association. Kirkintilloch has had no cinema at all! since 1966.

December 3rd saw the reopening of the Essoldo, Maida Vale, modernised inside and out, with seating reduced from 1,182 to 471. The old building was originally famous as the Kilburn Empire music hall. Opening film was *Catch 22*, booked for an indefinite run. News came the same month that the Imperial, Pateley Bridge, Yorkshire was to be demolished and replaced by a school. The blow will not fall very hard – the cinema had been closed for six years! (All the same, as long as a building exists there always remains the chance that one day . . .) The big news of the month (for London, if not for Pateley Bridge) was undoubtedly the opening of the first ABC twins in the West End by the EMI Group, on the 21st – a brave pre-Christmas date to choose. Sited in the

shell of the former Saville Theatre, the access to ABC 1 (616) is from street level, and to ABC 2 (501) about a storey's height below. Both are in very modernistic decor, and each has its own licensed bar. Cost of conversion was around £600,000. Opening films: ABC 1, *There's a Girl in My Soup*; ABC 2, *The Railway Children*.

Towards the end of the month the Essoldo, Lenton Abbey, Nottingham, reopened with *Carry On Loving*, having been redeveloped from an old-style to a modern luxury house. The reduction in the number of seats – as in the case of the Maida Vale Essoldo – was startling: 1,098 to 437.

Last opening of the year was the Star Group's renovated Scala, Walton Street, Oxford – (well I remember taking unofficial leave from school to see Janet Gaynor in *Seventh Heaven* at the old cinema – to find three masters also indulging in an orgy of emotionalism three rows behind!) Now it is twins – Studio 1 (250) and Studio 2 (141). Periscopic projection has been installed, and Studio 1 incorporates the floating screen principle. A feature of the conversion was its speed – eight weeks' closure only. Opening programmes were: Studio 1, *Anne of the Thousand Days*; Studio 2, *There Was a Crooked Man*.

Although this review is mainly concerned with the "commercial" cinema, mention must be made of the opening on the South Bank of the British Film Institute's National Film Theatre 2. This very attractive and comfortable younger brother of NFT 1, seating 165, forms part of a £125,000 extension scheme which by the time this survey appears may have resulted in the opening of a third – yet smaller – cinema, a restaurant and enlarged club premises.

Despite its modest proportions NFT 2 has facilities for screening films of any period and any size from 8-mm. to 35-mm., as well as earphone installations for commentaries and translations of foreign-language films. Opening programme was a feature film financed by the BFI's Production Board, *Loving Memory*, directed by Tony Scott, which won the Vivien Leigh award. The Institute's Regional Theatres also continued to expand, totalling, at the time of writing, 36.

Despite the shadows of rising costs, falling admissions, cut-backs in production, and – the latest menace – the CASSETTE, many plans are going ahead for building, conversion and modernisation during the coming months which should have come to fruition by the time these words are printed. The Tower of London cinema project, mentioned in my last review, still remains very much in the air and meanwhile beefeaters, traitors and others must exercise their patience a little longer.

Finally, the see-saw saga of the Cameo-Poly continues. It is always pleasant for a prophet to be proved wrong when his prophecies are nasty ones. Three years ago I reported threatened closure of this famous and unique old cinema: two years ago – reprieve: last year – threatened closure: this year, happily – reprieve, and for up to three years. But fortune, unfortunately, is fickle. Next year, once again – perhaps . . .

FILM MAGAZINES

A survey of today's situation
by Allen Eyles

The cover of *Film Weekly* – dated Feb. 28, 1931.

An inseparable part of growing up with the movies, along with Saturday morning pictures and wholehearted renditions of the ABC Minors Song, used to be the fan magazines. They were a thriving part of a time when cinema was *the* mass entertainment and TV was something the better-off neighbours had who might permit you to watch an old Hopalong Cassidy on a rainy afternoon in the school holidays.

I remember picking up *Film Fun* and discarding it quickly for its inept cartoon strip imitations of flesh-and-blood favourites. I then tried both *Picture Show* and *Picturegoer* for a few weeks. A choice being dictated by the limits of pocket money, I quickly settled on the latter. It seemed the more brightly written of the two, the more attractively laid out, and it certainly conveyed a love of films old and new to which I could respond.

Picturegoer was never completely trivial, and later its review pages came under the command of Margaret Hinxman, now film critic of *The Sunday Telegraph*. She (though not all of her other reviewers) was

60 highly discriminating and the magazine would occasionally go out on a limb to champion the cause of an unimportant-seeming film as well as deflate some of the bigger offerings. *Picturegoer's* "Seal of Merit" went to *Invasion of the Body Snatchers* which didn't even get a circuit release, and I was sufficiently impressed to seek it out at an independent cinema and find my efforts well rewarded. Similarly, the magazine's 4-star rating of *Come Next Spring* led me to another happy evening at the cinema. Furthermore, *Picturegoer* had pull-out supplements of reference material from time to time, and even today I find them of occasional use. I also took advantage of its readers' service which answered queries with a rubber-stamped "George" at the foot of the reply. Here indeed was the way to pinpoint the title of that vaguely-remembered film that was nagging away at you or, no doubt, learn the exact curvature of Ray Milland's raised right eyebrow.

Alas, those days of simple film education are past. It's true that the *ABC Film Review* continues in very healthy shape and I still enjoy its crossword, and that *Photoplay* survives. But both these are monthlies and the weekly dose of information and news in the easy-going form of *Picturegoer* has passed for ever. Its circulation dropped with the decline in habitual filmgoing, and its attempts to broaden its appeal with a flashier approach and more extensive coverage of pop music drove me into the arms of the newcomer *Films and Filming*. Happily, *Picturegoer's* reference files were transferred to *Woman* magazine and its Star Service is available at the drop of a stamped, addressed envelope at 189 High Holborn, London WC1, though for serious information the best source is the Information Department of the British Film Institute, available to members of that organisation. (Incidentally, the records of *Picture Show* were taken over by the BFI and form a useful base of research.)

Films and Filming does much to cater for the interests of the film fan with coverage of the current scene and nostalgic pieces on the past. But the point of this article is to indicate that the tradition of the fan magazine proper is alive and well but living in more obscure quarters. I am referring to the modest efforts of small groups of individuals who dedicatedly produce semi-professional magazines. Their shoe-string budgets obviously do not permit wide promotion, and most of them come from the United States. They deserve to be better known and a large number of would-be readers cannot be aware of them. In this country, they really only surface to public view – if at all – in the cinema bookshops of the Charing Cross Road.

These magazines are more than the equivalent of the old fan journals. They do not try to cater to a casual readership but instead assume a knowledge and interest in the minutiae of cinema history, tracing in great depth the careers of often almost forgotten artists. Here is where most of the basic research into the facts of the past is being conducted. The magazines comment on and directly encourage the revival of older films; they remind us that the contemporary cinema is only the tip of an iceberg of past achievement and are a welcome antidote to the excess of attention granted to new films in the better-known magazines. And at a time when the cult of the director is uppermost, these smaller publications work towards restoring a balance by their emphasis – in fan mag tradition – on the most visible element of the players. For, when one looks at a film like *The Big Sleep*, it is more than the style and talent of Howard Hawks that makes it as effective as it is; it is also the abilities of not only the stars but the supporting actors like Elisha Cook Jnr. and Louis Jean Heydt. It is the old stars and this kind of supporting player whose work is appreciated in the pages of the new fan periodicals.

Would *Sight and Sound* find space to interview Grady Sutton (a familiar face, if not a familiar name, to anyone who has watched a few old films)? Or interview Marie Windsor or Raymond Walburn? This is the *forte* of these magazines, which usually publish a list of film appearances as well. A prominent American critic once wrote of one of these magazines that it knew the facts about everything and the value of nothing. And it is true that the publication of facts for facts' sake can become a pointless mania without some criterion of artistic worth. The comment I have just quoted was levelled against *Films in Review*, and the critic was, broadly speaking, quite right. Yet this small, 68-page journal, which has appeared ten times annually with great regularity for some twenty years, is a valuable repository of information. It has carried an immense range of career articles, from popular choices like Jack Lemmon and Elizabeth Taylor to a wide range of silent stars like Pauline Frederick and James Murray. And, unlike many of its rivals, it will publish articles on directors (like James Whale or Michael Curtiz), on a writer like Frances Marion, and even leave Hollywood altogether to run a piece on Marcel Pagnol.

Here particularly the value of the work resides in the detailed filmographies that are a standard feature. The articles themselves are too often irritating in their obsession with details of scandal and marital discord at the expense of any intelligent comment on the films involved, and even the best work generally fails to relate the person under study to his or her work in an illuminating way. Also, the magazine prints film reviews that so over-reach the limits of commonsense in their indignation over the "moral degeneracy" of most current releases as to make hilarious reading. But it does have a fascinating end section of readers' letters which is a kind of meeting place for the exchange of information.

Also monthly and commendably regular in its appearance is *Film Fan Monthly*, now well past its hundredth issue. This is slim and low-priced and specialises in covering people who are less well-known and of lesser stature than those in *Films in Review*. This magazine was the one that interviewed Grady Sutton; it has also talked to Buddy Rogers and Ralph Bellamy in recent numbers, run appreciations of Jane Frazee and Leon Errol, as well as a multi-part index of the films of Johnny Mack Brown. Whereas the subjects of articles in *Films in Review* are always deserving of attention, I sometimes feel that many of *FFM*'s choices have a doubtful claim to artistic worthiness, but it's made apparent that someone still loves them and is displaying it effectively in words.

Screen Facts seems to have come to a halt, though it may just be that recent issues have escaped my notice. This was (is?) a very attractive publication with excellent, large illustrations and appealing caricatures of its subjects drawn by Al Kilgore. One particularly enjoyable issue was devoted entirely to Ann Sheridan, and in a long interview she conveyed with intelligence and warmth a great deal about how Hollywood worked when she was a star and what she thought of her films.

A newcomer, and something of a luxury item, is *Filmograph*, a quarterly printed on thick paper in brown ink and costing $2 per issue. So far it has interviewed Lois Wilson and carried pieces on Raymond Hatton, the Cisco Kids, Mae Murray and the like, as well as a splattering of more routine articles. By far the most intensive research I've found appears in *Views and Reviews*, ostensibly a magazine of the arts. The issues I've seen have mainly concentrated on classical records and the cinema, and its interest in the latter area so far seems to have focused mainly on lesser Westerns and detective films. It has zealously crusaded (and with some success) for the revival of Tim McCoy's work on 16 mm. in the States and written extensively about it; there have also been dossiers on selected Westerns and on Mae West films, as well as a several-part essay on the films from the novels of S. S. Van Dine. The editors are particularly scrupulous about correcting the most minor of errors from preceding issues.

Samuel K. Rubin's *Classic Film Collector* is, as its title indicates, an organ for news to interest film collectors. It is laid out like a newspaper and in its chaotically crammed pages there are all kinds of fascinating details about Hollywood's past. The dedication to cinema and to all-night sessions with the layout sheets and pastepot is splendidly evident.

These are just some of the American

Cover of *Picture Show* – dated Oct. 10, 1942.

Cover of *Picturegoer* – dated March 21, 1959.

62 publications that ought to be more widely read than they are. In Britain, this kind of magazine has not flourished. One exception is Anthony Slide's *The Silent Picture*, which lovingly examines aspects of the silent period. Recent issues have covered the silent work of director Raoul Walsh with a detailed filmography of his entire career; Lotte Reiniger's reminiscences on making a full-length cartoon, *The Adventures of Prince Achmed*, in 1926; Emil Jannings; Marion Davies; the early work of the Russian director Dovzhenko; and so on.

And for Western enthusiasts, there is the extraordinary newsletter, *Wrangler's Roost*, which covers aspects of the "B" Western and its stars and is issued *free* by its editor who only asks for a supply of stamped addressed envelopes.

This brings me – with great lack of modesty – to a magazine called *Focus on Film* which I edit. This was launched partly in respectful emulation of some of the American magazines I have described above but also partly as an attempt to bridge the gap between the "fan" and the "serious" readership. Since I do not find an interest in Claude Chabrol *and* Edward Everett Horton a contradiction in terms, I don't see why others should, but besides conveying the facts in our career articles we have tried to probe a little further into the precise qualities of each artist surveyed. Tom Milne's succinct piece on Tuesday Weld is a good example of this kind of balance well achieved. Major articles have covered such stars as Bob Hope, Lon Chaney, John Barrymore and Ronald Colman; supporting players like Charlie Ruggles and Margaret Hamilton; directors like Sergei Bondarchuk and Ken Hughes; writers like Donald Ogden Stewart and Wendell Mayes; and subjects like the American "B" Film. As far as possible, we choose subjects that have not been researched before by other magazines so as to add to the amount of knowledge available and, when we have gone over familiar ground, as in a John Ford issue, we have presented fresh material.

We try to make each piece the definitive study of its subject. When we selected Edward Everett Horton, it took twenty pages to cover his lengthy career in comment on his life and work, much of it by the actor himself in an interview with the writer, and to list full details of the enormous number of films that have invariably benefited from his appearance in them. Inevitably we make errors of omission and many of these are recorded in later issues as we discover them or readers point them out.

In addition, *Focus on Film* also takes an interest in current cinema. Selected new films are given lengthy reviews and short biographical sketches and lists of previous work are attached to cover the principal artists. In this way a deeper appreciation of a film should be possible with the background facts readily available. Like the other magazines mentioned in this piece, *Focus on Film* does not pretend to give complete coverage of the film scene; instead it works at filling in the gaps in film history. We were greatly encouraged by the comment of a little known intellectual journal, *The Brighton Film Review*, when it observed – somewhat sniffily – that *Focus on Film* seemed to have been put together in the dusty recesses of some library. So much dust has accumulated that it's about time it was shaken off! I hope this article will encourage you to take a look at some of the work being done, and by your support encourage those who do the work, often without any payment and always with dogged enthusiasm.

Films in Review, 210 East 68th Street, New York, N.Y. 10021, U.S.A. 10 issues per year. 90 cents per issue.

Film Fan Monthly, 77 Grayson Place, Teaneck, N.J. 07666, U.S.A. 11 issues per year. 50 cents per issue.

Screen Facts, P.O. Box 154, Kew Gardens, N.Y. 11415, U.S.A. Occasional. Current price not to hand.

Filmograph, 7926 Ashboro Drive, Alexandria, Virginia 22309, U.S.A. Quarterly. $2 per issue.

Views and Reviews, Suite 403, The Clark Building, 633 W. Wisconsin Avenue, Milwaukee, Wisconsin, U.S.A. Quarterly. $1.25 per issue.

Classic Film Collector, 734 Philadelphia Street, Indiana, Pa. 15701. Quarterly? Price not to hand.

The Silent Picture, 613 Harrow Road, London W.10. Quarterly. 15p per issue.

Wrangler's Roost, 29 Sheepcote Gardens, Denham, Bucks. Monthly. Free on receipt of s.a.e. or 30 cents International Postal Coupon.

Focus on Film, The Tantivy Press, 108 New Bond Street, London W1Y 0QX. Five issues per year. 30p or $1 per issue.

THE NEGLECTED ONES

The following eleven films are cross-referenced in the section Releases of the Year in Detail.

Milo O'Shea, as Mr. Zero, endures his wife's (Phyllis Diller) ceaseless nagging in the Universal–Rank release of Jerome Epstein's screen adaptation of the Elmer Rice stage play *The Adding Machine*, a film specially noteworthy for a number of brilliant performances.

A constant puzzle to those concerned about films is why a number of really bad movies get a general release and a number of really good ones are hardly seen after their première unveiling. It is not only grossly unfair to those who made the neglected movies, but also to the public refused the opportunity of seeing a film which they almost certainly would enjoy.

I am not going to list those movies released during the period covered by this volume which could be certainly classified as very bad or even disastrous – you'll find them easily enough in the "Releases of the Year" feature – but I will record a number of movies which have hardly been seen at all but which in various ways offer enough entertainment to deserve far wider showing than they have had or are likely to get. One or two, like *Pookie* and *Borsalino*, for instance, are really top-class movies, fully deserving of the success I'm quite certain they would have had if they had been released generally on one of the major circuits.

That these films have been unjustly neglected is fact; the reasons why I would not know, I only know there is something very wrong with an industry which on the one hand can complain of the lack of films and on the other hand reject a number of movies which in every way seem to me to be very good box-office. I can only suggest that if you do happen to see any of the following films being advertised you should make an effort to see them, for they are all, though often in diverse ways, not only entertaining but in fact quite outstanding productions of artistic or other merit.

Jack Lemmon and Catherine Deneuve were the co-stars in Warner–Pathé's *The April Fools*; as a couple of runaways from the Wall Street business atmosphere who leave their respective spouses in order to find what they hope will be a new and happy life together in Paris.

It is somewhat easier to understand why Columbia's *Castle Keep* never had a very wide showing, for it was, with its odd mixture of blood, thunder and beauty, a strange and rather uncomfortable film which refused to be slotted into any ordinary niche. But with all its failures it had a certain distinction, and a cast headed by Burt Lancaster.

Paramount's French release *Borsalino* was a quite outstanding gangster movie – brutal in its retailing of the ruthless gang rivalry of the 30's in Marseilles but made with a tongue-in-cheek manner which brought it to the edge of farce on occasions. Jean-Paul Belmondo and Alain Delon played the two young climbers to crooked power: and the title tune was memorable.

Fairly understandable, too, why Commonwealth United's *Julius Caesar* didn't get a circuit release, though it deserved, because of the cinematic treatment and performances from a starry cast (a cast including John Gielgud, Charlton Heston and Jason Robards – the latter shown with a reclining Richard Johnson) in the new adaptation of the Shakespeare history far better treatment than it received.

Even if *The Madwoman of Chaillot* was off-beat it had some wonderful stuff in it: a beautifully wrought adaptation of the witty Girandot play directed by Bryan Forbes, it starred Katharine Hepburn as the deliciously mad lady who defeats a gang of crooks who plan to despoil Paris of its underlying oil!

Still awaiting more than the isolated showing is UA's *Leo the Last*, the Irwin Winkler film which dressed up a rather ordinary little moral tale with some quite magnificent trappings. Marcello Mastroianni played the man who tries to play God but finds the gesture leads only to disaster.

The most astonishingly neglected film of all those in this section is Paramount's *The Out-of-Towners*, which I personally would put very high on any list of the funniest, brightest and wittiest comedies of this, last or any other year. Jack Lemmon and Sandy Dennis were right on top of their form as the two innocents who come to New York and within a few hours experience the disasters of any normal lifetime.

Quite outstandingly funny, and touching, too, was Paramount's *Pookie*, the comedy about a rather eccentric young girl (played beautifully by Liza Minelli) who latches on to a young student and leads him gently to the joys of love and sex and friendship.

Of all these films listed the most understandably not given a very wide showing was Fox's *The Magus*, for although it starred Michael Caine, as a British schoolteacher drawn into a strange mystery on a Greek island, it was perhaps too specialised, even too confusing, to have found more than limited public favour.

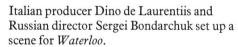

Italian producer Dino de Laurentiis and
Russian director Sergei Bondarchuk set up a
scene for *Waterloo*.

above right
Bondarchuk directs one of the more intimate
scenes in the film.

Napoleon (Rod Steiger, inset) starts on the
journey which will take him into exile.

THE MAKING OF AN EPIC

by John Webster

Ever since Fred Niblo directed the lavish 1927 production of *Ben Hur*, producers have been willing to gamble their reputations, their money and their health to make an "epic".

There have been great epics which made money at the box office; there have been epics which, to the puzzlement and despair of film companies, have flopped. Film people discovered long ago that a huge budget doesn't guarantee box office success. Neither does an arm-length list of stars above the title. For the producer, in terms of physical and mental energy, no other kind of production is as demanding. The problems and frustrations can make a nervous wreck of the calmest man. "You've got to know what you are doing when you embark on an epic," says Italian producer Dino de Laurentiis. It is the understatement of the year. De Laurentiis, however, knows what he's talking about. He is the man behind one of the greatest epics of all time: *Waterloo*. It was the battle which neither side could afford to lose – and no film company could afford to put on the screen.

The battle took place on June 18, 1815. It lasted almost ten hours and over 140,000 troops were involved in the terrible struggle for life – and victory. Of those who took part 52,000 died. It was a massive slaughter that cost Napoleon his empire and altered the course of history.

But until Dino de Laurentiis came along with his incredible plan, no one could afford the multi-million-dollar budget needed to film it.

For more than six years, the little Corsican tried fruitlessly to find a major American company to finance the project. The cost? $25,000,000. It would be the most expensive film ever made. Too expensive, everyone said. Then de Laurentiis went "cap in hand" to a Russian film company, Mosfilms, and the deal was done. They would join him for the monumental production. The deal? In addition to more than $10,000,000 of the costs, Mosfilm would provide 20,000 soldiers of the Red Army – twice the record 10,000 Yugoslav troops used by De Laurentiis in his *War and Peace* – as well as a full brigade of Soviet cavalry and the crack Moscow Militia with their fabulous white horses. All turned up for the 48 days of location shooting in the Ukraine.

It was the soldiers as much as the money which made *Waterloo* possible.

"You just couldn't afford to get that many people together in Hollywood or anywhere else," explained the film's director, Sergei Bondarchuk.

He's right. It was estimated that the *Waterloo* budget would have been trebled had the film been made in America.

After the deal was set with the Russians, it was not difficult for De Laurentiis to persuade both Paramount and Columbia Pictures to become his financial and distribution partners in the Western world. The film was set to go . . . and that's when De Laurentiis's problems really began.

The production required more planning, perhaps, than the battle itself. Months before filming began, with Rod Steiger playing Napoleon and Christopher Plummer as the Duke of Wellington, the 20,000 Russian soldiers (who were paid their usual 25s. a month) were drilled in the Upper Ukraine in the now outmoded bayonet and sabre fighting techniques and a special law was passed to get soldiers old enough to portray Napoleon's famous Old Guard.

Meanwhile, in a potato field eight miles from Uzhgorod, the ancient capital of Rutenia, the Waterloo battlefield was being duplicated. Soviet army engineers, labourers and farmworkers carved four miles of a road representing the Charleroi road in Belgium, levelled two hills, deepened a valley and built four farmsteads of Brabant and the entire village of Placenoit.

"Dino said he'd move mountains to make this picture," said Rod Steiger. "And he has – literally!"

Because it rained before and during the battle 16 miles of irrigation tubing was sunk into the ground to provide rain and mud to order. When the film was completed it was left there to irrigate real crops.

Well in advance, too, farmers planted special crops to match the vegetation that existed at Waterloo on June 18, 1815. These were wheat, rye and barley. The rye had to be up to a good height because Wellington kept his soldiers hidden in it. More than 5,000 trees were planted, all over 18 feet high. They and Wellington's historic elm, under which he spent most of the battle, were transported on huge trucks and planted with cranes!

And that wasn't all. . . . Because paintings and descriptions of the battleground showed it to be carpeted with flowers, especially red and white ones, production designer Mario Garbuglia arranged for the sowing of wild daisies, broom, poppies and tough grass which stood up under the feet of many men and horses.

While De Laurentiis and his unit watched the slow but sure progress on the field itself, 52 factories were making 28,000 blue French uniforms and red and grey English

70   uniforms. More than 1,000 officers' uniforms were made in Italy because they were needed early in filming at the studio and at the huge, ornate Royal Palace at Caserta, near Naples, which doubles for Fontainebleau, from which Napoleon departed for his first taste of exile.

More than a dozen cannon were brought from Italy to Russia, but the majority of the 1,400 period pieces used in the battle sequences were moulded in Russia. Authenticity was always the vital ingredient De Laurentiis asked for – and got.

Because all of the horses in the Russian cavalry were either bay or black, the Moscow Militia were called down to the Ukraine to stand in for the famous Scots Greys. The Greys were the cavalry regiment which, in the heat of battle, overcharged the French ranks and were slaughtered deep behind the French lines. Napoleon's legendary white stallion was a beautiful Arabian specimen bought for the film in Russia. The price? Over £4,000 . . .

Five Panavision cameras were shipped to Russia to film the battle simultaneously, some mounted on helicopters and others on 100-foot towers built at vantage points on the battlefield. An overhead trolley was installed across the two-mile field to carry a camera in giant pan views of the massive French cavalry attacks. Director Bondarchuk, throughout the location filming, communicated by walkie-talkie with Army commanders stationed in close contact with their men. Three dialogue coaches speaking English, Italian, French and Russian worked with the actors.

"It was very necessary," explained Director Bondarchuk, through an interpreter. "You see, I don't speak anything but Russian – but I had to know everything would sound all right!"

Bristling with activity, from dawn until dusk, the *Waterloo* location presented an awesome spectacle to the visitor. After a

Christopher Plummer as Wellington discusses a scene with Bondarchuk.

bumpy ride from Uzhgorod on a cobblestone road running past 19th-century farmhouses with slate and tile roofs, one arrived at a vast open field, marked by a sign BATEPAOO, with the English translation WATERLOO in smaller letters below. Then a left turn up the muddy dirt road – past the raw pine temporary buildings housing the camera equipment, costumes and props for the film – to the crest of the hill, from which one could see the full sweep of the battlefiled, dotted with thousands of moving men, frightening and beautiful at the same time.

Let us review one typical day. A Red Army guard, armed with only a walkie-talkie, stops your car because a big scene is about to begin shooting at the far end of the Charleroi road in the centre of the battlefield. Moments later, the entire battlefield erupts in smoke and fiery explosions. Brass cannon, with a frightening noise, boom the length of the field. There is a direct hit on Napoleon's headquarters, the French pub, La Belle Alliance. Smoke and flame pour from it.

Closer to you an explosion shatters the slate of La Haye Sainte, others hit Hougoumont with the same effect, and it's hard to believe that these explosions are the wizardry of special effects experts and not real cannon ball explosions. Five cameras are turning on the inferno.

"It's incredible," says Steiger. "I've never seen anything like it before."

Here and there, smoke and flame erupt directly at the feet of orderly columns of resplendent troops in reds, whites, blues and gold braid. Many fall, presumably dead. A cavalry company charges toward some cannon on your left through explosion after explosion. Horses, specially trained to fall by the unit's Italian and Yugoslavian stunt men, go down, their daring riders tumbling end over end, both lying realistically dead when they fall.

Then loud above the sound of the battle a public address horn blares "Schtop", and something else in Russian. The scene ends. It is during the lull that the guard lets your car through. At the end of the road, firemen are putting out the last traces of the fire. Beyond it, on a mound, Rod Steiger, the most convincing Napoleon the screen will ever see, sits in a canvas chair under a blue umbrella conferring through an interpreter with Sergei Bondarchuk.

Was Napoleon like this dirty, sweaty, ailing man?

"He was a physical wreck at Waterloo," explains Steiger. "He was dying; only half a man. I'm trying to make him human and believable."

So much for the battle – but what of the period when it was fought?

The world – then as now – was changing. The American and French revolutions had upset the order. As always, men sought to eliminate their differences by killing one another with the sword. Napoleon Bonaparte, madman or liberator – depending on whether one was an aristocrat fearing the guillotine or a commoner promised equality – had over-extended himself. Driven from Spain, then Russia, he had been forced to abdicate and King Louis XVIII was on the throne of France restoring the status quo.

But then came the news that Napoleon had escaped his prison on Elba and had marched a rabble army against Louis' troops, winning them over without firing a shot.

Renewed fear of Napoleon swept through the courts of Europe. Four nations girded to put down the idolised "madman" who was moving fast, as was his battle technique, to consolidate his "comeback".

Thus the stage was set – a hundred days after Napoleon's escape – for the biggest, bloodiest and proudest battle of the times. For Director Bondarchuk *Waterloo* represented the greatest challenge of his life. He was determined to make the film a universal and lasting indictment of war, without political implications of any kind. For him, the climactic moment of the film is not the violent clash of English and French troops in battle, but rather the moonlit, shadowy "field of dead" through which Wellington rides in lonely silence as he surveys the cost of liberating Europe from the fear of the "monster", Napoleon. To make this scene a telling experience for audiences, Bondarchuk used every single soldier the Red Army could provide – more than 18,000 men – to present a spectacle of carnage that covered the entire valley floor of his Ukrainian location.

"But 52,000 men died at Waterloo," an enterprising journalist pointed out. "Would not that number give a more historically accurate picture of Waterloo's dead?"

"No, the camera cannot physically encompass that many bodies," Bondarchuk replied and then, with a twinkle in his eye, added, "But 18,000 still makes a greater spectacle than 2,000 or 3,000 which is all that Hollywood would have been able to afford if they had done this film."

Of course, Bondarchuk is right. *Waterloo* is unique. And Producer Dino de Laurentiis must take most of the credit for bringing it to the screen.

Some of the tremendously spectacular
scenes of the battle itself.

WORLD ROUND-UP

Georges Franju's *La Faute de L'Abbe Mouret* (France).

Yves Montand in Jean-Pierre Melville's *Le Cercle Rouge* (France).

Perhaps it was never obvious, even in the golden years of the cinema, that a particular year was a landmark in its history. Perhaps it needs the distance of time to make the high points stand out. Certainly the cinema seems to be in the doldrums now and it is difficult to believe that we will look back in a few years' time upon the present and recognise it as the point at which something wonderful suddenly happened to films.

If this is a time of troubled economics, we are told that salvation lies around the corner with the video-cassette revolution. Apart from the fact that this particular revolution seems so long coming, scepticism is excusable. The appeal of a cinema in every home, the elimination of middlemen exhibitors and the parity of competition with television, understandably make the mouths of producers water. But, assuming all the legal and technical problems get sorted out, it is unlikely that the video-cassettes will provide a quick remedy for the cinema's ills. Like television, they may provide a financial shot in the arm by living on the pickings of the film past, but it will take a long time before they lead directly to any new film production. With 40 per cent of Hollywood's technicians unemployed and the American movie audience down to a quarter of its size in the 1940s, it calls for the pie-in-the-sky optimism of Richard Zanuck, shortly before he was deposed as President of Twentieth Century-Fox, to believe "the feature motion picture business will come back on a scale that will dwarf the golden era of Hollywood".

Of course the publicity machine would have us believe many things. Last year the success of *Easy Rider* led to the conclusion that it did not take a big budget to make a good film.

The moral should have been that whether a film is great or whether it stinks, audiences are indifferent to costs. Now we are told that all the replicas of *Easy Rider* died at the box-office and this must be taken on trust for they failed to arrive. Meanwhile cost-paring goes on, not so much because of the success of some cheap films but because the studios are no longer in the hands of the extravagant moguls of yesteryear but are now controlled by the accountants of the large corporations that have grown out of oil and hotels. If the businessmen can get a feature which would have cost $5m. last year made for $2m. this year, and can produce *Fiddler on the Roof* for half and *Cabaret* for a quarter of the cost of *Hello, Dolly!* and do this without any loss in quality, then they will deserve their rewards.

This year's standout success is *Love Story*, so the new line is that the romance film is back, sweeping across all the age barriers. Well, it may be; but it could be another of those cinematic summers with only one swallow. And who believes that producers are going to abandon sex themes in favour of romantic love? The decline of the sex film is still a figment of the wishful thinking of prudes and people like the retiring censor with the liberal image, John Trevelyan, who claimed to be suffering boredom from over-exposure. As yet the sex film does not appear to be any less durable than the Western and that shows no signs of dying out. It is suggested that youth films will shift from the campus to the drug scene with films like *Speed is of the Essence*, but this, too, would seem to be a passing, possibly belated, fancy.

What many of us would like to see is a string of first-rate comedies. They go on trying, of

Catherine Deneuve in Jacques Demy's *Peau D'Ane* (France).

Jean-Pierre Léaud and Barbara Laage in François Truffaut's *Domicile Conjugal* (France).

Annie Girardot in André Cayatte's *Mourir D'Aimer* (France).

Brigitte Bardot in Robert Enrico's *Boulevard du Rhum* (France).

Jeanne Moreau in Roger Pigaut's *Comptes à'Rebours*.

Jean Gabin and Simone Signoret in Pierre Granier-Deferre's *Le Chat* (France).

course. In Britain it seems there is a plan to revive fortunes by taking over the proven successes of the comedy series on television. This does not sound like a prescription for original movie comedies but we will not complain if it does put the industry on its feet again and leads to better things. In the US, a combination of the national mood and the cancer of "Laugh-In" has reduced humour to a witless, infantile level. With the death of Harold Lloyd bringing the great comedians of the past to mind, it is easy to become despondent about the prospects for the American comic film. The only consoling thought is that some of the most brilliant social comedies in the history of the cinema were made in the worst years of depression in the thirties.

Though there is more scope for gloom – the survival of and, conceivably, a swing back to censorship – there is no need for total despair. The cinema is far from dead. Even as it languishes in the major production centres, important films suddenly appear from new sources. Where will it be next? Peru? Greece? Egypt? Perhaps Formosa, for the Formosans go on average 66 times a year to the cinema as against the Americans' 7. Perhaps it will be nearer home with such diverse projects as the Polanski–Tynan–Heffner *Macbeth* or Solzhenitsyn's *The First Circle* directed in Denmark by the Pole, Aleksander Ford, who is now based in Israel. Wherever it is, around the world, old hands and new are striving to make good films.

*   *   *

FRANCE

While the number of French films made last year went down from 153 the year before to 140, the trend has been towards bigger films made in association with European or American partners – particularly Paramount and Columbia. Running against the worldwide trend, and for the first time in over a decade, audiences did not fall off over the previous year but actually rose slightly. Even if crisis has never been far away, there is now much hope.

As elsewhere, it is not the films which travel well which necessarily do best at home. For years the most popular domestic films have been the comedies starring Louis de Funès and he has now taken over the prolific mantle of Fernandel. His recent films include *The Atlantic Wall*, *La folie des grandeurs*, *L'homme orchestre*, *Le gendarme en balade* and *Jo*, an adaptation of the stage success *The Gazebo*.

Following *Borsalino*, the gangster film is in great vogue. Lelouch's *Simon the Swiss* with Jean-Louis Trintignant and Charles Denner has done well but many critics are alienated by the high polish of Lelouch's technique. Jean-Pierre Melville has also succeeded with *The Red Circle* which stars Montand, Delon, Bourvil and Périer, but again, some critics feel the film is too portentous and that Melville has sold himself short in going for a winner. There is some suggestion that the day of the sex films is already past and that they have been overtaken in popularity by the romantic films such as Jacques Doniol-Valcroze's *La Maison des Bories*, Henry Chapier's *Sexpower* and the films of Truffaut and Rohmer.

Some of the older directors have re-established themselves with huge box-office successes: René Clément with *Rider on the Rain* and the ex-lawyer André Cayatte with *Die of Love* which marked a return to the style of hard-hitting dramas of miscarried justice such as *Justice est Faite* with which he began his career twenty years ago. Both directors have since gone off at tangents: Clément with *The House under the Trees*, about an American couple living in Paris whose young children are kidnapped and starring Faye Dunaway; Cayatte with a science-fiction story set 9,000 years ago, *La nuit des temps*, in which he intends to use a cast of non-professional Indonesians shot through distorting lens.

Apart from commercials for after-shave lotions, Godard continues to make political films for non-cinematic showing, but other directors who would find survival much more difficult if not impossible outside France, continue to thrive. Eric Rohmer has now made five out of the six of his highly literate moral tales with *Claire's Knee* which won the coveted Louis Delluc prize and stars a heavily-bearded Jean-Claude Brialy, Aurora Cornu and Beatrice Romand. Jacques Demy has contrived another of his confections, *Donkey Skin*, this time from a Perrault fairy tale with Deneuve as the princess, Perrin as the prince, Seyrig as the fairy godmother and also Presle, Ledoux, Piteoff and Jean Marais for whom the affinities with Cocteau's *La belle et la bête* must have induced strong nostalgia. After adaptations from Mauriac, Bazin, Feuillade and Cocteau, Georges Franju went to Zola for *The Fault of Abbé Mouret* with Francis Huster as the Abbé. After getting way out of his depth with the dull and trite *L'enfant sauvage*, Truffaut recovered by returning in *Domicile conjugal* to the character of Antoine Doinel who had served him so well in *The 400 Blows* and *Stolen Kisses*. Truffaut would appear to have exhausted this vein of lightweight charm and it remains to be seen

Liliana Cavani's *The Cannibals* (Italy).

Ingmar Bergman's documentary (about his island) *The Farö Document* (Sweden).

if he can move on to another level and find another rich source of material. Marguerite Duras is more fortunate in having her own novels to draw on and this she did again with *L'écriture bleue*, an adaptation of *Abahn, Sabana, David*.

Another woman director, Nadine Trintignant, is making *Mi-temps*, with Mastroianni and Deneuve, about an architect and his wife who lose their child. Her husband, Jean-Louis Trintignant, also plans to direct *Une journée bien remplie* about a mentally retarded, fifty-year-old baker. Trintignant's acting career continues with Doniol-Valcroze's *L'homme au cerveau greffé*.

Most of the top stars are in great demand with Alain Delon, Jean-Paul Belmondo and Catherine Deneuve at the head of the list. A number of older, but equally familiar faces, have had a good year. Yves Montand's reputation has grown with *Z*, *L'aveu* and *The Red Circle*, and Jean Gabin and Lino Ventura keep on turning. Gabin appears with Simone Signoret in Pierre Granier-Deferre's *Le Chat*. The new Brigitte Bardot appeared in *Les novices* and *L'ours et la poupée* and she appears with Ventura in Robert Enrico's adventure of the gay twenties, *Boulevard du rhum*. Though she has made two films, including *Monte Walsh*, in Hollywood, Jeanne Moreau had not been in French studios for two years before she returned in Roger Pigaut's *Comptes à rebours* which also stars Serge Reggiani, Signoret and Charles Vanel. We shall be looking out for a number of interesting productions: Chabrol's *Le visiteur de la nuit* with Michel Bouquet, Stéphane Audran and François Périer; Alain Resnais' *Marquis de Sade* with Dirk

Bogarde as the Marquis; André Delvaux's *Le rendezvous à Braye*; Alexandre Astruc's *Les affinités électives* based on Goethe's novel; Verneuil's *The Chase* based on the novel by David Goodis with Belmondo, Omar Sharif, Hossein, Renato Salvatori and Dyan Cannon; Jacques Deray's *Doucement les basses* with Alain and Natalie Delon and Paul Meurisse; Jean-Paul Rappeneau's *Les mariés de l'an II* with Belmondo, Jobert, Antonelli, Auclair, Frey and Brasseur; Michel Delville's *Räphael ou le débauché* with Maurice Ronet and Françoise Fabian; Marcel Carné's *La force et le droit* with Charles Denner; Gerard Brach's *The Boat* with Michel Simon; and the Pole Walerian Borowczyk's *Blanche*, also with Michel Simon, described as a story of medieval savagery in which sublime and brutal passions rock an isolated castle to its foundations.

ITALY

Carlo Ponti has declared that "the Italian industry without America does not exist" and, like much of the rest of the world, it is currently suffering from the Hollywood 'flu. There is still much activity. The big domestic successes have been *The Night Visitors*, *A Prostitute Serving the Community Within the Law*, Campanile's prehistoric farce, *When Women Had Tails*, Elio Petri's *Investigation of a Citizen Above Suspicion* with Gian Maria Volonté, and the timid comedies about sex and religion such as *The Priest's Wife*, *The Married Priest* and *The Stripping Nun*. The spaghetti westerns and gangsters refuse to bite the dust: Leone and others carrying on with *Once Upon a Time in America*, *Duck You Suckers*, *Kill Him!*, *Head Down!*, *Let's Go to Kill*,

Comrades, Big Reward for Butch Cassidy and *Violent City* which features such Hollywood heavies as James Coburn, Rod Steiger, Charles Bronson and Telly Savalas. Alberto Sordi and Nino Manfredi carry the burden of local comedy with *Where There's War There's Hope, So Long Italy, Hello Abysynnia* and *The President of the Borgorosso Football Club*.

Apart from further collaboration with Hollywood and the filming of Monicelli's *Mortadella* with Loren in New York exteriors, the Italians continue with Soviet co-productions. An interesting development is the ten one-hour television serial episodes of *Anna Karenina*, again with Loren, from which a feature film will be distilled. After *Waterloo* and *The Red Tent*, the super-colossals continue with Gillo Pontecorvo's *Queimada*, Blassetti's *Simon Bolivar*, Eriprando Visconti's *Strogoff*, Comencini's *Casanova's Childhood and First Adventures* and Castellani's *Leonardo*. The giants among the directors continue to be active. With the success of *Death in Venice*, Luchino Visconti has had the most recent acclaim. He has temporarily abandoned *The Driver's Seat* from a Muriel Spark story in favour of the long anticipated story of Marcel and Albertine from Proust's *Remembrance of Things Past* ("I can't take everything: I have to leave something for other directors!") The film should get this year's Oscar for the most phenomenal publicity lift-off with the speculations about the cast including what must be the final suggestion of a Garbo appearance.

Antonioni has gone from *Zabriskie Point* to Brazil to film, under the tentative title *Technically Sweet*, on a modest budget of $1·6m. and trying to resist Warners'

insistence upon holding the final cutting rights. De Sica, who as a director had almost sunk into oblivion since his major successes of the late forties and early fifties has come back with *The Garden of the Finzi Continis* and is to make two further films with his old collaborator, Cesare Zavattini, one, a love story *We'll Call Him Andrea*. Fellini is working on *Rome*, a multi-episode film which he describes as "an autobiographical kaleidoscope of my early years in the capital" with appearances by stars Sordi, Magnani, Mastroianni, Fabrizi and Rascel as well as by authors Gore Vidal, Alberto Moravia and Muriel Spark. Fellini seems all the time to fall deeper into nostalgia and personal fantasy: perhaps there is some hope of a break in the report that he approached Streisand with a view to filming *Much Ado About Nothing*.

Fellini, who has a commitment to make four more specials, feels that he cannot express himself within the limits of television. He may be reacting to the fact that the black-and-white showing of *The Clowns* killed its intended Italian theatrical release in colour. Other directors do not share these inhibitions about television and Rossellini with *Socrates*, Olmi with *The Scavengers* and Bertolucci with *The Spider's Strategy* have had highly pleasing experiences. Rossellini has now turned all his attention away from the cinema to television, and Bertolucci, who has had a major cinematic success with *The Conformist*, has welcomed the chance to experiment and declared that he finds "a deeper breath of freedom in television than in the cinema".

There are numerous other productions of interest: Dallamano's *Dorian Gray* with Helmut Berger; Ettore Scola's *May I*

Sergei Bondarchuk as Astrov in Andrei Mikhalkov-Konchalovsky's *Uncle Vanya* (Russia).

Akira Kurosawa's *Dodeska Den* (Japan).

78 *Introduce Myself?* with Mastroianni; Zeffirelli's *Brother Son, Sister Moon* based on St. Francis of Assisi; Lattuada's *The Man Who Came For Coffee* with Tognazzi and *White, Red and Green* with Loren; Bellocchio's *In the Name of the Father* with Yves Beneyton and Lou Castel; Bolognini's *Bubu de Montparnasse* from the romantic, turn of the century, French novel; Nelo Risi's *A Season in Hell* with Terence Stamp as Rimbaud and Jean-Claude Brialy as Verlaine; Patroni-Griffi's *'Tis a Pity She's a Whore*; Dino Risi's *She* with Vitti in a multi-role; Monicelli's *Bourvard and Pecuchet* from Flaubert with Vittorio Gassman; Enzo Muzii's *A Pink Spot*; Tinto Brass's *The Cry* and *The Vacation* with Vanessa Redgrave and Franco Nero; and Elio Petri's *The Working Class Goes to Heaven*.

SWEDEN

The fortunes of Swedish cinema have been variable in the past year. While nearly 4 per cent of the cinemas closed during the year, receipts rose by just over 1 per cent. The number of Swedish features dropped from 34 the year before to 24, though the Swedish share of receipts jumped 5 per cent to nearly 20 per cent. Well ahead of its nearest rivals, the family film *Pippi Långstrump on the Seven Seas*, and the sex information film *The Language of Love* attracted the largest audiences. With other box-office successes in *The Vicar* and *The First Stone*, the sixty-year-old director, Torgny Wickman, believing that audiences are in no danger of tiring of sex films, has embarked on *More About the Language of Love* and *Language of Love III*. He has also completed *Fear has 1,000 Eyes*.

Enough has already been written about *Blushing Charlie*, the comedy by Vilgot Sjöman which followed his sensational *Curious* films and his box-office flop, *You're Lying*, and about *The Touch*, which Bergman made with his usual crew in his usual manner despite over $1m. of American backing and despite using a foreign actor, Elliott Gould, and working in English for the first time. Another of the older directors, Arne Mattsson, who had his big international success back in 1951 with *One Summer of Happiness* but who has since fallen foul of the critics, has answered them with *Ann and Eve*, the story of a female critic who decides for purely personal reasons to drive a film director to suicide. Jarl Kulle, the leading actor whose first attempt at directing *The Bookseller Who Gave Up Bathing* was so successful, has followed up with a comedy, *The Minister*, in which he also stars. The young film-maker Johan Bergenstråhle's *Baltic Tragedy* concerns the handing back to the Soviets after the Second World War of a large number of German soldiers who had escaped to Sweden. After his social dramas, *The Corridor* and *A Dream of Freedom*, another young director, Jan Halldoff, has turned to black comedy with *Dog Days*. Second features have been made by Susan Sontag whose *Brother Carl* stars Geneviève Page, Torsten Wahlund, Keve Hjelm, Gunnel Lindblom and Laurent Terzieff and by Stellan Olsson who has followed his interesting début, *Between Us*, with *Deadline*. Other new films include: Per Berglund's *Beyond the Line of Duty*; Arne Stivell's *The Midsummer Dance*; Torbjörn Lindquist's *Sound of Näverlur*; and Gunnar Höglund's *Do You Believe in Swedish Sin?*

U.S.S.R.

Apparently unaffected by television, cinema attendances continue to rise in the Soviet Union and this year are expected to top 5,000 million. About five features and fifteen shorts are released every week, and the Russians are still researching into three-dimensional cinema which is a sign of their optimism for the medium. The most recent system projects eight to ten sequences simultaneously to produce a single three-dimensional screen image which does not require polaroid spectacles.

Several genres seem to be eternally popular: the war film, e.g. Ozerov's *Liberation* dealing with the last two years of the Second World War; the homages to Lenin, e.g. Georgiev's adaptation of the play *The Kremlin Chimes*; the opera film, e.g. Victor Titov's version of Prokofiev's *Love of Three Oranges* with Tamara Nosova and Boris Amarantov; and the biographical pictures with *Goya* and *Tchaikovsky* being followed by *I, Francis Skorina* about a sixteenth-century Byelorussian philosopher, and *Lieutenant Basil* about a more recent Ukrainian war hero. Another biographical feature of interest is the two-part life of the great singer *Fyodor Chaliapin* which Mark Donskoy, who established international fame over thirty years ago with his *Maxim Gorky* trilogy, has begun and will partly shoot in France and Italy. Another veteran, Sergei Gerasimov, has made a love story, *By the Lake*, around one of his favourite themes, youth in contemporary society, while the much-admired wild-life photographer Alexander Zguridi has gone into the Indian jungles and villages to make a co-production, *Black Mountain*. Among the films by younger directors, the new version of Chekhov's *Uncle Vanya* by Andrei Mikhalkov-Konchalovsky stands out. Konchalovsky made a fine début with *The First Teacher* and followed up with a beautiful version of Turgenev's *A Nest of Gentlefolk*. Vanya is played by Innokenty Smoktunovsky, the Russian film *Hamlet*, and Astrov is played by the great actor and director of *War and Peace*, Sergei Bondarchuk. Two other features deserve mention: *The Ambler's Race*, the first directorial assignment of cameraman Sergei Uresevski and *Bluebird* by Vasily Livanov, an actor who has had many leading roles but who has now gone over to making cartoons with considerable success.

JAPAN

From an international point of view, the major event of the last year has been the return to film-making after five years of Akira Kurosawa with *Dodeska-den*, his first film in colour. Some other veteran directors have also made comebacks in independent productions. Shohei Imamura made a semi-documentary review, *Post-war History in Japan*, about a bar madam who caters for foreign servicemen; Masaki Kobayashi made a period drama, *Let's Stake Our Lives*; the late Tomu Uchida completed a swashbuckler, *Shinken Shobu* before his death; and Kon Ichikawa filmed the romance of a French youth and Japanese girl in *Pourquoi*. The attempt of some of the top stars such as Toshiro Mifune to follow the directors into independent production with star-studded pieces (*Machibue* and *The Walking Major*) have been neither critical nor box-office successes. And while Kurosawa has had a critical success, *Dodeska-den* is struggling to recoup its costs

despite the director's efforts at personal promotion for the first time in his career. Kurosawa has called for an overhaul of the major production companies and the block booking system and has urged the injection of government finance.

There have been a number of outstanding films such as Yamada's *Where Spring Comes Late*, the story of a coal-mining family who cross country to start a new life on a dairy farm, and two anti-war films, *The Militarists* and Yamamoto's *Men and War*. Shinoda has made one of the lavish period spectacles, *The Scandalous Adventures of Buraikan* with Tatsuya Nakadai and Shima Iwashita. Other independent productions of note have come from Oshima, the intriguingly-titled *The Story of a Young Man Who Left His Will on Film*; Yoshida, *Heroic Purgatory*; and Wakamatsu, *Shinjuku Mad*.

However, the most successful genres are the gangster, gambling and sex films. *Bullet Wound*, *Showdown at Nagasaki*, *The Clean-up*, *Womanboss*, *Wolves of the City*, *Operation Rat*, *Showdown in Blood*, *Kamikaze Kop*, *Mini-skirted Gambler* and *Sexphobia* are among the string of titles of films which have sustained the industry and provoked the police. The deaths of Uchida and Eiji Tsuburaya, the special effects expert of *Godzilla*, *Mothra*, *King Kong*, have been a serious loss to the Japanese horror movie. None the less the monsters keep appearing in films such as *Space Amoeba* and *Gamera vs. Jiger*, the former a staunch friend of children and the latter a hideous monster bent on wrecking the Japanese World Expo site.

Another death of significance to the Japanese cinema was that of the leading novelist and swordsman Yukio Mishima,

who made the world headlines when he committed harakiri after taking over a military camp. Ten of Mishima's novels had been filmed and two, *The Temple of the Golden Pavilion* and *Enjo*, had inspired two of Ichikawa's finest works. *Thirst*, published in Japan in 1950 but only recently issued here as *Sun and Steel*, was filmed by Kurahara in 1968 and has Ruriko Asaoka as the lovely widow who falls in love with a young gardener.

CZECHOSLOVAKIA

The troubled history of Czechoslovak cinema since summer 1968 continues to be shrouded in some doubt. What we do know is that there has been bureaucratic pressure and reorganisation of the management of the state industry and that a number of films have been refused distribution. This would seem to have been the fate of Schorm's *The Seventh Day, the Eighth Night*, Menzel's *Larks on a String*, Kachyna's *The Ear*, Sirovy's *Funeral Rites*, Jakubisco's *Birds, Orphans, Fools* and Bocan's *The Decoy*. Other films have started with one director and finished with another. Jasny began directing *Dogs and People* but finished with only a script credit, the direction going to Schorm. *The Murder of Mr. Devil*, earlier announced as Nemec's films, was directed by Ester Krumbachová who had worked on the script.

The character of Czech cinema would have changed in any case with the death of Trnka and the break-up of the long partnership of Kadár and Klos. The team which had made many features over the past twenty years including the international success of *The Shop on the High Street*, ended their partnership with *Anada*, a wide

80 screen, colour film, co-produced with the Americans and starring the Yugoslav actress Milena Pravic. Kadár has stayed in the States to continue film-making but Klos has returned to his teaching duties at the Prague Film School. Milos Forman is also still abroad and made his first US film *Taking Off*.

The new leadership at the Czech studios has debunked some past successes and declared itself against art for art's sake and in favour of entertainment. The emphasis is on comedies, fairy tales, children's films and films for television. Examples: Lipsky's *Four Murders are Enough, Dear*, a gangster comedy; Moskalyk's *Grandmother*, a romantic version of a classic fairy tale; Hanibal's *The Ponies of Karlovy Vary* for West German TV; Podskalsky's comedy *The Devil's Honeymoon*; Cech's musical *The Holy Sinner*; and Karel Zeman's fantasy *On the Comet*. Papoušek has followed *Ecce Homo Homolka* with *Hogo Fogo Homolka*, a tragi-comedy about the death of great-grandfather Homolka, using the same actors, Helená Ruzicková, Josef Hušak, Josef Sebanek, Marie Morlová and the Forman twins. Another sequel on the Homolka family fortunes is anticipated.

There has been a great increase in the number of colour films and it seems to be the intention to move towards a bigger scale of production, particularly in the co-productions with the East Germans on 70 mm. Two films in this category are Brynych's *Oasis* and Cech's *The Great White Road* based on stories by Jack London. Two more East German co-productions are Sequens's *The Duel of the Vultures* and Lipsky's *The Straw Hat*.

Other films likely to be of interest are: Gajer's *Catherine and Her Children*; *Well, Hello*, the directorial début of the young actor Vit Olmer; Hobl's *The Great Unknown*, three psychological fantasies; Schmidt's *The Bow of Queen Dorothy*; Solan's *The Master did Not Ask for Anything* with the great Slovak actor Josef Kroner; and *The Bride*, the first feature of pop singer, actor, songwriter, poet, Jiří Suchy.

WEST GERMANY

When film critics withhold their prizes to draw attention to the precarious state of the industry, it would seem that in West Germany the cinema is in worse shape than elsewhere. There are still many closures and it is not encouraging that, apart from sex films, currently the most successful genres are schoolboy and "mad aunt" comedies. The sex films go on with *The Nude Countess*, *Confessions of Sweet Seventeen, Bordello*, etc., and the big question is will the West German film industry survive if there is a decline in the popularity of the cheap sex film? Perhaps hope lies in the horror film, a genre which gave German cinema an international reputation back in the twenties. Three examples: Haro Seno's *Purgatory*; Harry Kumel's *Blood on Your Lips*, described as a horrorgasm; and Hans Geissendoerfer's *Jonathon* which has vampires and political overtones in a story of unsuccessful revolution in 1975. (It sounds as if the East Germans could also be off on a horror kick for their lists include *The Screech Owl Pit* and *Mohr and the Ravens of London* among such predictable titles as *The Dead Will Remain Young* and *At Noon the Boss Walks In*.)

Two directors who may be worth watching are Peter Fleischmann and Rainer Werner

Werner Hertzog's *Even Dwarfs Started Small* (West Germany).

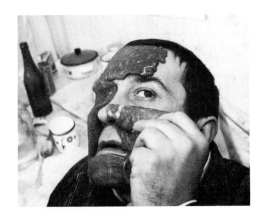

Kozomara and Mihic's black comedy *The Crows* (Yugoslavia).

Carlos Saura's *Garden of Delights* (Spain).

Fassbinder. After a bitter first feature on fascism and anti-semitism, Fleischmann has made a problems of youth picture, *Havoc*, with United Artists backing. Fassbinder, whose *Katzelmacher* was described as anti-theatre and in debt to the minimal cinema of Straub, has made a perfect killer story, *The American Soldier*.

Other films likely to be of interest: Franz Josef Spieker's *Kuckucksei im Gangsternest*, a wild satire on the *nouveaux riches*; Ulrich Schamoni's *Wir-Zwei*, a straightforward love story about the disillusionment of the man when he finds his former girlfriend is now a staid housewife; Hans Juergen Syberburg's *San Domingo*, adapted from Heinrich von Kleist's classic novel and mixing realistic and surrealistic sequences.

YUGOSLAVIA

Like most European cinemas, the Yugoslav is supposed to be in a temporary crisis, a creative lethargy. Our notion of Yugoslav film is dominated by partisan dramas, stark and cruel action and a pessimistic tone. Many films are still concerned with bizarre aspects of the war such as Mimicca's *The Nourishee* in which the inmates of a concentration camp set aside their rations to build up the nourishee who is earmarked to kill a brutal Capo, and Djordjević's *Cyclists* which was inspired by the first partisan "motorised" unit in 1941 using captured German army bicycles. The traumas of the war and the present would seem to be reflected in such titles as Petrović's *Moribund Spring* and Čengić's *The Role of My Family in World Revolution*. The work of other directors often has a crazy, schizophrenic quality as, for example, in Radivojević's *Bats in the Belfry* and Kozomara and Mihic's *Crows*, a black comedy which it is not easy for outsiders to penetrate.

Despite the apparent malaise, new directors have been getting opportunities; apart from Radivojević, there is Pleša's *Lilika*, Fannelli's *Way to Paradise* and Galić's *The First Love*. And the production schedules would seem to hold much of promise in Babaja's *Odour, Gold and Incense*, Pavlović's *Red Crop*, Janković's *A Bloody Tale*, Velimirović's *Blood Feud*, Drašković's *Knockout*, Fadej's *He Who Sings Means No Evil* and Hadzic's *Wild Angels*. Coming from Dusan Makavejev who made *Switchboard Operator* and who has been away studying in the US for the past two years, *WR or the Mysteries of the Body* is likely to be an interesting curiosity at the very least. WR stands for Wilhelm Reich whose writings such as "The Function of the Orgasm" have inspired Makavejev's new film. It is unlikely to be any ordinary sex film.

HUNGARY

Hungarian cinema does not seem to be going through one of its more exciting phases, partly, perhaps, because Miklós Jancsó is away in Italy filming with Monica Vitti, Pierre Clémenti and Daniel Olbrychski. The old directors, such as Zóltan Fábri with *The Toth Family*, keep going and there are still directorial débuts such as Sándor Simó's *The Bespectacled*. Some of the directors who began their careers in the late fifties are also showing strongly: János Herskó with *Requiem in the Hungarian Manner*, Tamás Banovich with *Lovely Hungarian Comedy* and Pál Zolnay with *The Face* which aims at various levels of emotion and ideology in the story of a young communist at the end of the war. The team

82 that produced *Ten Thousand Suns*, Ferenc Kosá, Sándor Csoóri and Sándor Sára have made a Hungarian–Rumanian–Slovak co-production, *Judgement*, about Gyorgy Dosza, the leader of the rebellion of the serfs in 1514.

If any cinema is obsessed with love, it is the Hungarian. Apart from Márton Keleti's *Dreams of Love*, there is István Szabó's *A Film About Love* which integrates personal emotions and historical events and Károly Makk's *Love* with Lili Darvas, Mari Torocsik and Ivan Darvas. Based on a short story by Tibor Dery, *Love* deals with the nostalgic memories of the pre-1914 world of a dying, old woman and the efforts of her daughter to keep her happy with stories of the success of her son as a film director in Hollywood when he is, in fact, a political prisoner.

POLAND

Last year's hope that Polish cinema was about to enter a purple patch has not been fulfilled. While the first works of some young directors attracted much critical attention, it was Kazimierz Kutz's folk ballad, *A Taste of Black Earth* about the uprisings in Upper Silesia in 1919–21, which won most domestic praise, and the most popular Polish films abroad were Wajda's *Landscape After the Battle*, Chmielewski's *How I Unleashed the Second World War*, Piotrowski's *The Star of the Season* and Majewski's *Lokis*.

Most films are still set in the closing stages of the war or in the early post-war period. Zbigniew Chmielewski's *Angel's Face* centres on a concentration camp for children. Piotrowski's *The Trap* depicts the efforts of a small town to prevent the retreating Nazi army destroying a coal-mine. Jan Rybkowski's *The Return* is a story of unfulfilled love in the migrations which took place just after the war. Passendorfer's *Operation Brutus* deals with the resistance to the new regime in 1946–47. Scibor-Rylski's *An Echo of Evil* is a mountain adventure concerning Ukrainian nationalist bands. The rest of the films are for the most part either period films or contemporary comedies. The historical pieces include the Petelskis' *Nicolaus Copernicus* made to mark the 500th anniversary of the astronomer's birth; Lesiewicz's *Boleslaus the Bold* about an eleventh-century king; and Roziewicz's *The Romantics*, a story of love and disillusion in mid-nineteenth-century Prussia. The comedies include Jan Batory's *A Cure for Love* and Tadeusz Chmieleski's *I Don't Like Mondays*.

Andrzej Wajda has described his latest film, *The Birch Wood*, as "a farewell to a romantic outlook". Made for television, it is set in the thirties and is about a young man dying of tuberculosis who returns to his brother's home in the forest and meets a vital, peasant girl. The result is a curiously bewitching pastoral. It will be interesting to see in which direction Wajda turns next. Other noteworthy films: Zanussi's *The Family Life*, Haupe's *Landscape With a Hero*, Solarz's *A Challenge* and Lenartowicz's *Calm Flat*.

Knud Leif Thomsen's *Jazz All Around* (Denmark).

Andrzej Wajda's *The Birch Wood* (Poland).

RELEASES OF THE YEAR
IN PICTURES

(You will find more detailed information about the films illustrated in a later section of this volume—The Year's Releases in detail)

Universal's *Airport* was one of those big, glossy, all-star movies which, in the direct "Grand Hotel" tradition, offer plenty for your money; and very entertaining it was, too, with its several intertwined personal stories seen against the background of an American Mid-West airport struggling against one of the worst blizzards in years. Van Heflin (i) played the mental case planning to blow his plane up with a bomb – seen with him, Maureen Stapleton. Helen Hayes (ii) was the dear old lady who knows all the best ways of airways free-riding – with her, John Findlater. George Kennedy (iii) was the maintenance man whose efforts to move a snowed-up plane can mean life or death for another one trying to land, and (iv) Dean Martin played an egotistical pilot, brother-in-law to the dedicated, harassed airport manager (Burt Lancaster) on whose shoulders rest most of the responsibilities.

84

If brutal in its realism, CIRO's *They Shoot Horses, Don't They?* was at the same time a brilliantly detailed re-creation of a now almost-forgotten period: the Big American Depression and all that it brought in its wake. Jane Fonda (inset) played one of many pathetic entrants in a typical Hollywood Dance Marathon, struggling to the edge – and in some cases beyond the edge – of human endurance before a sadistically applauding audience for the all-important money prizes to be won by those tough enough to stay the course to the end.

Another view of the American scene, this time a contemporary one, was given by the widely popular Frankovich production for Columbia of *Bob and Carol and Ted and Alice,* which with amusing insight examined some of the up-to-date mores and morals involved in a story about two young married couples who start out as very good friends and proceed from that point! The leading couple were played by Natalie Wood and Robert Culp.

Elia Kazan also examined modern American Society in his interesting, though less than wholly successful, adaptation of his own novel, *The Arrangement* (for Warner–Pathé), which was about an extremely successful – American! – man who, with wealth, wife and mistress suddenly realises the futility of existence and tries, less than determinedly, to take a suicide's way out: subsequently deciding to sort things out the less spectacular, harder way.

The colour question as it disturbs the American conscience was the subject, in one way or another, directly or obliquely, of a number of films, among the best of which was Columbia's *The Liberation of L. B. Jones*, a careful and balanced story about the way that a basically honest, high-principled Southern American lawyer (Lee J. Cobb) becomes unwillingly involved in a nasty case of racial prejudice when an affluent negro undertaker (Roscoe Lee Browne) is murdered by two white cops, one of whom (Anthony Zerbe) is having an affair with the undertaker's fascinating but faithless wife (Lola Falana).

MGM's . . . *tick . . . tick . . . tick . . .* was concerned with the difficulties of a coloured American deep south sheriff (Jim Brown) whose efforts to keep honest law and order are complicated by the racial prejudice which everywhere surrounds him. With him in this scene, George Kennedy.

A happier, more lovingly set scene was that of Memphis in 1905, created by director Mark Rydell in his Warner–Pathé film *The Reivers*, with its slim story about a boy losing his illusions and growing up against a beautifully detailed, nostalgic background of the life of the period. Star of the film, playing the boy's mentor, was Steve McQueen.

Yet another facet of American life was examined with care and perception in Columbia's *Loving*: the story of a (typical?) North US suburban family: the father an ambitious, hard-drinking, sex-seeking, basically insecure business executive whose unhappy wife sees the marital gulf widening all the time and so many of her neighbours in the same sort of troubles. George Segal played the husband, Eva Marie Saint the wife.

Another story of America's more recent past was in MGM's *The Moonshine War* which, set in the days of prohibition and gangsters, told a story of one of the periodic flare-ups in the long-lasting war between the authorities and the Moonshiners, or illicit spirit distillers of the Southern States. Richard Widmark, for the distillers, was opposed by government agent Patrick McGoohan.

There were no political implications or any other serious undertones in Columbia's quite charmingly old-fashioned *A Walk in the Spring Rain*, a vehicle for one of Ingrid Bergman's now quite rare screen appearances. She played a sedately married woman, a professor's wife, who is tempted towards marital infidelity when she comes to stay for a while in the quiet rusticity of the Great Smoky Mountains and meets a down-to-earth character (Anthony Quinn) who quickly falls in love with her.

The ubiquitous Mr. Quinn was seen again in roaring form in the extremely amusing, musical comedy-style Stanley Kramer film, *The Secret of Santa Vittoria*, which was set in a small town in Northern Italy and was based on a factual case of villagers hiding a million bottles of wine – their entire wealth – from the Germans when the latter took over the town at the fall of Mussolini. Sergio Franchi played the Italian Army deserter who suggests the perfect hiding place and Virna Lisi was the Countess who helps the plot along.

Apparently one of the most successful Westerns of the year at the box-office was the meticulously authentic *A Man Called Horse*, which related the story of an English milord (Richard Harris) in the Dakotas in the 19th century who, taken prisoner by the Sioux while out hunting and made a slave, climbed, by a long, slow and extremely painful process, from that position to become an acknowledged member and "brave" of the tribe.

The similarly titled Columbia Western *A Man Called Sledge* starred James Garner as a villain, a "wanted" bandit, involved with like undesirable characters in plot and counter-plot to steal the weekly half-million golden output of the rich mine near the town so oddly named 3W's.

A larger scale, bloodier struggle for gold was the focal point of John Guillermin's *El Condor* in which the opponents were those within the fortress of the title, with the gold, and those without but wanting it! In a cast which included such Western familiars as Iron Eyes Cody and Lee Van Cleef, Patrick O'Neal (shown dealing with attacking Apaches) played the soldier in command of the fort.

More gold – this time fashioned into a native-revered Madonna statue – and the efforts by the crooks to steal it was the heart of the story of Fox's *Joaquin Murieta*, in which Ricardo Montalban was involved in some very rough stuff indeed in the turbulent California of the mid-1800s.

Most rewarding for the real Western film fan was the fact that Big John Wayne, that rough, indestructible rider of the range, took to his celluloid saddle on several occasions during the period: once for Batjac–Warner's *Chisum*, in which in true Grit-ish manner he defeated the machinations of all kinds of baddies and triumphantly maintained law and order.

And in Carthay Center's *The Cheyenne Social Club* we had two fine old Western stars for the price of one: James Stewart and Henry Fonda as a couple of Texas cow-hands who discover at the end of the 1,000-mile trek they make to take up the former's inheritance that it is a bawdy and not boarding house which has been left him by his brother: and a fully and prettily staffed (inset) brothel at that!

Even more comic and less conventionally Western was Warner's *The Great Bank Robbery* in which Texas ranger Clint Walker (seen succumbing to the aggressive wooing tactics of Kim Novak) stands between the many plots to rob the local bank.

92

Another of these less conventional, more insistently comic Westerns was MGM's *Dirty Dingus Magee*, in which Frank Sinatra played a small-time crook way out West and Michele Carey was the very pretty Indian who becomes his companion.

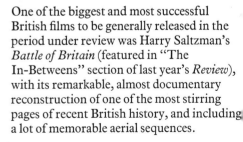

George Hilton, a new Western name, seems, as the hero of the European-made Western *For a Few Bullets More*, to be in a pretty unpleasant situation while he's on the mission to grab a million dollars in gold – and several other baddies have the same thing in mind.

One of the biggest and most successful British films to be generally released in the period under review was Harry Saltzman's *Battle of Britain* (featured in "The In-Betweens" section of last year's *Review*), with its remarkable, almost documentary reconstruction of one of the most stirring pages of recent British history, and including a lot of memorable aerial sequences.

94

Very much on the ground was CIRO's consistently tense and gripping story of Pacific island warfare, *Too Late the Hero*, in which Cliff Robertson played the American officer seconded to lead a suicidal English military sabotage mission against a Japanese camp and its radar establishment – a deadly trek from which only the American and one survivor, the indomitable cockney character played by Michael Caine, return to within sight of base – and there have to run the final gauntlet.

Crooked artist David Hemmings watches reactions to his portrait of the girl whose love he has shamelessly exploited as he plans to rob her employer in MGM's *The Walking Stick*.

Britain's representative Michael Crawford collapses during the last few yards of the Marathon race in Michael Winner's *The Games* for Fox, a story of and behind an Olympics meeting in which more than the athletics and athletes are involved.

Peter Sellers kisses his pretty prisoner Sinead Cusack in Warner–Pathé's *Hoffman*, in which he played the gentle, middle-aged businessman who falls madly in love with one of his prettier and younger employees, whom he blackmails into spending a week with him in his flat – and it all ends up like a fairy story!

Love more kinky and far less pleasant was the motivation of Alan Gibson's *Goodbye Gemini* for CIRO, with Judy Geeson and Martin Potter playing identical twins with a vague suggestion of incest, who come to London and get involved with a lot of particularly nasty characters and through them with double murder and suicide – a story that left an unpleasant taste in the mouth in spite of its lush production values and technically polished direction.

96

Two of the *Toomorrow* musical group who give the title to a quite happy little UA musical which ranged from the London College of Art to spies from Outer Space and was both written and directed by Val Guest.

More unhealthy relationships were to be found in MGM's odd little movie *My Lover, My Son* – a title which rather illustrates the point! Romy Schneider played the all too possessive Momma and Dennis Waterman the cosily cossetted son, and it all ends in murder most (melodramatically) foul.

Unpleasant, too, in atmosphere was Eagle's *Groupie Girl*, which told a story of one of those silly little girls who follow the Pop Groups around "collecting" (or having sexual relations with) as many of their members as they can. This rather lurid story had Esme Johns thrown out by one Group's leader (Jimmie Edwards) and winding up in the arms of the law.

The start of it all . . . The Baron, Curt Jurgens, and his faithless wife (new star Geneviève Gilles) offer the British car salesman-mechanic (played by Michael Crawford) a lift outside the Casino and so lay the seeds for the long and chequered liaison that is to follow in Fox's *Hello–Goodbye*.

Another angle of the contemporary Pop scene was in Avco–Embassy's *The Man Who Had Power Over Women*, in which Rod Taylor played the manager of Pop people – and one unpleasant young star in particular – who becomes immersed in his clients' sordid troubles.

Columbia's *The Buttercup Chain* suffered from the kind of uncertainty of object and outlook which afflicts the four young people with whom it was concerned; the story weaving its way from a fairy-tale opening to a tragic ending. Two of the quartet were Jane Asher and Leigh Taylor-Young.

Though the period covered in this feature was generally a sensationally sexy and otherwise adult one in the cinema, there was a leavening of movies appealing to the younger generation. For instance, that fine actor Lionel Jeffries turned script-writer/director to bring to the screen a charming and careful adaptation of the Victorian classic for youngsters, *The Railway Children*, the story of three likeable youngsters and their quite eventful sojourn in a cottage bordering on a railway cutting in rural Yorkshire. The children were played by Gary Warren, Jenny Agutter and Sally Thomsett, one of whose more solid achievements is to stop a train before it ploughs into a landslide.

Disney's range of offerings was wide, from animal stories and warm little tales of man-and-animal friendships to short and feature cartoons, the latter being represented by *The Aristocats*, the story of a very blue-blooded Paris-based Puss who, with her family of three small kittens, becomes the object of envy of the animal's wealthy and adoring owner's greedy butler and is marooned by him many miles away in the country. However, the villain's plan is duly thwarted, thanks to the resources of O'Malley (left) and his Alley Cat pals (inset).

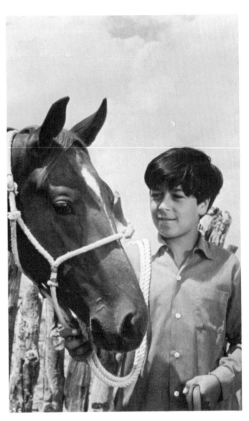

Even funnier was the shorter cartoon feature *It's Tough to be a Bird*, an amusing ornithological survey of our feathered friends made with great style and lots of wit.

Two examples of boy and pet friendships which are a favourite recurring Disney subject were *Hang Your Hat on the Wind* (a) and *Smoke* (b). The first was a film about a young Indian boy and the horse which, having captured it, he comes to love and which he finally wins for himself. The boy was played by Ric Natoli, a young Navajo. Ronny Howard played the lad in the second film, an adaptation of a William Corbin novel about a boy who finds a wounded Alsatian dog and nurses him back to health, and then through his canine friend grows up and comes to a closer understanding of his elders.

A real animal, "Charlie", was the hero of *Charlie, the Lonesome Cougar*, one of the Disney studio's series of real-life films (with fictional trimmings) about various animals.

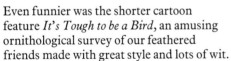

Disney's *The Boatniks* was aimed at the whole family rather than specifically its younger members and was a quite charming little farce-comedy of particular appeal to all who love "messing about with boats". Among the stars: young Robert Morse and old favourite Don Ameche.

Fantasy, thrills and fun – of a kind! – were all in Hammer's *When Dinosaurs Ruled the Earth*, which was all about the breathless adventures of dawn-of-world glamour girl Victoria Vetri (a shapely newcomer from Eastern Europe, see above) who at one point in the story finds herself in a dinosaur's nest, accepted as one of the beast's prettier progeny.

David Niven, the wheel in one hand, his favourite tipple in the other, as *The Extraordinary Seaman*, a weird little thriller from MGM about World War Two in the Pacific with Niven in charge of a British ship not listed at the Admiralty or elsewhere, but very real to all the motley crew who sail in her!

David Greene's UA film *I Start Counting* was a neat, unpretentious but gripping British thriller about some sex murders, seen against a convincing background of a suburban council estate. The film was also concerned with the growing up of the 16-year-old girl most deeply involved – a part played most beautifully by newcomer Jenny Agutter (inset).

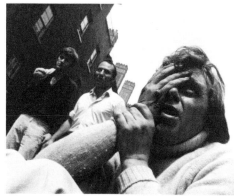

Investigating David Hemmings takes possible information-supplier Roland Culver for a wind-swept, rainy sea-front walk in Columbia's *Fragment of Fear*, a very professional thriller about the mysterious murder of an old lady in Pompeii which leads her puzzled and worried nephew a long chase until . . . The tail, twisted or otherwise, either infuriated or delighted you – according to personal taste.

Night After Night After Night was a thriller from Butcher's about the tracking down of a psychopath killer, with several red herrings neatly salted before the final (surprise. . . ?) revealing of the guilty man.

The Irving Allen/MGM film adaptation of the Mark Hebden novel *Eyewitness* never quite became an outstanding thriller, although it did come quite close to it, with its intriguing story about a little boy living on Malta (Mark Lester) who is such a natural romancer that when after seeing a political murder and, as the only witness, becoming the next on the assassins' "death" list, he cannot convince anyone – including sister Susan George – that he is speaking the truth. Inset: the villain's plans for the end of the boy but from which he manages to escape.

Executioner George Peppard prepares to carry out the personal sentence he has passed on suspect spy Keith Michell in the Columbia film of that title, a highly complicated story of Russian and American and British spies weaving their intricate webs of intrigue and murder.

More international espionage in John Huston's Fox thriller *The Kremlin Letter*, a technically almost faultless and generally exciting condensation and adaptation of the Noel Behn book about the ruthless underground struggle of the several countries involved to gain possession of an incriminating letter written by an indiscreet US diplomat to the Russians, in which he promises them help in any action they may decide to take against the Chinese! In the first scene the American spy team of George Sanders, Dean Jagger, Barbara Parkins and Patrick O'Neal is briefed by their leader Richard Boone (centre). In the second scene with Sanders and O'Neal, the plot progresses in strange ways!

Roger Moore faces up to his problems in one of the first films to be made under the Bryan Forbes production plan for Associated British. As the worried fellow in the title, *The Man Who Haunted Himself*, the ex-"Saint" begins to wonder if he's going off his trolley as one strange event follows another, all adding up to the self-doubts that the mysterious enemy are anxious to implant in him.

Another of these early Forbes films for Associated was also a thriller, *And Soon the Darkness*, a beautifully atmosphered murder mystery – albeit a somewhat leisurely paced one – set in a quiet piece of Northern French countryside in the high summer and concerning holidaying nurse Pamela Franklin's attempts to discover what has happened to her suddenly vanished cycling companion.

Patricia Heywood (as "Nanny"), Robert Swann (as "Soldier") and Ursula Howells (as "Mumsy") play one of their strange, ritualistic "games" in the modestly made, utterly unbelievable but highly effective (and rather sadly neglected – at the box-office) black comedy thriller for Fitzroy–CIRO, *Mumsy, Nanny, Sonny and Girly*, in which a bizarre and frightening family play with their selected "guests" until they tire of them, whereupon they happily "send them to heaven" – hence the head that bubbles on the stove.

Woodfall's *Kes* was a sad illustration of the way that a really good film of wide appeal – and "Kes" was all that and more, in fact it was a small masterpiece – can be unjustly neglected by the cinema bookers. For, internationally acclaimed as it was, this moving, amusing story of a Barnsley schoolboy and the hawk he catches, trains and finds giving him a new and vivid interest in life, had a struggle to get more than isolated showings and was never generally released in the normal sense. A wonderfully directed film (by Ken Loach) including a number of quite unforgettable sequences. David Bradley played the boy and Colin Welland was the understanding schoolmaster.

Another unusual, highly personal (and probably almost certainly financially unsuccessful movie) was John ("Funnyman") Korty's *riverrun*, a visual poem about the inter-reactions of an old salt, a sea captain home from the sea (John McLiam), his beloved daughter (Louise Ober) and the young man (Mark Jenkins) she is living with and helping in his struggles on a small and dismal farm, all of which helps to accentuate the tensions that lead to the final outburst of violence.

Some rather odd casting gave Mick Jagger the leading, straight-acting role in UA's *Ned Kelly*, a sort of strip cartoon version of the story of the famous Australian bushranger, and one of the less successful technical experiments of the year.

Certainly more successful in part, if perhaps not overall, was Joseph Strick's gallant effort to capture the difficult, literary flavour of Henry Miller's bawdy autobiographical book, *Tropic of Cancer*, with its eroticism and foul language. Rip Torn played the writer, seen here with Phil Brown.

Another film certainly needing the new climate of censorial tolerance was Fox's screen adaptation of the Mart Crowley play about homosexuals, *The Boys in the Band*. The four boys in this scene of anger are played by Reuben Greene, Cliff Gorman, Peter White and Laurence Luckinbill.

A nice example of one way in which the film is going, the undisciplined, underground way, was illustrated by Robert Downey's wild and weird swipe at The Establishment, *Putney Swope*.

Don Stroud (right) screams in terror as his unstable and unlikeable pal (Gordon Thomson) gets his just desserts at the hand of the mounties in *Explosion*, a story of two young Americans unable to take the strains of modern life who make this an excuse to explode into violence.

  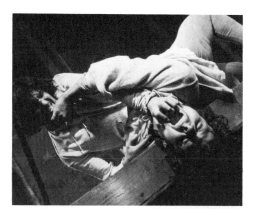

And so to the chiller-thrillers, one of the most consistently successful genres of this or any other cinematic year. Robert Quarry, as *Count Yorga, Vampire* in the American International film of that title.

The clever mixture of violence and eroticism which are such important elements in so many of the new school of horror films, illustrated by two scenes from Anglo's *Cry of the Banshee*.

Monster David Prowse, looking like a do-it-yourself Frankenstein creation, presides over little – but certainly well endowed – Kate O'Mara in Hammer's *The Horror of Frankenstein*.

Christopher Lee as everybody's favourite bloodsucker – Count Dracula: in Hammer's horror piece *The Scars of Dracula*. And you'd have to have seen the film to know what is terrifying the bedded couple Christopher Matthews and Anoushka Hempel in another scene from the movie.

 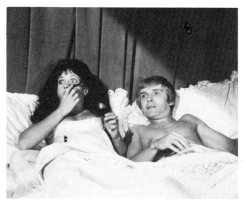

110

Peter Cushing gets to work on Ingrid Pitt in Hammer's *The Vampire Lovers*, a new screen adaptation of Sheridan le Fanu's vampirish little classic called "Carmilla". And Miss Pitt walks away from the body on the stairs . . .

III

Sandra Dee gets a grisly shock in Anglo's *The Dunwich Horror*, in which she becomes captivated by a nasty piece of work called Wilbur, who persuades her to help him with his sexual and other horrible rites and, finally, is raising Old Nick himself!

Vincent Price and Peter Arne confront each other in Anglo's *The Oblong Box*, an adaptation of one of Edgar Allan Poe's famous tales of terror.

112

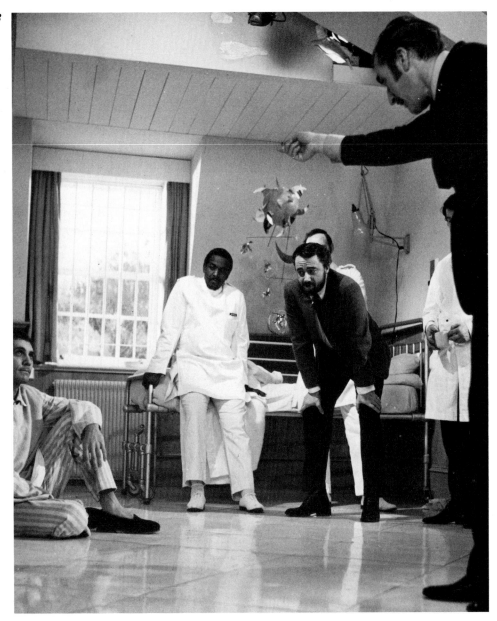

A little bit of grave robbing in *Ravaged*, a chiller-diller about beauty-grafting, which in spite of having English dialogue started life in France with the title "La Rose Ecorchée".

A strange little film, far enough out of the rut to make a wide success impossible, was Alan Cooke's Columbia film *The Mind of Mr. Soames*, in which Terence Stamp played the part of a man with the mind of a child who becomes the object of constant medical and scientific surveillance and experiment until he rebels and breaks out of the claustrophobic circle. Among the kindly tormentors, Robert Vaughn and Nigel Davenport.

Tremendously successful both sides of the Atlantic, Fox's *M*A*S*H* represented an entirely new departure in black, anarchic, crazy comedy, with its war story about a group of young doctors and nurses determinedly carrying on their private lives, coupling and joking among the broken, bloody bodies they go casually to work on. The film introduced several new comedians to the screen, including Elliott Gould, Tom Skerritt and Donald Sutherland.

Tony Curtis as one of the three modern musketeers in CIRO's comedy *Suppose They Gave a War and Nobody Came,* a modern-style, vaguely M★A★S★H-like comedy about three American soldiers who (in peacetime) decide to foster community relations with a nearby town to their camp and end up by creating a little war of their own.

CIRO's *Take the Money and Run* was very much of an exercise for American comedian Woody Allen, who worked from his own script (sharing credit for it with Mickey Rose) and directed himself as star of this consistently, if quietly satirically funny biographical story of a young man who has the ambition but not the ability to become one of America's top-listed wanted criminals.

Entirely conventional, but deliciously amusing, was Columbia's adaptation of the bubbling, witty stage play success *Cactus Flower*, in which Walter Matthau, Ingrid Bergman and Goldie Hawn (her first starring role in the cinema) as a marriage-shy New York dentist, his coolly lovely nurse and trusting young mistress respectively all gave superb performances.

Obviously not overjoyed at Robert Wagner's rescue of abducted Barbara Rhoades is Mary Tyler Moore in the Universal comedy *Don't Just Stand There*.

116

Essentially British in its humour was Warner–Pathé's *Some Will, Some Won't*, a story of a practical joker who leaves £600,000 to four people – but leaves it on conditions. . . ! Ronnie Corbett played the timid little nephew who stands to get a quarter of the inheritance providing he can pluck up enough courage to rob his own bank at gunpoint!

Inextinguishably British in style, humour and story are those everlastingly successful "Carry On" films of which the 1970 release was *Carry on Up the Jungle*, with all the old gang of comics working hard and well, including Joan Sims and Kenneth Connor.

And nothing could have been more English than *All the Way Up*, the screen version of the David Turner stage play "Semi-Detached" with its farcical story about the little cockney insurance salesman (Warren Mitchell, right) who has visions of grandeur and ruthlessly uses his family (including wife Elaine Taylor, centre, and daughter Pat Heywood, left) to translate those visions into reality.

118 Robert Morley as ship's captain and Harry Secombe as the pools winning passenger who appears at the ship's dance dressed in identical manner to him, are two of the players who keep the fun coming in a further comedy medical chapter from Betty Box, *Doctor in Trouble*.

David Warner as the unfortunate young man in *The Engagement*, a short comedy in which with ever mounting panic he goes from place to place trying in vain to raise the money to pay off the taxi in which he is travelling and which goes on ticking up the shillings which he hasn't got to settle the bill.

Marty Ingels and Catherine Spaak in a scene from UA's comedy *If it's Tuesday, this must be Belgium*, an allusion to the typical American package tour of Europe which it satirises.

UA's *One More Time* was a second "Salt and Pepper" film and something of a sequel to that comedy, with Sammy Davis Jnr. playing Charlie Salt and Peter Lawford as Chris Pepper, both equally involved in a complicated comic crookery plot.

Charles Chaplin's 1928 feature *The Circus* was re-issued this year with a new musical sound track of his music and even with a theme song (sung by Chaplin, too!). One of his less widely-known long pictures, it contains some rich gags and one or two quite outstandingly classically funny sequences. The girl watching him and spoiling his feast: Merna Kennedy – the ill-used equestrian star of the show put on by her villainous daddy.

Richard Lester's special brand of humour was to be seen again this year in his UA film *The Bed Sitting Room*, a black and sick comedy set in the world that survives the holocaust of World War Three. And it isn't so hard – or shouldn't be – to guess the identity of the figure coming out of No. 10!

122

Jack Hawkins played a renegade Englishman in UA's *The Adventures of Gerard*, based on the famous Sir Arthur Conan Doyle stories about a silly swaggering swordsman's highly unlikely adventures during Napoleon's Spanish campaign.

An unusual film was Peter Medak's *Negatives*, for the Walter Reade Organisation, which was about the world of fantasy built by the couple who live above an antique shop (owned by the husband's father, who is dying in hospital) from which they obtain the props for their sexual explorations – a situation split down the middle with the arrival on the scene of a lodger. The three involved were Peter McEnery, Diane Cilento (shown with a wax figure) and Glenda Jackson.

Another unusual film was Samuel Fuller's *Shock Corridor*, shown in Britain in 1970 after previously being banned from public showing here for some five years. It was the story of a reporter who, in order to investigate a murder in a lunatic asylum, has himself committed to it; but by the time he has pinned the murder on the correct suspect has himself been driven off his trolley.

Also destined for a "minority audience" was Robert Stevens's CIRO film *Change of Mind*, which managed to introduce into its story two topical themes in giving the story of a brain transplant a racial prejudice angle by making a negro the recipient of a white man's grey matter! The unfortunate man was played by Raymond St. Jacques, shown with Susan Oliver as the wife who won't accept the brain as her husband because it is now housed in a black body!

124

Many critics and concerned moviegoers came to think – maybe wishful thinking – that the bottom for permissive period movies was reached in early 1971, and whatever followed could only show a rise in movie standards. One of the films most widely critically savaged during that period was Fox's *Myra Breckinridge*, a not over-tasteful adaptation (to put it diplomatically) of the Gore Vidal novel about sex change in which Raquel Welch played the unpleasant title role of the man-cum-girl.

Another film which did possibly good business at the Box Office at the same time was Fox's *Beyond the Valley of the Dolls*, the story of a girl trio pop group who become involved in the debased lunatic fringe of the film city with its dope, orgies, kinky sex and other unpleasant facets of the debased seventies!

The motivation of Border Films' *Games that Lovers Play* was a duel between two "famous London Madames" as to which had the most irresistible girls, the chosen champions being (left) Penny Brahms as Constance Chatterley and Joanna Lumley as Fanny Hill. And the Games? Well, the inset picture might give you a rough idea if you hadn't already got a pretty clear one in mind.

126

The – obviously not seriously intended – presumptuous title of Richard Schulman's film *All About Women* was the catchy and box-office-slanted label for a light-hearted romance about three girls and their daily lives and, more important, the amorous part of them!

Not, as you might suppose, a scene from another German sex education movie, but one in fact from a British suspense thriller called *Taste of Excitement*, from Monarch Films; the story of a girl on the way to her South of France holiday who sees a murder on the cross-channel boat and thereafter becomes ever more terrifyingly deeply involved in its aftermath. Lovely Eva Renzi the girl; the man, David Buck.

Donovan Winters, whose documentary "Sunday in the Park" took five years to make and was also released this year, certainly took a great deal less time in making his *Come Back Peter*, the story of a young man with a strong erotic imagination who has quite a time with the Chelsea chicks before he wakes up to far less erotic realism. Christopher Matthews had the imagination; Yolanda Turner was one of the girls imagined.

Early 1971 saw the emergence of a small, sudden flood of cinematic spine-chillers, included in which was Hammer–MGM–EMI's *Lust for a Vampire*, a title which became more easily understood when you saw the shape of some of the vampires – including beautiful little blood-sucker Yutte Stensgaard.

128

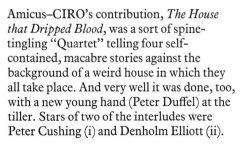

Amicus–CIRO's contribution, *The House that Dripped Blood*, was a sort of spine-tingling "Quartet" telling four self-contained, macabre stories against the background of a weird house in which they all take place. And very well it was done, too, with a new young hand (Peter Duffel) at the tiller. Stars of two of the interludes were Peter Cushing (i) and Denholm Elliott (ii).

Another "House" thriller was MGM–EMI's *House of Dark Shadows*, the story of a mysterious stranger who turns up at the door of the gloomy mansion of the title, in the Maine countryside, and claims he's the British cousin of the family – which, when accepted as fact and he moves in, leads to a series of horrible killings.

Transformation scene: Ingrid Pitt, as the youth-seeking, wicked old Countess, accidentally discovers the startling rejuvenating effect of a young girl's blood upon her skin; the half of her face where the blood has touched growing clear and youthful, the other, untouched, remaining old and wrinkled – and so she gets the terrible idea which is to lead to a lot of the horror and chills in Alexander Paal's film for Rank, *Countess Dracula*.

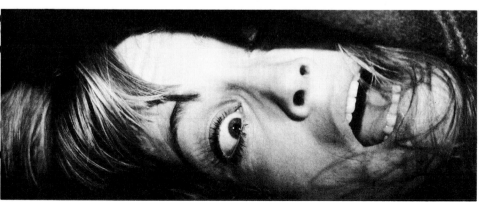

Struck dumb with terror, teacher Suzy Kendall is attacked by the killer who has already raped two schoolgirls (and murdered one) in the George Brown–Rank film *Assault*, a straightforward, consistently tense murder thriller.

130

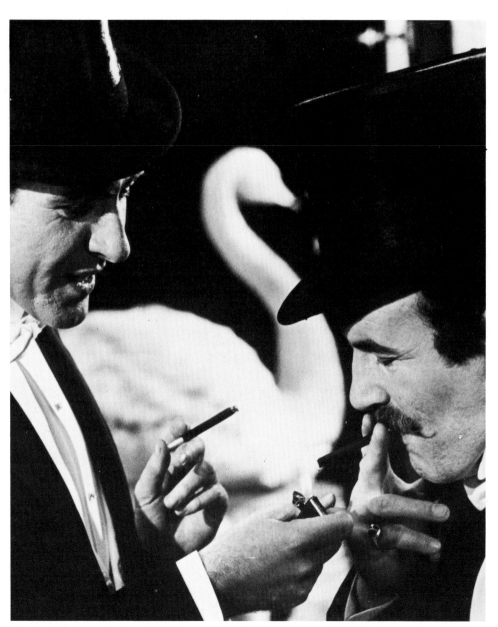

The great Baker Street sleuth (Robert Stephens) and his medical aide (Colin Blakely) in festive mood in Billy Wilder's original, amusing, exciting yet completely in-key Wilder addition to the Sherlock Holmes–Doctor Watson stories, *The Private Life of Sherlock Holmes*, a story of two cases, neatly conceived, wittily executed, which Sir Conan Doyle *didn't* write.

The artful Christie (Richard Attenborough – a fine character performance) arrives at the police station to lay information about the murder he himself has committed but of which he has carefully slanted suspicion against his sub-normal lodger Evans (John Hurt, below, a subtle and quite outstanding performance) who is subsequently arrested, condemned and hanged for the crime (of which long after he was officially declared innocent). From Richard Fleischer's Columbia film *10 Rillington Place*, an extremely careful reconstruction of the case made on the actual location, including the old, tumbledown house in which the several bodies were eventually discovered and led to the uncovering of Christie's horrible guilt.

Comedy: Goldie Hawn, the English girl who became a star of the popular American TV show "Laugh-In", came back to GB to co-star triumphantly in Columbia's screen adaptation of Terence Frisby's long-running stage comedy success, *There's a Girl in My Soup*. She played, quite deliciously, the American teenager who is picked up by a middle-aged lecher (Peter Sellers) and with a series of verbal swipes quickly reduces him not only to size but considerably below it!

In UA's *They Call Me MISTER Tibbs* we're re-introduced to the coloured cop character we first met on the screen in "In The Heat Of The Night". But this new film was on another level and was completely different in most other ways: telling a straightforward murder story about the killing of joy-girl Joy and the sifting of suspects until the final revelation that the killing was done by Mister Tibbs's preacher pal.

Peter Lawford and Jerry Lewis were co-stars in the latter's Columbia comedy *Hook, Line and Sinker*, in which Lewis played the dupe of his wife and her doctor friend. They, in love with each other, plan to get rid of him so they can spend the rest of their nasty little lives happily together!

134

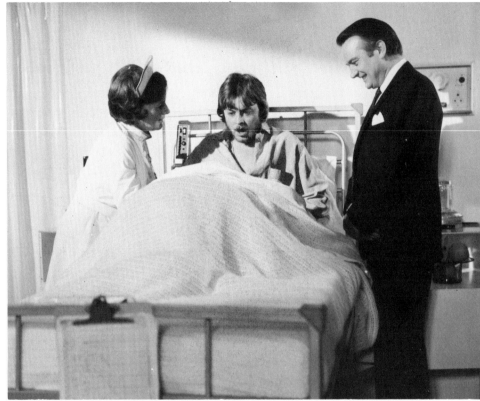

The 20th "Carry On" film from the evergreen Gerald Thomas–Peter Rogers team of blue-tinted celluloid laughter-raisers was *Carry on Loving*, in which the mickey was well and truly (and very broadly of course) taken out of the Marriage Bureau business. Among the team of funsters involved was Kenneth Williams, seen here being taken by surprise when his quiet housekeeper, Patsy Rowlands, suddenly becomes a real man-eater!

Nobody could claim, or obviously would want to, that *Percy* was the most tasteful or subtle comedy ever to be made by that very professional duo Betty E. Box and Ralph Thomas, but this story of the first penis transplant and the new owner's efforts to track down the women who knew the donor's details . . . imagine? . . . had plenty of rude laughs of the kind that usually strikes golden echoes at the box-office. Hywel Bennett played the recipient, Denholm Elliott (right) the doctor who breaks new ground, and Pauline Delaney was the nurse.

Hayley Mills played the teacher from the North who comes down South and is here taught a thing or two by several sex-hungry Southern males; including man-about-town smoothie Noel Harrison, whose sophisticated assault on the virgin citadel is the one that eventually pays off and takes – though not for keeps – the girl in Columbia's *Take a Girl Like You*.

Though premiered quite a long time ago, it wasn't until the beginning of 1971 that Fox's gay, spectacular and generally entertaining musical *Hello, Dolly!* was generally released. Barbra Streisand – shown leading "the escape from Yonkers to Manhattan" – was the star of this new musical adaptation of the Thornton Wilder straight play called "The Matchmaker", a period comedy of Jewish life in New York.

Jocelyn Lane on the pillion of Jeremy Slate's motor-bike in MGM–EMI's *Hell's Belles*, a story of young motor cycle hoodlums in America and the long pursuit by one of another who has stolen his machine.

Peter O'Toole, with cheerful French companion Philippe Noiret, in Dimitri de Grunwald's *Murphy's War*, the exciting Peter Yates-directed adventure story about the crazy, fighting-Irish sole survivor of a German U-boat attack on a British merchantman at the end of the war who becomes obsessed with destroying the sub and its crew, and finally, ironically, succeeds after the bigger war has ended.

The Nazi sentry appears not to appreciate paratroop captain Rock Hudson's killing treatment of him in UA's *Hornets' Nest*, a World-War-Two story set in Italy and detailing his efforts, assisted by some tough youngsters who have survived a German massacre of their village, to blow up the dam which was the American officer's original mission.

How black can you take your black comedy? Not everyone was repelled by the macabre laughter of British Lion's adaptation of the late Joe Orton's stage play *Loot*, which was largely about a couple of louts who rob a bank and then use the coffin of one's just-deceased mother to hide the proceeds, callously stuffing the body down serving hatches and sundry other places as they try to hide it, and the money, from bumbling 'tec Richard Attenborough. Hywel Bennett played one of the young horrors. Lee Remick was the nurse with her eye on the main chance.

Black, too, was the American (MGM–EMI) comedy *The Travelling Executioner* which, set in the deep South, was a story of the way a pretty killer (Mariana Hill) spoils everything for the touring executioner, with his portable electric chair, to the extent of finally putting him in it as a condemned killer!

Lee Marvin (right) and Jack Palance as the old-time cowboys in Fox's *Monte Walsh* who come to the reluctant realisation that times are changing and the easy-going, law-free frontier world they knew of the 1880's is vanishing for ever. A good Western with an added sociological depth.

The old maestro himself, "Big John" Wayne, was the star of Fox's routine, but expert, thoroughly entertaining Western *Rio Lobo*, in which Wayne played the ex-Union Army Colonel who after the Civil War doggedly tracks down the men from his own troop whose greed had led them into a plot to assist the enemy to hi-jack the gold train which he had been assigned to guard. With him in the wagon, pretty newcomer Jennifer O'Neil.

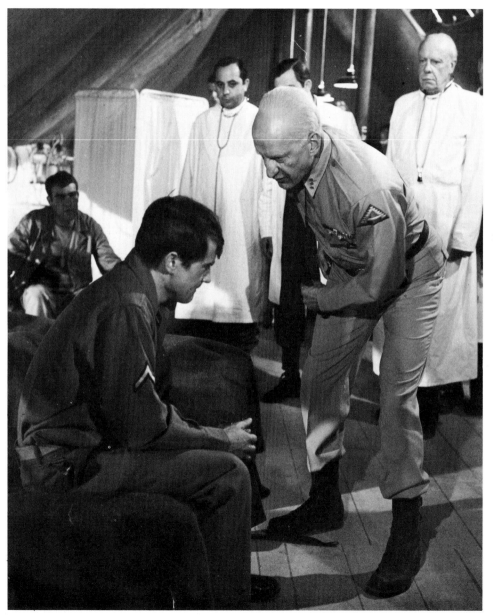

The famous scene where General Patton, in a field hospital in Sicily, smacks an inmate across the face and accuses him of malingering: one incident in the stormy career of one of America's most controversial World War Two figures brought powerfully and effectively to the screen by Fox in their large-scale film, *Patton: Lust for Glory*, in which George C. Scott gave a great performance in the title role and walked off with the 1971 "Oscar".

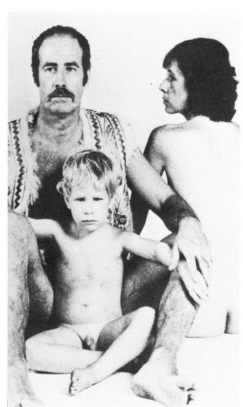

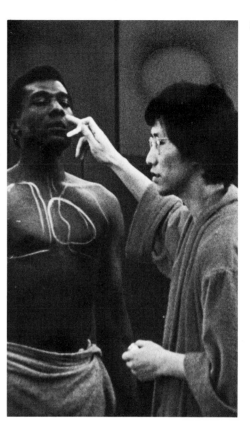

A performance, too, was the best thing about CIRO's with-it comedy, *Say Hello to Yesterday*, the story of a conventional, pretty young wife from the Cobham stockbroker belt who comes to town for the day to shop and allows a young and nutty waster to pick her up, bully, embarrass and finally seduce her! But Jean Simmons as the temporarily wayward wife gave a tender and convincing performance in a never very credible part.

Contemporary's rather odd American film *A Married Couple* was an "actuality drama" in which director-producer Allan King took his cameras into the house of the Edwards family and stayed there for weeks as he watched the break-up of the couple's seven-year-old marriage.

Another unusual film was Kestrel's *The Body*, a fascinating semi-documentary about the human body and its environment, including a quite extraordinary sequence in which the camera did a kind of Cook's tour of the body's interior.

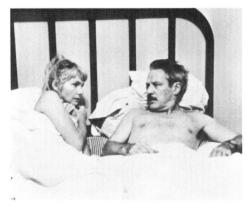

One of the most brilliant of this year's unusual films, however, was certainly *Wanda*, which marked the screen début as writer-director-star of Barbara Loden (Mrs. Elia Kazan in private life) in a *tour-de-force* story about a hopelessly ill-equipped woman who drifts away from her marriage, into crime and finally to sad, utter futility.

A pointer to the possibly changing climate in movies and movie tastes was Fox's British production *One Brief Summer*, released early in 1971; for this romantic drama about

top-drawer people, with its background of lovely English country houses, Rolls and E-types, etc., was refreshingly old-fashioned and free of sexual titillation or sadism! In fact it was the story of a middle-aged banker who falls in love with his possessive young daughter's schoolfriend and, disastrously, marries her, a disaster considerably assisted by the daughter. Father and daughter were played by Clifford Evans and Jennifer Hilary. Inset: the girl, played by pretty newcomer Felicity Gibson.

Anglo-German British spy Michael York faces a suspicious Anton Diffring on board the *Zeppelin* of the title in the Warner release which had a historical background of the development of the German airships as a weapon of terror warfare on this country during the First World War.

Adventurers Charles Bronson – clasping Michèle Mercier – and Tony Curtis in one of the many tight spots from which they happily emerge, either singly or as a team, in Columbia's fine old slice of entertaining Hollywood hokum, *You Can't Win 'em All*. It all took place in Turkey, where Curtis goes to recover one of his family's ships, pressed into German service during the First World War.

Wildest, loveliest Scotland was the unusual and fascinating background to British Lion's adventure story *When Eight Bells Toll*, the screen version of the Alistair Maclean thriller about gold-smuggling. Anthony Hopkins (left – threatening one of the villains, Jack Hawkins) played the young British Navy agent assigned the task of smashing the gang, which he does with a fine assortment of lethal weapons!

Joseph L. Mankiewicz is a highly literate, intelligent director whose work (both writing and directing) will surely one day in retrospect be critically more highly valued than it generally is today! Typical example was his *There Was a Crooked Man* for Warner, a story of a superficially pleasant but utterly ruthless rogue (Kirk Douglas) and his plans for escape from the Arizona State jail in 1880. Henry Fonda played the reforming prison governor: and beneath all the fun were some acid comments on human nature.

Very popular small-screen series were the basis of two of the year's most successful British large-screen comedies. Not only did Frankie Howerd's *Up Pompeii!* for Anglo–MGM make a great success on its own account but it subsequently encouraged its makers to announce a whole series of "Up" comedies following in the "Carry On" tradition. Sharing this miniature orgy with explosive slave Howerd and a pretty Romanesque lass is sensual senator Michael Hordern.

Almost, if not quite, as successful was the adaptation of Columbia's *Dad's Army*, the series about the old World War Two Home Guard in which Arthur Lowe (as Captain Mainwaring), Clive Dunn (as L/c Jones) and John Le Mesurier (as Sgt. Wilson) repeated their generally hilarious television roles.

Franco Nero as the Gypsy and Joanna Shimkus as the Virgin, watching him with disturbing longings, in the beautiful London Screenplays film on the D. H. Lawrence story, *The Virgin and the Gypsy*, which was given just the right treatment by director Christopher Miles, who magnificently re-created the time and the place as described by the author.

Brilliant Bryan Forbes took time off from his – subsequently surrendered – arduous job of managing ABC's production programme to make within it a remarkably sincere and altogether superior personal film, *The Raging Moon*, the story of a tragic-ending romance between two physically afflicted young people, played beautifully by Forbes's own wife Nanette Newman, and Malcolm McDowell.

Jerzy Skolimowski's somewhat hybrid *Deep End*, for Connoisseur release, was a strange, fascinating and in part brilliant movie. The story of a young London public baths attendant who falls desperately in love with his slightly older, far more sophisticated opposite number in the "Women's" section, it had depth, truth, humour and, finally, confected drama. Too, it had a couple of remarkably good performances by newcomer John Moulder-Brown and Jane Asher in the leading roles.

146 Directed with enough fluency and imagination to give promise for the future, though a little rough around the production edges, new director Barney Platts-Mills's *Bronco Bullfrog* was a tragi-comedy about an East End borstal boy who runs away with his girl-friend when neither of their parents will approve or help their romance. Made on location in some of the sadder areas of London, largely by an amateur cast.

Two other new directors, Donald Cammell and Nicolas Roeg, shared the credits for Warners' *Performance*, which ran into extremely variable critical comment when first shown. A story of the confrontation of two highly contrasting worlds, those of Pop and Crime, it had a fascinatingly baroque treatment of a story about a gangland killer on the run (James Fox, giving one of his best performances) who finds refuge with an erstwhile pop-star, Mick Jagger, until the latent hate between them bursts into final violence.

Not so many films are made mainly for or about youngsters, and on looking back this year seems quite a vintage one, headed as it was by the brilliant *Kes*. Also about a small boy and his hawk was Paramount's *My Side of the Mountain*, which against a Canadian Rockies background in all its splendour related the adventures of a boy who runs away from his Montreal home and spends a year in the wilds in order to prove his capacity for living alone and off the land. The boy was played by Teddy Eccles.

In the same category was Tigon's adaptation of the Anna Sewell children's classic of the 1870s, *Black Beauty*, the story of a horse and its changing fortunes between the time it is separated from its young master – played by Mark Lester – until finally reunited with him.

UA's *The McKenzie Break* was yet another P.O.W. "Escape" story, though this one did have certain novel angles in that the camp was situated in Scotland and the escapers were German prisoners; notably a very dedicated young Nazi submarine captain who is prepared to get his men and himself back into action even at a high cost of the lives of the other (Army and Luftwaffe) inmates. The film in fact boiled down to a personal battle of wits and strength of character between this young man and the Irish captain sent by "Intelligence" in Whitehall to keep order and thwart the suspected escape plans.

Disney's films are always tailored for the "Family Trade" with the youngsters very much in mind and in spite of the title, *The Barefoot Executive* was no exception, for the hero was a boy and the comic was a very clever chimp, the two forming a pretty well unbeatable team even when pitted against American Big – Television – Business.

A neat adaptation of a stage success, CIRO's *Lovers and Other Strangers* was a quietly amusing story of a wedding (that of two young people who have already been living together, unknown to their parents, for more than a year) which in the course of the preparations and the actual event uncovers a great many family skeletons in the marital cupboards. Gig Young played the father of the bride.

In Warners' *The Last Warrior* Anthony Quinn – dancing with Shelley Winters – played the hard-drinking, simple, but not unintelligent American Indian who, tired of the treatment meted out to him and his fellow Indians at the hands of the colour-bar-conscious whites, starts a modern Indian Uprising: and it all added up to a slightly sour comedy built on a serious modern problem.

148 Another comedy which was based on a serious problem was UA's *The Landlord*, in which a young socialite takes over a tenement in a Negro ghetto district for a super-lark but is brought down to earth by his black tenants. Beau Bridges played the young man – seen with his mother (Lee Grant) and his girl-friend (Marki Bey, centre).

Grand National's *The Gay Deceivers* was one in a minicycle of films dealing with American draft dodging: in this case two youngsters pretend to be homosexuals to avoid being called up and are then driven into continuing the masquerade long after the joke has worn thin for them. The two young men were played by Larry Casey (left) and Kevin Coughlin: the quizzical-looking recruiting officer in the centre is Jack Starrett.

As tough, incisive and coldly brutal as any American effort in the same category, Michael Klinger's *Get Carter* for MGM was a British gangster piece about a London professional killer who goes back to his home-town Newcastle to find out the facts of his elder brother's sudden death, and when he discovers it was murder, sets out methodically to wipe out all those who took part in the killing. The film had the advantage of a smooth, convincing portrait of a casual assassin from Michael Caine.

Stanley Baker as the bank manager tempted into robbing his own bank in a big way by lovely and loose customer Ursula Andress – in Dimitri de Grunwald's neatly tailored crime comedy-thriller *Perfect Friday*.

Columbia's *A Severed Head* was a smooth and sophisticated comedy about a sextet of characters, three men and three women, who cynically switch partners as they dance around in a wholly superficial and selfish measure of pleasure: neatly directed and beautifully acted by a cast including Ian Holm (outstanding in the main role), Jennie Linden and Lee Remick.

Richly comic, in the old sense of crazy comedy, was Warners' *Start the Revolution Without Me*, which, sometimes reminiscent of such films as those once made by Abbott and Costello, "sent-up" Dumas and his stories against a riotously funny background of the French Revolution. Two superbly funny performances were supplied by Gene Wilder and Donald Sutherland.

Plenty of near-the-knuckle comedy, too, in CIRO's *The Statue*, in which sculptress Virna Lisi's husband David Niven gets the idea that the huge statue his wife has made of him for exhibition in Grosvenor Square is modelled from him with the exception of one vital member and that, he jealously thinks, was modelled from some other man – and sets out to find the model!

If you ever got the idea that glamour was a more or less modern invention, Hammer set out to explode the myth when they made their Stone Age epic *Creatures the World Forgot* and put luscious and largely unclad Julie Ege into the star brackets.

Following in the "sleeper" footsteps of *Easy Rider* and others of the same kind, British Lion's *Joe* was a great success in America and received a considerable, if slightly less critically acclaimed, reception in Great Britain. The story of the violent dangers that lie waiting in the generation gap, it drew a terrifying picture of modern American society – and carried an ominous threat for a future Britain!

New star John Hansen, centre – yes, centre – with John Tompkins (right) and Quinn Radeker in Edward Small's adaptation of the book *The Christine Jorgensen Story*, a story about a a sex change (you see!) in which young Mr. Hansen played both male and female facets of the character.

James Beattie, playing Jess Willard, takes one of James Earl Jones's best punches on the chin in the great fight climax of Fox's *The Great White Hope*, the story of the rise and faltering and final fall (was he pushed?) of the great coloured world champion Jack Johnson (called Jefferson in the film). Jones's performance in the title role was one of the more memorable of the year.

A renewed interest by the moviemakers in Victoriana in general and the Brontës in particular has resulted in new screen adaptations of two of their novels, the yet to be seen (at the time of writing) *Wuthering Heights* and British Lion's *Jane Eyre*, in which Susannah York (in background) played the tragic little lass whose love for the gloomy, handsome Rochester (George C. Scott) outlasts all impediments (including the mad wife – Jean Marsh, bottom left) to finally triumph.

Joan Plowright (as Masha), Jeanne Watts (as Olga) and Louise Purnell (as Irina) as the *Three Sisters* of the title in Alan Clore's British Lion cinematic record of the superb Laurence Olivier-directed stage production of the Chekhov classic.

Colour prejudice played a big part, too, in Columbia's comedy *Watermelon Man*: the central comic situation of which is the waking one morning of a white insurance agent to find he has changed into a Negro during the night, and the sadly comic situations which follow. Godfrey Cambridge played the changed, Estelle Parsons his incredulous wife!

Julian Mayfield and Max Julian in Jules Dassin's *Uptight*, an up-dated variation on O'Flaherty's story of *The Informer*, switching the scene from Ireland to America and bringing in a racial angle by making it a Negro who sells out his pals for money but nothing but woe and, finally, death.

Best of the several Pop Festival films was Warners' *Woodstock* which covered the scene of the three-days youthful get-together at considerable length and in great detail.

Not many British director-producers have attempted to make Westerns, a fact which gave an added interest to Michael Winner's *Lawman* which, while gathering a number of highly variable critical notices, was generally judged to be a pretty thorough recapture of a classic film type in its story of a stern, straight lawman – played by Burt Lancaster – who is one day called upon to take seven convicted criminals out of a hostile town to the justice he is determined they shall face in a neighbouring place.

UA's *Sabata*, an Italian Western, had the advantage of having Lee Van Cleef in the main role, that of a cool, dead-eyed gunman able to outwit and outgun the villain's private army and so walk off with a $65,000 booty.

Walt Disney's *The Wild Country* was, in contrast, a completely conventional Western, telling – well – a story of a pioneering family from Pittsburgh who are almost defeated in their efforts to make good in wildest Wyoming but eventually conquer all the man-made and natural obstacles to make succeed – thanks largely to their two brave young sons.

Ralph Nelson's Avco–Embassy film *Soldier Blue* certainly had a unique angle in paralleling the terrible Sand Creek Massacre of 1864 (of Indians – men, women and children by the US Army) with the headline-hitting Vietnam business of 1970 and excusing the horrifying bestiality of the scenes of carnage by claiming that they were intended to stir the viewing public's conscience. Candice Bergen and Peter Strauss played the two fugitives from an Indian ambush whose flight reveals their respective characters.

154

Racial prejudice played a large and unusual part in another Western, London Screen's *The McMasters*, in which kindly rancher Burl Ives opposes frantic villain Jack Palance over the former's selling at a nominal price of half his ranch to the young Negro he has brought up and is now home from the wars – the American Civil one.

The tragic story of the Sheriff of Jenkins County (played by Gregory Peck), whose downfall is brought about by his passion for a young girl, daughter of a bad character running an illicit still – comes near to its tragic end in Columbia's *I Walk the Line*, the movie version of Madison Jones's perfect little story *An Exile*.

What Do You Say To A Naked Lady? is a good question: some of the suggested answers were to be found in the UA film of that title made by Allen Funt in his collection of candid-camera sequences in which various people are confronted by the problem in the flesh.

Vixen was that rarity, a Canadian film. It was all about a very sexy holiday enjoyed by a set of visitors and some of the residents of a vacation spot high in the Canadian Rockies.

Jean Seberg is caught up in a good deal of brutality and becomes involved in a very odd love affair in the turbulent America of the Civil War period in Avco–Embassy's *Macho Callahan*.

More Western-style brutality and ruthlessness in Scotia–Barber's *A Town Called Bastard*, a doom-laden story of Mexico at the end of the 1905 rebellion, when dictator Diaz searches out the defeated leaders, and the lovely lady Alvira (Stella Stevens) as diligently searches for the man who made her a widow, with the grim idea of taking a deadly revenge.

Parental problems of today was the theme of Avco–Embassy's *The People Next Door*, which was about a normal family who are suddenly confronted by the fact that their daughter is a hopeless young drug addict and suspect her brother as the one who has been responsible! Eli Wallach and Julie Harris played the parents (i), Stephen McHattie and Deborah Winters the children (ii).

156

Rod Taylor as a thick-ear type amateur 'tec out for revenge for the killing by the baddies of their former pretty prostitute employee Suzy Kendall, after Taylor had rescued (aiding the scene, Theodore Bikel) her once from a watery grave and fallen in love with her in Fox's *Darker Than Amber*.

Samuel Goldwyn Junior's UA film *Cotton Comes to Harlem* may well have been a trend-setter, for it was a cops and robbers story, confined almost wholly to Negro characters on both sides of the law-line and set against a fascinating background of the real Harlem.

One of the most artistically satisfying films of the year was Joseph Losey's *Figures in a Landscape* for Fox. A superbly photographed, wholly visual and altogether magnificently handled story of two escaped prisoners (Robert Shaw and Malcom McDowell) on the run, pursued relentlessly by a helicopter until the climactic battle between man and machine.

NGC's *The Baby Maker* was an unusual story of a modern marital experiment: an affluent childless couple persuading a young girl to move in with them so that she can bear the husband's child, which the couple will then adopt as their own. Barbara Hershey played the girl, Collin Wilcox-Horne and Sam Groom the couple.

Ma Barker (Shelley Winters) with the eldest of her horrible brood of sons (Don Stroud) in MGM's *Bloody Mama*, the brutal, bloody story of the Barker Family Gang which Ma Kate led in a series of crimes which culminated (in the film) in a slap-up battle between the besieged family and the cops. Long refused any censor's certificate, the film with – controversial – cuts was given a 1971 general release.

158

Avco–Embassy's *C.C. and Company* was yet another in the considerable number of movies built around that apparently very considerable problem, the law-breaking, US hoodlumish motor-cycle gangs.

The old star and the new one: Cecil Kellaway and Elliott Gould share a ruminative scene from Columbia's *Getting Straight* in which Gould played an ex-student back at his old school preparing for a teaching degree and becoming aware that the young people he supports are, knowingly or not, supporting nihilism.

The making of a masterpiece – American amateur moviemaker Gideon Bachman takes a film of Federico Fellini making his *Satyricon* film – and emerges with a fascinating, revealing portrait in depth of the baroque manner in which Fellini works. Connoisseur's *Ciao, Federico!*

Alain Delon (right) as the hired killer,
Francois Perrier (centre) and Nathalie
Delon in Scotia-Barber's *The Samourai* –
or *The Killer* – a grim story of the Paris
underworld and a portrait in depth of a
professional killer.

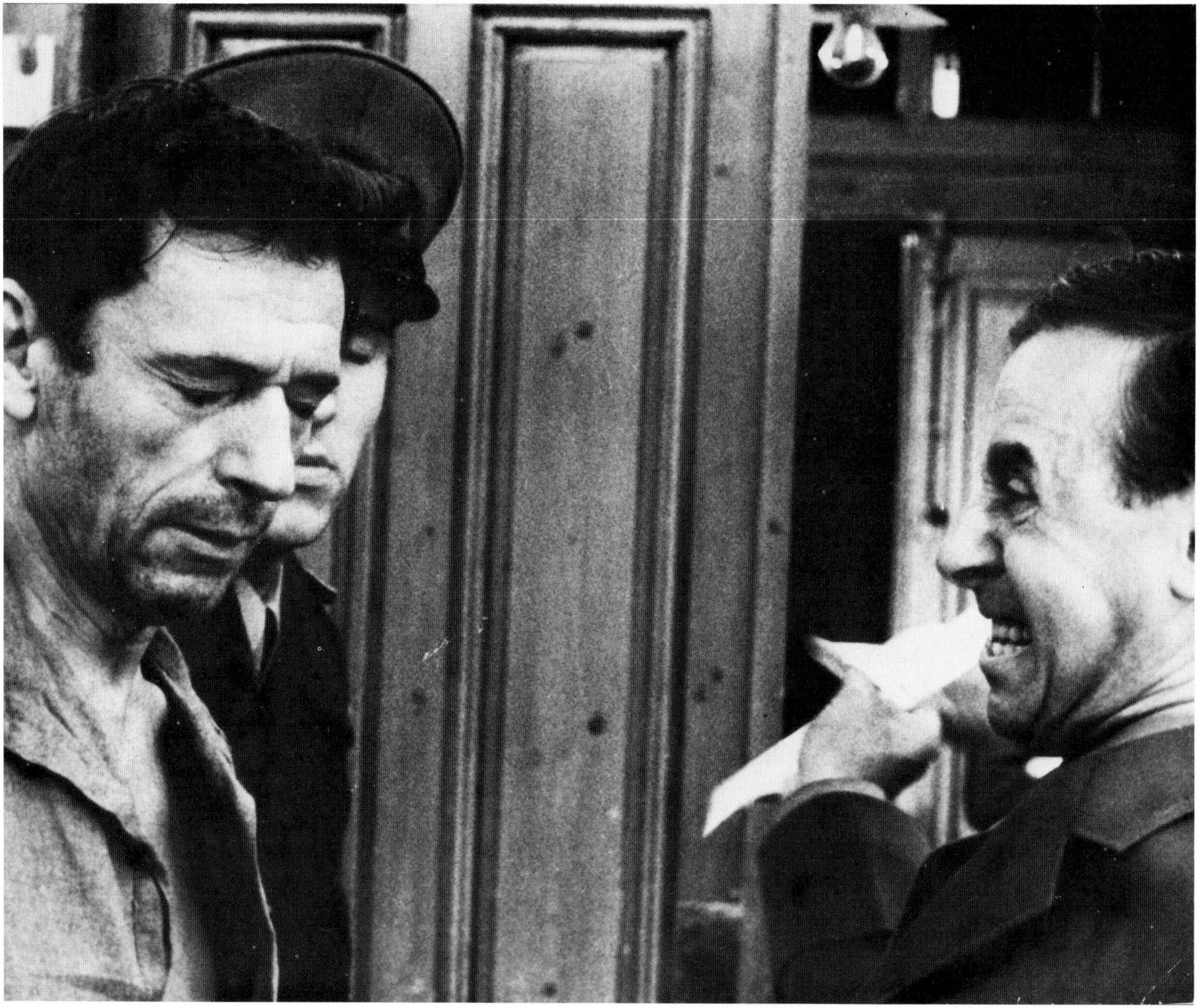

THE CONTINENTAL FILM

I think I should preface this section with a word of warning: and self-defence! I have for convenience divided it up into sub-sections, placing the various films under headings denoting the country of origin. But it is no longer easy (nor has it been for several years now) always to say if a film is actually French, Italian, Spanish or German in origin in view of the considerable number of often complicated European international co-productions which are made. So if you find a film listed in the French section, whereas you feel it really should be Italian, you'll have to excuse the misplacing and put it down to my ignorance! I have in all cases categorised the film on the evidence available at the time of selection.

Following the enormous success of *Z*, the same team (director-star-cameraman) produced *L'Aveu*, another grim political document, only this time rather surprisingly showing the other side of the same coin. Whereas *Z* showed the corruption of a right-wing Fascist State, *L'Aveu* was set in a Communist country (Czechoslovakia in fact) and was based on the true story of a dedicated party member who for sordid and never easy-to-understand reasons of State is arrested, tortured and forced into public confession of crimes of which he is innocent. It was a grim, harrowing film of great power and conviction, with Yves Montand again in the leading role of the victim.

Another, highly contrasting, outstanding film from France was François Truffaut's

L'Enfant Sauvage – The Wild Boy, in which with almost clinical detail and in cool, documentary manner he traces the facts of a strange case which occurred in France in the 18th century, when a small, quite wild boy was discovered in the woods, caught, abused by a curious and unsympathetic society, and finally taken in hand and trained at least towards a civilised state by a good young doctor – played with quiet conviction by Truffaut himself. The boy, a remarkable performance, was played by Jean-Pierre Cargol.

France now contributes regularly a number of excellent gangster films, including this year Henri Verneuil's *The Sicilian Clan*, with Jean Gabin back in his oft-played role of old master crook: this time he was head of a Sicilian family which takes its crime and honour with great seriousness, so that when a member of the gang seduces one of Gabin's son's wives it is poppa himself who clears the matter up . . . the hard way as you will see! Lady in dire distress is Irina Demick.

Though made in 1966, it was not until 1970 that Jean-Luc Godard's *Two or Three Things I Know About Her* was shown in England. A typical Godard film, it hung all sorts of complaints against, and criticism of, contemporary society on a story about housewives who become part-time prostitutes in order to earn money for luxuries, two such loose little ladies being played by Marina Vlady and Anny Duperey.

Dominique Sanda as the young wife, *A Gentle Creature*, driven to despair and self-violence in Robert Bresson's excellent though strangely uncommitted adaptation of a Dostoievsky short story about a young girl who marries a pawnbroker.

Made, apparently, in France but wholly Jewish in content was Claude Berri's rather charming little comedy about love and marriage, *Marry Me! Marry Me!*, which he wrote, directed, produced and in which he played the leading role. This scene is shared by English teacher Prudence Harrington, with whom Berri has a pre-marriage interlude and who alters all his wedding plans – for a while!

With his great fertility of comedy ideas amounting to inspiration, Pierre Etaix is often sadly under-valued, but he is undoubtedly one of the greatest comic talents working in the medium of the cinema today and his *Le Grand Amour* was a good example of the quality of his work, for he wrote, directed and himself starred in this hilarious and bubblingly inventive story of a happily married man who suddenly falls in love – and then out of it again!

Secret French Prostitution Report was a screen adaptation of the Dominique Dallayrac book called "Dossier Prostitution", an examination of the whole field of this old, old profession: illustrated by various facets of the relationship between vendor and customer.

Annie Girardot and Jean Yanne as the married couple in Gerard Pirès' sly, satirical and pretty crazy Franco-Italian *Erotissimo*, which in its larky, technically flashy way took a long hard look at the current craze of selling everything by sex. It did so by relating the story of a worried, neglected wife trying to recapture the amorous attentions of her spouse by means of various widely advertised erotic merchandise, unaware that his neglect stems purely from the worry that a tax inspector has caused him.

166

(opposite) Claude Sautet's *Les Choses de la Vie – The Things of Life* was a brilliant film by virtue of its painstaking attention to the smallest detail and its remarkable realism, especially with regard to its treatment of the car crash which forms the climax and tragedy of a slim story about a man, his ex-wife and his mistress. And beautifully acted, too, from Michel Piccoli and Romy Schneider downwards to the tiniest bit player.

Highway Pickup was a rather untypical Julien Duvivier crime thriller about a young woman whose greed for wealth leads her to murder, to blackmail and final destruction at the hands of the man she is trying to use for her further evil ends . . . ! Catherine Rouvel played the beastly beauty, Robert Hossein one of her unfortunate dupes.

Senta Berger, Louis Jourdan and Bernard Blier as three of the people involved in Edouard Molinaro's intricate spy thriller *To Commit a Murder*, revolving around a plot to get a brilliant young nuclear scientist out of France and into Mao's hands!

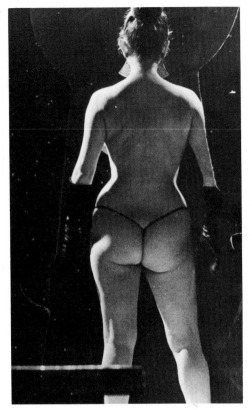

Gala's *Girls for Pleasure* was another film based on the facts of the Dominique Dallayrac book *Dossier Prostitution* and was a largely pictorial examination in some – sordid – depth of the oldest trade in the world.

René Gainville's *Alyse and Chloe* (English sub-title "The Lesbian Lovers") was a not untastefully treated story of the problem of a girl who is attracted away from her boyfriend by a lesbian businesswoman and the turmoil that follows, mental and physical, as they struggle against each other and their own appetites.

One of the oddest little films to emerge from Italy was Salvatore Samperi's *Grazie Zia*, which quite obviously expected to be taken seriously, but which had a somewhat pretentious story of an unusually lovely lady doctor who becomes sexually and otherwise obsessed with her nasty nephew, a psychiatric cripple who plays erotic games with her and finally brings her to the decision, the only possible way out for both of them is death – murder and suicide! Lisa Gastoni was the doctor, Lou Castel the patient.

Vittorio de Sica's *Sunflower* was a real old-time tear-jerker, with its story of love and leaving, search and finding, sacrifice and sorrowful ending. Marcello Mastroianni played the North Italian soldier sent to the Russian front and Sophia Loren was the girl he left behind.

170

Erika Blanc, the Emmanuelle in Cesare Canevari's *A Man for Emmanuelle*: a girl so depressed by the state of the world that she sets off on a tour of her lovers for consolation, but finds only final disillusionment in their embraces. Ben Salvador played one of the disappointments.

Superbly Southern-Italian every celluloid foot of the way was Pietro Germi's voluble, noisy, frenetic comedy *Serafino*, which was all about a young hill shepherd whose only real interest in life is seduction, and who puts in plenty of lively, amusing practice during the course of the film.

Some of the fire in *Burn, Boy, Burn!*, a film all about a sad seaside holiday at the end of which wife Françoise Prévost realises her husband will never understand her wild affair with a young student at the same resort.

The car and the guns may be authentic US, but Saverio Seto's *Mafia Mob* was an otherwise wholly Italian-made American gangster thriller set against a carefully confected background of prohibition-era Chicago!

172

Edmund Purdom supplied the commentary, in English, for Luigi Scattini's documentary about the place that magic of various black and white kinds still holds in this modern computerised world of ours – *The Satanists*.

More ambitious, more internationally cast and generally of greater conviction was an earlier Italian-made, English-talking gangster movie called *Machine Gun McCain* (*Gli Intoccabili* in the original Italian) which had a story about a Mafia-involved plot to rob a Las Vegas hotel. Among the American members of the cast, and in the title role, was John Cassavetes.

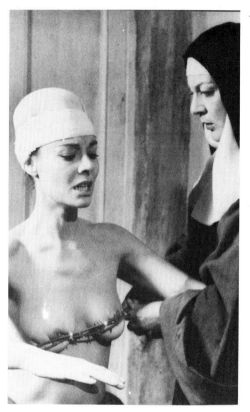

Though Britain saw but few new Italian films during the period in review, one at least was a masterpiece, Ermanno Olmi's quite perfect *One Fine Day*, the third movie in which he revealed his pre-occupation, if not obsession, with observing man at work and the manner in which his work permeates his whole existence. This time (again using a wholly amateur cast) he portrayed the problem of an advertising executive, successful and dedicated, whose moment of truth arrives with a car accident in which he knocks down and kills a man. Brunetto del

Vita as the man: Lidia Fuortes as his mistress.

British Anne Heywood played the title role in *The Awful Story of the Nun of Monza*; the story in question, claimed to be from the Vatican's secret files, being about a Milanese Nun who in 1608 was raped by the man she had succoured. Having subsequently fallen in love with him and borne his child, she was tried by the Papal authorities and condemned to be walled up alive in the convent walls! In fact the film was less sensational than all this might lead you to believe.

174

The German films we saw in Britain in the period under review were hardly outstanding: in fact, from the examples that were imported one might be – obviously mistakenly – led to think the whole industry there was concerned entirely with sex and sex-education subjects. Typical of the latter, by the way, was Oswalt Kolle's *Female Sexuality*, which illustrated various feminine sex problems and added intervening mini-lectures for good measure.

Run, Virgin, Run was a sex comedy about a village which wins the national award for the "output" of babies and the eventual revealing of the secret of success: a man and not the wind as is originally credited as the reason! Those involved included Helga Tölle, Joav Jasinski and Michaela Martin.

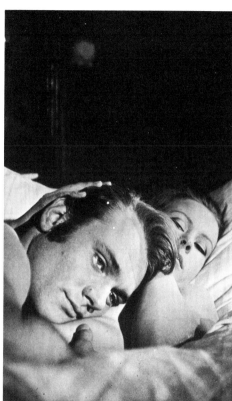

More sexual rompings – participants in this illustrated case being Ivan Nesbitt and Angelica Ott – in *The Blonde and the Black Pussycat*, in which the object of those most involved appears to be divided between getting the girls and gaining the vast estate which is finally inherited by the most unlikely (?) suspect!

Elbow Play was another film mainly concerned with the arts of seduction, more especially the success one can have by serving milady's cup of tea in the nude!

176

Butcher's *Guess Who's Sleeping With Us Tonight* was most aptly titled, for this German film was concerned almost completely with a series of sexual romps shared by a still very much sexily interested mamma, her three well-aware daughters and a butler, truly prepared to serve . . .

Neat twist in the German sex comedy *Wild, Willing and Sexy* was that the five girls involved in the embrace of that title (four "professionals" and a fifth working-girl who inherits a farm and persuades the quartet to help her run it) was the plan they evolve to get the hard work done, doling out their favours in return for a little ploughing, sowing or reaping or whatever, a scheme that pays off very happily for all concerned.

A very suitable scene from the E. J. Fancey German-made *Guess Who's Coming for Breakfast*, an up-dated adaptation of the Guy de Maupassant story *The Nieces of Madame Colonel*.

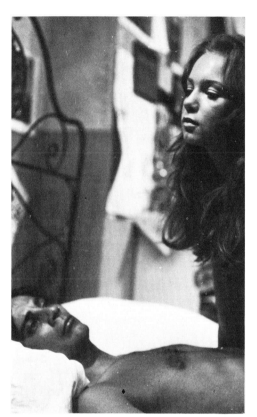

Anybody's – a title which in the
circumstances tells the whole story! –
introduced new Swedish sex star Marie
Liljedahl in a story about the erotic
adventures of two women while on holiday.

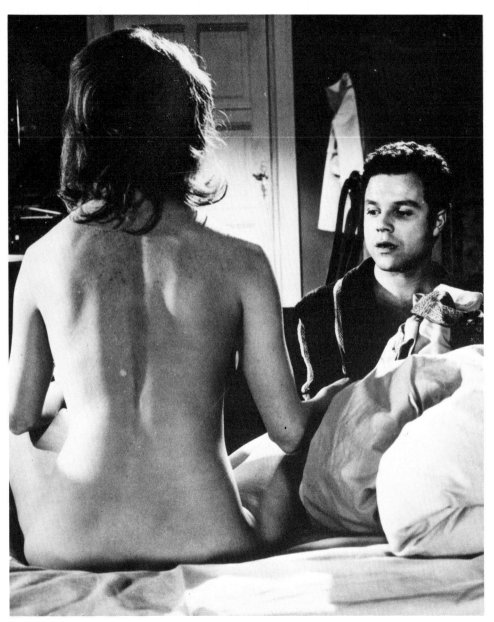

Denmark's Annelise Meineche, one of the world's few women directors, came up with a sequel to her highly successful "Seventeen" in *The Song of the Red Ruby*, which carried on the sex saga of the former book's hero (played in both films by Ole Søltoft), who, now chubbier but as sexually hungry as ever, manages to get in quite a lot of seductions (including that illustrated of Gertie Jung) before settling down to marriage and his career as a concert pianist.

Ingmar Bergman's *A Passion* was the continuation of his bleak philosophical outlook on life, with its story – set against a cold, grey island off the Swedish coastline – as a further illustration of the thesis that Hell is The Other, the Self and Life itself! It was a story told slowly, powerfully and uncinematically yet always absorbingly. Max Von Sydow played the man and Liv Ullmann and Bibi Andersson (not in this scene) the women.

One of the most outspoken and visually explicit sex education films yet to be shown on British screens, and one of the most earnest, was the Darville Organisation's *The Language of Love*, in which a cosy quartet of Scandinavian experts on the subject discussed various facets of sex with the aid of some pretty vivid pictorial interpolations.

Miracle's *Bamse* centred on a "teddy bear" found in a wrecked car, a toy through which a young man finds out that his father, who was killed in the wreck, had a young mistress. At first hating her, he grows, reluctantly, to desire her. Those most involved were Folke Sanquist and Ulla Jacobsson.

Ole Soltoft, the chubby young Danish star already seen in two similar pieces of comedy-erotica (*Seventeen* and *Song of the Red Ruby*) again played the virginal young man whose initiation into the joys of sex is followed by a number of amorous adventures in Gala's rather jolly *Bedroom Mazurka*, in which he played the young schoolmaster who must be married quickly if he is to step into the shoes of the retiring headmaster: and amusingly enough it is the latter's lovely wife who shows him how! And how!

Though she has got her boots on – and nothing else – she's certainly not dead! Pia Anderson in the E. J. Fancey film from Denmark, *She Died With Her Boots On*, a story of a nasty photographer and his equally horrid aunt who plan a wretched future for the girl they lure into their orbit as a photographer's model.

Anna Gaël as Nana the courtesan and actress who travels from man to man, breaks hearts and otherwise plays the old game in Miracle's *Take Me, Love Me* . . .

Denmark's woman director Annelise Meineche was responsible for Gala's *Without A Stitch*, the story of a sort of sexual pilgrimage made across Europe by Anne Grete, who is advised to undertake it by her doctor when she goes to him to complain that her boy-friend isn't as satisfactory as she feels he ought to be. Niels Borksard played one of her tutors.

One of the outstanding film comedies of the
year from any source was Akira Kurosawa's
dazzling *Sanjuro*, with its beautifully
stylised choreography and its wonderfully
crazy story about a magnificent samurai –
played with great style and superb sense of
comedy timing by Toshiro Mifune – who
with wit and sword comes to the aid of a
rather silly but sincere group of young men
fighting corruption in their city.

Toshiro Mifune was also the star of the
period's other Akira Kurosawa film,
Yojimbo, a more serious – and bloodthirsty –
tale along vaguely similar lines in that here
again the giant samurai brings peace and
justice to a place seething with crime, by the
quickness of his wit and the power of his
sword.

184

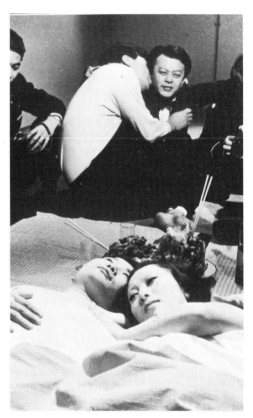

Another brilliant Japanese film was Nagisa Oshima's *The Boy*, which at the same time as telling the story of a small boy who becomes a professional road accident victim (Tetsue Abe) for his small-time criminal father (Fumio Watanabe) when his mother (Akiko Koyama) has to give up the role, offered a profound examination of human nature.

Though shown *after*, Nagisa Oshima's *Death By Hanging* was made *before* both his successful *The Boy* and *Diary of a Shinjuku Thief*. It was a very oblique and difficult film which in essence was a cinematic pamphlet against the death penalty. Initially documentary in style, it switched to fantasy and even humour as it told a story about a young Korean who rapes and murders and then though executed just won't die! Yun-Do Yun played the murderer (left) and Akiko Koyama the girl.

Scenes from Jerzy Hoffman's Polish spectacular *Colonel Wolodyjowski*, which was just about the most expensive and largest-scale film ever made in that country. Superbly photographed, it related a chapter of 17th-century Polish history, when the almost legendary hero of the title fought and defeated the Turks.

Ulivi Dogan, Julia Kotsch and Errol Tash (in foreground) in the somewhat ambiguously titled New Realm film *I Had My Brother's Wife*, a story of a poor peasant's struggle to exist in a Middle Eastern country.

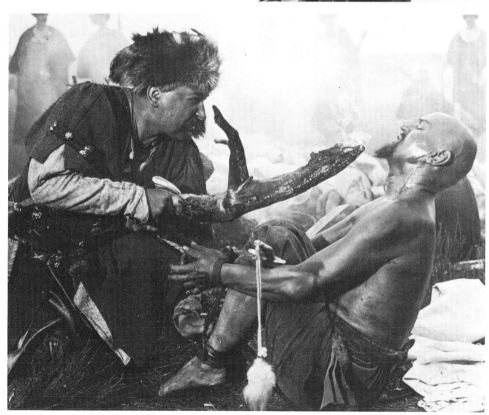

186 Connoisseur's *Asterix the Gaul* – or *Asterix le Gaulois* – was an amusing transcription to the cinema screen of an extremely popular French newspaper and book strip cartoon – with considerable political implications, best understood in its country of origin.

René Clément's thriller *Rider on the Rain* was about a woman (Marlène Jobert) who is raped by an intruder and then kills the rapist when he returns for a second helping! Disposing of the body and thinking there are no witnesses to the crime, she suddenly finds a mysterious American (Charles Bronson) tailing her and when she confronts him, she finds out he knows exactly what has happened . . .

Miracle's *House of Pleasure* was another amorous chapter in the sensual story of previously cinematically established Sexy Susan (Terry Torday) who on this occasion manages to provide a most welcome service to her Emperor, Napoleon.

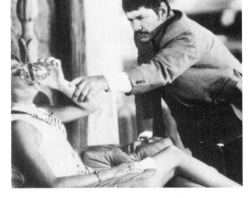

More French crime – but presented in much lighter vein – was in Claude Lelouch's UA film *Simon the Swiss*, a polished but needlessly intricately composed story about an ex-lawyer turned expert crook who plans and carries, successfully, through (until fate takes a final ironic hand) a faked kidnapping and ransoming of a small boy.

Sabine Sun, Phillipe Nicaud and Jean-Claude Bouillon in SF's Jean-Claude Dague film *The Sextrovert* which was largely concerned with a jealous girl's efforts to split up the budding romance between her girl-friend and the latter's new boy-friend.

The magical atmosphere of Fair Enterprises' Jean-Gabriel Albicocco fantasy *The Wanderer*, based on the Alain-Fournier love story which has become a French classic for younger readers.

Peter Zadek's Connoisseur release *I'm An Elephant, Madame* obviously had a great deal to say about German traditions and form of education, but it said it in such a gimmicky, surrealistic way that it was always difficult to sort it all out and draw firmly satisfactory conclusions.

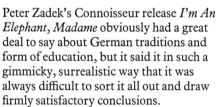

Suzy Kendall, patient, in Paramount's Alberto Lattuada film *Fräulein Doktor*, the story of a very busy lady spy during the First World War who wins plenty of victories over the Allies through her espionage but is finally defeated by addiction to drugs.

188   A very much updated and otherwise modernised version of the old German fairy story, "Hansel and Gretel", *Hands Off Gretel!* was the story of a bewitching witch (Barbara Klingered (right), using her Rolls-Royce as a boudoir) who nearly – but finally not quite – steals the innocent Hansel (Dagobert Walter) from his previously rather old-fashioned-thinking girl-friend (Francy Fair) below.

Anna Moffo and Gianni Machia in the E. J. Fancey release of *Love Me, Baby, Love Me*, the story of a happily married woman who during her husband's absence falls for the wiles of a young man who makes his living by blackmailing women but who, finding he really loves *her*, relents and crosses her off his list of victims.

Eagle's *The Gallery Murders* was the story of an American author vacationing in Italy who sees a murder and so becomes unwillingly involved in a series of maniacal killings.

True to the pattern of his previous films, including the censor-shaking *I Am Curious* duo, Vilgot Sjöman's *Blushing Charlie* included plenty of nudity (male and frontal) and politics ("Hoorah For Cuba") in its basically not unamusing story of a man who takes a pregnant girl into his home and gets so used to having her there he is disappointed when she finally leaves to marry the father of her child.

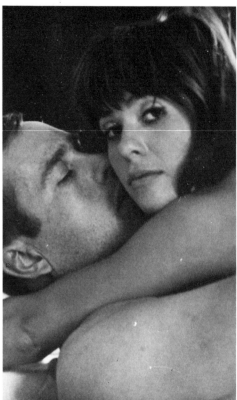

The E. J. Fancey release *My Swedish Meatball* was the story of some amorous rompings between a couple of Swedish couples while they are on holiday in Normandy: at the end of which male egos are dented when the two men find that instead of playing with the girls the girls have in fact been playing around with them!

Jörn Donner's film *Portraits of Women* had, possibly fictional, autobiographical allusions in its story of a pornographic film-maker who returns to his native Finland to add to his output but becomes so enamoured, and involved, with three girls that in the end his movie goes almost literally down the drain. Donner, as well as directing and writing the screenplay, took one of the leading roles in the movie.

Originally made for television – and on closer inspection almost obviously so – Ingmar Bergman's *The Rite* was the story of three strolling, world-famous players who, when brought before the magistrate on a charge of obscenity and reduced to pathetic vulnerability by his probings of their private lives, together utterly defeat him when allowed to confront him with their art. A story full of deeply fascinating implications. With Ingrid Thulin as the woman, Erik Hell as the magistrate.

Monica Nordquist in Crispin's *Swedish Love Play*, a story of a girl about whom an older woman as well as men become greedily possessive.

192 As with last year these two formerly separate features are now combined.

First of all, the *1970 OSCARS*, those little statuettes of merit awarded each year with due ceremony by the *American Academy of Motion Picture Arts and Sciences* and announced last April.

Best Film
PATTON, 20th Century-Fox.

Best Foreign Language Film
INVESTIGATION OF A CITIZEN ABOVE SUSPICION, Vera Films SPA (Italy) Columbia.

Best Direction
FRANKLIN J. SCHAFFNER, for *Patton*.

Best Acting Performance (Male)
GEORGE C. SCOTT, in *Patton*.

Best Acting Performance (Female)
GLENDA JACKSON, in *Women in Love*.

Best Supporting Actor
JOHN MILLS, in *Ryan's Daughter*.

Best Supporting Actress
HELEN HAYES, in *Airport*.

Best Screenplay
RING LARDNER JUNIOR'S *M*A*S*H*.

Best Story and Screenplay
FRANCIS FORD COPPOLA and DEMUND NORTH'S *Patton*.

Best Cinematography
FRED A. YOUNG, for *Ryan's Daughter*.

Best Editing
HUGH S. FOWLER, for *Patton*.

Best Costume Design
NINO NOVARESE, for *Cromwell*.

Best Visual Effects
A. D. FLOWER and L. B. ABBOTT, for *Tora! Tora! Tora!*

Best Sound
DOUGLAS WILLIAMS and DON BASSMAN, for *Patton*.

Best Musical Score
FRANCIS LAI'S *Love Story* (original).

Art Direction and Set Decoration
URIE McCLEARY, GIL MAURICE LTD., ANTONIO MATEOS, PIERRE-LOUIS THEVENET, for *Patton*.

Best Documentary Feature
BOB MAURICE'S *Woodstock*.

Best Documentary Short
JOSEPH STRICK'S *Interviews With My Lai Veterans*.

Live Action Short Film
JOHN LONGENECKER'S *The Resurrection of Broncho Billy*.

Animated Short Film
NICK BOSUSTOW'S *Is It Always Right to be Right?*

Now to the British equivalent of the American Oscars, *The Society of Film and Television Arts Annual Awards* of the feminine statuettes known as *Stellas*.

Best Film
BUTCH CASSIDY AND THE SUNDANCE KID, 20th Century-Fox.

Best Actor
ROBERT REDFORD, for *Butch Cassidy, Tell Them Willie Boy is Here* and *Downhill Racer*.

Best Actress
KATHARINE ROSS, for *Butch Cassidy* and *Tell Them Willie Boy is Here*.

Best Direction
GEORGE ROY HILL, for *Butch Cassidy*.

Best Screenplay
WILLIAM GOLDMAN, for *Butch Cassidy*.

Best Cinematography
CONRAD HALL

Best Editing
J. C. HOWARD and R. C. MEYER

Best Soundtrack
DON HALL, DAVID DOCKENDORF and WILLIAM EDMUNDSON, all for *Butch Cassidy*.

Best Film Music
(The Anthony Asquith Award)
BURT BACHARACH, for *Butch Cassidy*.

Best Art Direction
MARIO GARBUGLIA, for Columbia's *Waterloo*.

Best Costume Design
MARIA DE MATTEIS, for *Waterloo*.

Best Supporting Actress
SUSANNAH YORK, in *They Shoot Horses, Don't They?*

Best Supporting Actor
COLIN WELLAND, in *Kes*.

AWARDS AND FESTIVALS

Most Promising Newcomer
DAVID BRADLEY, in *Kes.*

Best Animated Film
HENRY NINE 'TIL FIVE.

Best Specialised Film
THE RISE AND FALL OF THE GREAT LAKES.

Best Short
SHADOW OF PROGRESS.

The Robert Flaherty Award
SAD SONG OF YELLOW SKIN.

The annual awards of the *Writers Guild of G.B.* were announced on March 11 as follows:

Best British Documentary or Short Film
MICHAEL BARNES'S *Who Killed the Sale?*

Best British Comedy Screenplay
TERENCE FRISBY, for *There's a Girl in My Soup.*

Best British Original Screenplay
BARNEY PLATTS-MILLS, for *Bronco Bullfrog.*

Best British Screenplay
KEN LOACH and TONY GARNETT'S *Kes.*

Carrying no actual awards but always interesting is the result of the *Motion Picture Herald*'s annual poll of the most popular stars, voted for by exhibitors of America and Canada who list them according to what they consider to be their drawing powers at the box-office. The 1970 list announced in January 1971 was as follows:

1. Paul Newman. 2. Clint Eastwood.
3. Steve McQueen. 4. John Wayne.
5. Elliott Gould. 6. Dustin Hoffman.
7. Lee Marvin. 8. Jack Lemmon.
9. Barbra Streisand. 10. Walter Matthau.
For the record the next fifteen were:
11. Robert Redford. 12. George C. Scott.
13. Sidney Poitier. 14. Dean Martin.
15. Raquel Welch. 16. Richard Burton.
17. James Stewart. 18. Peter Fonda.
19. Julie Andrews. 20. Katharine Hepburn.
21. Elvis Presley. 22. Jane Fonda.
23. Jon Voight. 24. Elizabeth Taylor.
25. Alan Arkin.

Now to some of the various International Film Festival Awards. This list doesn't pretend to be complete but it does contain most of the important festivals in a long and increasing list of them (many of which are non-competitive, like Edinburgh).

Cannes
The 1971 awards announced at the end of the Festival, on May 27, were as follows:
Grand Prix: Joseph Losey's *THE GO-BETWEEN*, with Julie Christie, Alan Bates and Margaret Leighton.
Runners-Up: *DEATH IN VENICE* and *TAKING OFF.*
Jury's Special Prize: Divided between *TAKING OFF* and *JOHNNY GOT HIS GUN.*
Special Prize: *DEATH IN VENICE.*
Best Actress: KITTY WINN in *Panic in Needle Park.*

Best Actor: RICARDO CUCCIOLA in *Sacco and Vanzetti.*
Secondary Awards to *LOVE* (Hungarian) and *JOE HILL* (Swedish).
Award for a Director's First Effort: to NINO MANFREDI for *By Grace Received* (Italian).

Bergamo 1970
Grand Prix: *VALERIE AND HER WEEK OF WONDERS* (Czech.)
Runner-up Gold Medals: *THE CYCLISTS* (Yugoslav); *BRONCO BULLFROG* (Great Britain); *A DREAM OF LIBERTY* (Sweden).

Chicago 1970
Best of the Festival: *THE GREEN WALL* (Peru).
Award of Merit: *A BALTIC TRAGEDY* (Sweden).
Award for Most Imaginative Film Exploration: *THE FRUIT OF PARADISE* (Peru–Belgium).
Best Actor: STIG ENGSTROM in *You're Lying* (Sweden).
Best Screenplay: *THE FALCONS* (Hungary).
Best Black and White Cinematography: *THE FRUIT OF PARADISE* (Czech–Belgium).
Best First Feature Film: *MISSISSIPPI SUMMER* (USA).
Critics Award: *THE GREEN WALL* (Peru) and *THE FRUIT OF PARADISE* (Peru–Belgium).

Cracow (International) 1970
Grand Prix: *PEACE AND RESISTANCE* (Japan).
Silver Dragons: *THE DAY THEY*

194   THE 1970 "OSCAR" WINNERS . . .

1. George C. Scott, for his performance in the title role of *Patton*.

2. Glenda Jackson for her performance in *Women in Love* (though in fact this portrait is from another of her films, *The Music Lovers*).

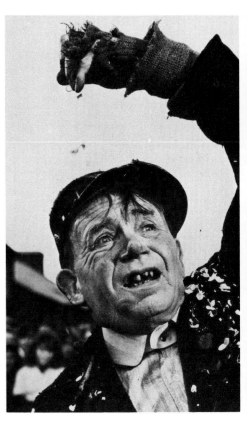

3. John Mills, Best Supporting Actor, for his part in MGM's *Ryan's Daughter*.

4. Helen Hayes, Best Supporting Actress, in Universal's *Airport*.

MOVED (USSR); *DR. SPOCK AND HIS BABIES* (USA); *100 YEARS OF RIGHT* (Cuba); *ANOTHER DAY* (France).
City of Cracow Special Prixe: *THE SON* (Poland).
CIDALC Silver Medal: *THE MOVEMENT* (Great Britain).
Osiris Statuette: *WHAT RIGHTS HAD A CHILD?* (United Nations).

Cracow (National)
Grand Prix: *THE SOIL ALWAYS YIELDS BREAD* (Polish T.V.).

Silver Lajkoniks: *THE SON* (mini studio Cracow unit); *THE TESTAMENT* (Polish T.V.).

Karlovy Vary 1970
(July 15–26)
Grand Prize: *KES* (Great Britain).
Jury Prizes: *BY THE LAKE* (USSR); *BLACK ANGELS* (Bulgaria).
Special Jury Awards: *TASTE OF BLACK EARTH* (Poland).
Special Awards: *GOTT MIT UNS* (Italy); *ON THE WAY TO LENIN* (East Germany).
Best Actor: MATTHIEU CARRIER in *La Maison Des Bories* (France).
Best Actress: NATHALINE BELECHOROSTIKOVA in *By the Lake* (USSR).
Worker Referendum Vote: *A BLOODY TALE* (Yugoslavia).

Venice 1970
(August 19–Sept. 1)
Italian Critics Prizes – Pasinetti Prizes: *THE CLOWNS*, by Federico Fellini; *WANDA*, by Barbara Loden.
Spanish Critics Prize – Luis Buñuel Prize: *THE SPIDERS STRATAGEM*, by Bernardo Bertolucci.
Timon Award: *THE CLOWNS*, by Fellini.
Best Short: *ELOQUENT PEASANT* (Egypt).

Mannheim 1970
Josef von Sternberg (original film award): *IMAGE, FLESH, VOICE* (USA).
Catholic Award: *HOSPITAL* (USA).
FIPRESCI: *RIGHT ON* (USA).
Interfilm: *RIGHT ON* (USA).

First Prize: *LA FINDES PYRENEES* (France); *OMNIA VINCIT AMOR* (German).
Other Jury Prizes: *BETEJEZETLENUL* (Hungary); *REINLICHKEITSERKIEHUNG* (Germany); *SYN* (Poland); *TIMES FOR* (Great Britain); *OLNEY A SAO PAULO* (Brazil).

San Sebastian 1970
Golden Shell Award for Best Feature: *ONDATA DI CALORE* (Italy).
Golden Shell Award for Best Short: *STAR OF BETHLEHEM* (Czech).
Silver Shell Awards – First: *ERSTE LIEBE* (Germany).
Silver Shell Awards – Second: *SEX POWER* (France).
Best Actor: INNOKENTI SMOKTUNOVSKI in *Tchaikowsky* (Russia) and ZOLTAN LATINOVITS for *Utazas a Koponyam Korul* (Hungary).
Best Actress: STEPHANE AUDRAN in *Le Boucher* (France).
Special Mention: *TCHAIKOWSKY* USSR).

Panama 1970
Best Picture: *THE GREEN WALL* (Peru).
Best Director: MAXIMILIAN SCHELL for *First Love* (Germany).
Best Actor: ELLIOTT GOULD, for *Getting Straight* (USA).
Best Actress: DOMINIQUE SANDA, for *First Love* (Germany).
Best Screenplay: ARMANDO ROBLES, for *The Green Wall*.
Best Cinematography: SVEN NYKVIST, for *First Love*.

Julie Andrews, in the title role of Paramount's *Darling Lili*, the story of a musical star who became a spy and duped handsome soldier Rock Hudson.

A Roman orgy in *Fellini-Satyricon*, Federico Fellini's vast, extravagant, self-indulgent, almost overwhelming succession of artistic cinematic pyrotechnics which parallels the decadence of today with that of ancient Rome.

Richard Burton as Henry VIII and Geneviève Bujold as his Queen, Anne Boleyn, in the screen adaptation of the Maxwell Anderson play *Anne of the Thousand Days*, a rich chapter of English history.

Alec Guinness, magnificent as King Charles I, and Dorothy Tutin as Queen Henrietta Maria in Columbia's *Cromwell* – in which Richard Harris plays the title role.

THE IN-BETWEENS

This feature was introduced a few years back in order to cover those otherwise unlisted films which are often on special release for long periods: the gap between première and general release sometimes being as much as several years.

All the films illustrated have been premièred or road-shown but have not yet had a general release, or at this moment do not have a date for one. When they *are* released they will be duly noted in that section of some future annual.

Anne of the Thousand Days. Rich, beautifully coloured, and generally credible recreation of a few pages from a chapter of colourful English history: the wooing, winning and condemnation to the headman's axe by Henry VIII of the lovely young Anne Boleyn. Done with restraint (only two beheadings, one small torture scene!), a pleasing lack of ketchup and reliance on the performances, in which it is well served by Richard Burton's thoughtful, credible portrait of the king, and Geneviève Bujold's quite astonishingly impassioned and exciting one of Anne. Fine support from Irene Papas, Anthony Quayle (Wolsey), John Colicos, etc. Rest of cast: Michael Hordern, Katharine Blake, Valerie Gearon, Michael Johnson, Peter Jeffrey, Joseph O'Conor, William Squire, Esmond Knight, Nora Swinburne, Vernon Dobtcheff, Brook Williams, Gary Bond, T. P. McKenna, Denis Quilley, Terry Wilton, Lesley Paterson, Nicola Pagett, June Ellis, Amanda Jane Smythe. Dir: Charles Jarrott. Pro: Hal. B. Wallis. Screenplay: John Hale & Bridget Boland, based on the Maxwell Anderson play. (Universal–Rank.) (Pan & T.) 146 mins. Cert. A.

Cromwell. Excellent Ken Hughes condensation and clarification to terms of visual cinema of a stirring and complicated chapter of British history, with some finely organised battles, political debates and other landmarks. With Richard Harris a forceful dictator and Alec Guinness – a great performance – superbly subtle and deep as King Charles. Rest of cast: Robert Morley, Dorothy Tutin, Frank Finlay, Timothy Dalton, Patrick Wymark, Patrick Magee, Nigel Stock, Charles Gray, Michael Jayston, Richard Cornish, Anna Cropper, Michael Goodliffe, Jack Gwillim, Basil Henson, Patrick Holt, Stratford Johns, Geoffrey Keen, Anthony May, Ian McCulloch, Patrick O'Connell, John Paul, Llewellyn Rees, Robin Stewart, Andre Van Gyseghem, Zena Walker, John Welsh, Douglas Wilmer, Anthony Kemp, Stacy Dorning, Melinda Churcher, George Merritt, Gerald Rowland, Josephine Gillick. Dir: Ken Hughes. Pro: Irving Allen. Screenplay: Ken Hughes. (Allen–Columbia.) (Pan & T.) 140 mins. Cert. U.

Darling Lili. Julie Andrews as a spy who sings and cheerfully and lovingly pumps information out of handsome Rock Hudson (an Allied Major) in order to pass it on to her bosses. It all ends with a gay auto-chase through Paris (where the movie was largely made) and an air attack on a train – the aerial dogfight scenes are among the best ever shot. Rest of cast: Jeremy Kemp, Lance Percival, Michael Witney, Jacques Marin, Andre Maranne, Gloria Paul, Bernard Kay, Doreen Keogh, Carl Duering, Vernon Dobtcheff, Ingo Mogendorf. Dir & Pro: Blake Edwards. Screenplay: Blake Edwards & Wm. Peter Blatty. (Paramount.) (Pan & T.) 136 mins. Cert. U.

Fellini-Satyricon. The largely unfortunate inevitable outcome of the maestro's progression towards self-indulgent cinematic pyrotechnics, throwing story and all else very much to the winds of chance in order to concentrate on visual extravagance; an explosion of the macabre, brutal, creepy and only occasionally beautiful image, set against a background of cardboard BC Rome and vaguely reminiscent of the unfinished Petronius story of a decadent society. Cast: Martin Potter, Hiram Keller, Salvo Randone, Max Born, Fanfulla, Mario Romagnoli, Capucine, Alain Cuny, Giuseppe Sanvitale, Hylette

Ryan's Daughter faces up to priest Trevor Howard in the very long and leisurely but gloriously photographed MGM film about the Irish troubles directed with endless artistry by David Lean.

Harry Secombe adding his comedy touch to CIRO's *Song of Norway*, the Andrew and Virginia Stone musical based on the life-story of Scandinavian composer Edvard Grieg.

Albert Finney, a magnificent portrait of miser Ebenezer *Scrooge*, the Ronald Neame/ Fox musical adaptation of the famous Dickens classic *A Christmas Carol*.

The Japanese airplanes start their surprise attack on Pearl Harbor in the careful, spectacular reconstruction of that event in Fox's *Tora! Tora! Tora!*

Adolphe, Donyale Luna, Magali Noel, Gordon Mitchell, Lucia Rose, Joseph Wheller, Eugenio Mastropietro, Danica La Loggia, Antonia Pietrosi, Wolfgang Hillinger, Elio Gigante, Sibilla Sedat, Lorenzo Piani, Luigi Zerbinati, Vittorio Vittori, Carlo Giordana, Marcello Di Folco, Luigi Montefiori, Elisa Mainardi. Dir (& Screenplay with B. Zapponi & B. Rondi): Federico Fellini. Pro: Alberto Grimaldi. (Grimaldi–UA.) (Pan & D.) 129 mins. Cert. X.

Ryan's Daughter. David Lean's very long, leisurely tale from a screenplay by Robert Bolt, about a young Irish publican's daughter in love with love, who marries the best available man, a middle-aged, widower schoolteacher, and finding his love far below the passionate, sensual heights she had expected, turns to a shell-shocked young British Army officer in the nearby camp (for this is the time of the Irish "troubles" of 1916) with whom she has a violent affair. Because of this she is suspected of being the informer who gives away the gun-running gang, is stripped and has her hair clipped by the local villagers. And with her lover dead, sets out to Dublin. . . . But this slim story is told by David Lean with a background of exquisitely photographed settings of the lonely, craggy Irish coastline, in roaring storm (a magnificent, utterly unforgettable sequence this: terrifying in its power and its realism) and occasional, water-washed calm: giving the film a breathtaking beauty. A very sensitive, impressive performance by Sarah Miles as Rosy, the daughter, an amazing one by John Mills as the village idiot, and fine work by Trevor Howard, Leo McKern and Robert Mitchum.

Rest of cast: Christopher Jones, Barry Foster, Archie O'Sullivan, Marie Kean, Yvonne Crowley, Barry Jackson, Douglas Sheldon, Philip O'Flynn, Owen O'Sullivan, Gerald Sim, Des Keogh, Niall Toibin, Donal Meligan, Brian O'Higgins, Niall O'Brien. Dir: David Lean. Pro: Anthony Havelock-Allan. Screenplay: Robert Bolt. (Faraway–MGM.) (70 mm Super Pan & Metrocolor.) 206 mins. Cert. AA.

Scrooge. A new and this time musical adaptation of the Charles Dickens classic, *A Christmas Carol*, with its perfect capture of the cosy, sentimental, boisterous, lavish Victorian Christmas spirit: with Albert Finney giving a remarkable performance of the old miser of the title brought to see the Christian light by the ghosts of Christmas Past (Edith Evans), Present (Kenneth More) and Future and his own, heavily chained old partner who is now in Hell (Alec Guinness, delightful). Rest of cast: Michael Medwin, Laurence Naismith, David Collings, Anton Rodgers, Suzanne Neve, Frances Cuka, Derek Francis, Roy Kinnear, Mary Peach, Paddy Stone, Kay Walsh, Gordon Jackson, Richard Beaumont, Geoffrey Bayldon, Molly Weir, Helena Gloag, Reg Lever, Keith March, Marianne Stone. Dir: Ronald Neame. Pro: Robert Solo. Screenplay: Leslie Bricusse (who also wrote the music and lyrics). (Cinema Center–Fox.) (Pan & T.) 118 mins. Cert. U.

Song of Norway. Beautifully photographed musical story of the life of Norwegian composer Edvard Grieg, with Norwegian singing star Toralv Maurstad playing the role. Rest of cast: Florence Henderson, Christina Schollin, Frank Poretta, Oscar Homolka, Elizabeth Larner, Robert Morley, E. G. Robinson, Harry Secombe, Frederick Jaeger, Henry Gilbert, Richard Wordsworth, Bernard Archard, Susan Richards, John Barrie, Wenke Foss, Ronald Adam, Carl Rigg, Aline Towne, Nan Munro, James Hayter, Morocco, Avind Harum, Rolf Berntzen, Tordis Maurstad, Erik Chitty, Charles Lloyd Pack, Robert Rietty, Rosalind Speight, Ros Drinkwater, Tracy Crisp, Cyril Renison, Manoug Parikian, Richard Vernon, Ernest Clark, Eli Lindtner, Ilse Tromm, Dave Brandon, Peter Pocock, Ray Ford. Dir (& Screenplay): Andrew L. Stone. Pro: Andrew & Virginia Stone. (ABC–CIRO.) (Super-Pan & D.) 141 mins. Cert. U.

Tora! Tora! Tora! That was the Japanese battle cry at Pearl Harbor as their planes swept in from the sea to devastate the great American Fleet that lay closely clustered there. And this film coldly and factually and extremely ably reconstructs this page of U.S. history, taking us behind the planning and operational scenes of both sides of the combatants. Add this to *D-Day the Sixth of June* and *Battle of Britain* and a few others as a real historical document on celluloid. Cast: Martin Balsam, Soh Yamamura, Jason Robards, Joseph Cotten, Tatsuya Mihashi, E. G. Marshall, Takahiro Tamura, James Whitmore, Eijiro Tono, Wesley Addy, Shogo Shimada, Frank Aletter, Koreya Senda, Leon Ames, Junya Usami, Richard Anderson, Kazuo Kitamura, Keith Andes, Edward Andrews, Neville Brand, Leora Dana, Asao Uchida, George Macready, Norman Alden, Walter Brooke, Rick Cooper, Elven Havard, June Dayton, Jeff Donnell, Richard Erdman, Jerry Fogel, Shunichi Nakamura, Carl Reindel, Edmon Ryan, Hisao Toake. Dir: Richard Fleischer (American sequences) & Toshio Masuda, Kiuji Fukasaku (Japanese sequences). Pro: Elmo Williams. Screenplay: Larry Forester, Hideo Oguni, Ryuzo Kikushima. (Kurosawa–Fox.) (Colour.) 144 mins. Cert. U.

Waterloo. Sergei Bondarchuk's almost miraculous, certainly incredibly vast, handling of the story of this famous historical battle in which the tight-lipped, secretive, unemotional Lord Wellington beat the volatile, wily but now ailing conqueror Napoleon and so shaped history. A tremendous, breathtaking, magnificently photographed spectacle which almost dwarfs the participants, though both Christopher Plummer (as Wellington) and Rod Steiger (as Napoleon) give performances of great care and considerable insight. Rest of cast: Orson Welles, Jack Hawkins, Virginia McKenna, Dan O'Herlihy, Rupert Davies, Philippe Forquet, Gianni Garko, Ivo Garrani, Ian Ogilvy, Michael Wilding, Sergei Zakhariadze, Terence Alexander, Andrea Checchi, Donal Donnelly, Charles Millot, Eughenj Samoilov, Oleg Vidov, Charles Borromel, Peter Davies, Veronica de Laurentiis, Vladimir Durjnikov, Willoughby Gray, Roger Green, Orso Maria Guerrini, Richard Heffer, Orazio Orlando, John Savident, Jeffry Wickham, Susan Wood, Ghennady Yudin. Dir: Sergei Bondarchuk. Pro: Dino de Laurentiis. Screenplay: H. A. L. Craig. (De Laurentiis–Columbia.) (Pan & T.) 132 mins. Cert. U.

FILM FUTURE

For almost the whole of this volume we are concerned with those films which have been generally released or otherwise unveiled to the public gaze! To redress the balance a little I have, as always, for the last several pages turned to the future, presenting a preview of some of the films you'll be seeing during the next three, six or even twelve months.

This survey of Film Future isn't claimed to be complete nor for that matter to be *very* comprehensive. But in all cases I have asked the companies for information on their future films and this is the material with which they replied. I suppose on an average some 300 new films are shown in Britain in a year so the 100 illustrated here do represent a very fair proportion of that product.

And this is a propitious moment once again to pass my very warm vote of thanks to the film companies for the immense and enthusiastic assistance they give me every year with the compilation of *Film Review*, without which help the book could never be produced at all. I can't name names for various reasons, but I would like to say how grateful I am to everyone for their help.

Richard Burton, playing the title role in Nat Cohen's EMI–MGM film *Villain*, the story of a psychotic East End gangster who in the end pays the price of his crimes.

Dominic Guard as the 12-year-old who carries the love letters between farmer Alan Bates (left) and Julie Christie (right), the proud and wealthy heiress in EMI–MGM's period (1900) piece *The Go-Between* which won the Grand Prix at the 1971 Cannes Film Festival.

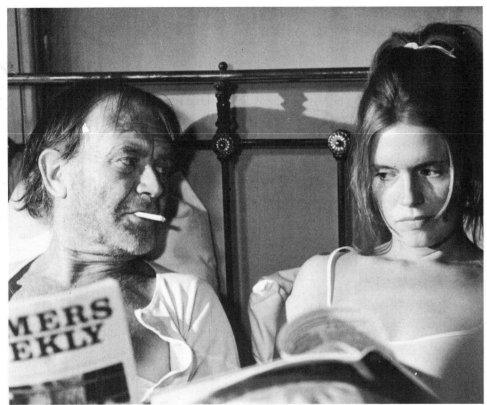

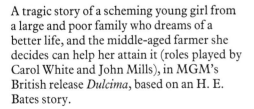

A tragic story of a scheming young girl from a large and poor family who dreams of a better life, and the middle-aged farmer she decides can help her attain it (roles played by Carol White and John Mills), in MGM's British release *Dulcima*, based on an H. E. Bates story.

George C. Scott as Harry Garmes, a former Chicago gunman now living quietly in Portugal who is lured into taking on one last job, driving an escaped criminal, and is soon involved in a very deadly business indeed in MGM's *The Last Run*.

With the proceeds of a bank robbery, some $8,000 in cash, William Holden, as the cowboy who has turned outlaw, starts to make his hazardous escape in MGM's Western *The Wild Rovers*.

Pop star Joe Cocker, the soul singer from Sheffield whose last tour of the United States (in 1970) is documented in MGM's *Mad Dogs and Englishmen*.

Some pretty violent things take place in U.A.'s *Adios Sabata*, a story of the turbulent period in Mexico during the Juarez regime; with Yul Brynner (centre) as a ruthless bounty hunter.

Milo O'Shea (centre) stands between the old tailor (Zero Mostel – right) and the enraged "Angel" (Harry Belafonte) in U.A.'s *The Angel Levine*, a fantasy-comedy from a short story ("The Magic Barrel") by Bernard Malamud.

William Watson tries to force Oliver Reed to return Candice Bergen to her husband in U.A.'s *The Hunting Party*, the story of a grim and ruthless revenge taken by the girl's rich and powerful, and twisted, husband.

204 Rod Steiger, riding high on the shoulders of his admirers, plays a surprised idol of the Mexican revolutionaries in U.A.'s *Duck You Sucker*. James Coburn plays the mastermind who becomes his pal and partner.

Woody Allen returns to the screen in another, largely one-man comedy effort in U.A.'s *Bananas*, the story of a bumbling Manhattan misfit who decides to throw everything up to join the anti-government forces in a South American revolution. With Allen, shapely Louise Lasser.

Murray Head, Peter Finch and Glenda Jackson, the three stars of U.A.'s *Sunday, Bloody Sunday*, the story of a triangular love relationship in which all three hang on to their involvements with each other, frightened to break them in case there is nothing better!

Topol repeats his tremendously successful stage performance in U.A.'s film of the musical *Fiddler on the Roof*.

Broadway stage producer Walter Matthau talks stage-struck Barbara Harris towards ideas of seduction in Paramount's *Plaza Suite*, a Neil Simon adaptation of his own very successful stage musical.

Poor little (reincarnated) orphan-Annie – in fact Barbra Streisand, who's thrown out of the establishment because of misbehaviour in Paramount's *On a Clear Day You Can See Forever*, a musical fantasy in which at the suggestion of psychiatrist-professor Yves Montand, she reveals details of her past lives!

Meet Mr. Webfoot Waddle, the duck playing the title role in the Walt Disney comedy *The $1,000,000 Duck*, which is about a very rare bird, a duck that really lays golden eggs and because of this gift looks like completely upsetting the world's monetary systems!

David Tomlinson, who has starred for Disney in the past, again heads the list of players – with Angela Lansbury – in *Bedknobs and Broomsticks*, a musical fantasy mixing live people with cartoon characters – as illustrated

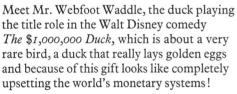

206

Sidney Furie's *Little Fauss and Big Halsy* for Paramount is a story of motor cycle racing in the States, and the effect on some of the young people involved. Michael J. Pollard (left) and Robert Redford play two of the key characters.

CIRO's *The Derby* is a story of what is virtually unknown in Britain, the world of the professional, highly competitive roller skating race tracks.

The Grisson Gang (including, l. to r. Irene Dailey, Don Keefer, Ralph Waite, Tony Musante and Joey Faye) count the ransom money in Robert Aldrich's CIRO film based on a James Hadley Chase kidnap crime thriller.

Walter Matthau as a 72-year-old character endeavouring to get some required information from Penny Santon in *Kotch*, the ABC Pictures comedy-drama, released by CIRO.

That superb real-life husband and wife team of Paul Newman and Joanne Woodward are together again in Paramount's *WUSA*, the story of an itinerant disc jockey who becomes enmeshed in the politics of his right-wing radio station.

Elliott Gould, one of the fastest-rising stars of recent cinematic years, gets the final honour of playing in a Bergman film, *The Touch*, the maestro's first American production, in which Gould is cast as an archaeologist in Sweden. Photo is by Bo-Eric Gyberg, and the film will be a CIRO release.

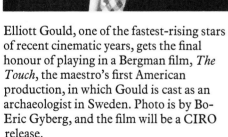

Dustin Hoffman came to England to make the CIRO release *The Straw Dogs*, a story about a young couple (Susan George plays the wife) who go to live in Cornwall with the idea of having a quiet life, but once there quickly find it anything but peaceful!

Oliver Reed as the priest who is defeated by the duplicity of his own kind in Warners' *The Devils*, a story of 17th-century France.

Jealous Marcello Mastroianni, as the loser all along the line, in Warners' Italian production *Jealousy – Italian Style*, a triangle comedy-drama with a tragic climax. Object of his desire, Monica Vitti.

Ian Bannen as the homicidal psychotic attacking the terrified baby-sitter, Susan George, in Fantale-British Lion's suspense thriller *Fright*.

Katharine Hepburn as Hecuba, Queen of Troy, and Vanessa Redgrave as Andromache, her daughter-in-law, as they are about to be led off into captivity by the Greek soldiers in Michael Cacoyannis's *The Trojan Women*, for Josef Shaftel.

Ron Moody (as the villain) and Jack Wild (of "Oliver" renown – the victim) are reunited in Columbia's *Flight of the Doves* – the Doves in question being the two children fleeing across Ireland towards the hoped-for sanctuary of their grandmother's cottage.

Looking like a younger Lyndon Johnson, Sean Connery strides into the sunlight in Columbia's crime thriller *The Anderson Tapes*, about a million-dollar robbery in New York's fashionable Upper East Side.

Columbia's *Horseman* has an unusual story and a seldom used background, being about the "Buzkashi" (described as the most violent sport in the world) which is played in Afghanistan.

Mia Farrow as the blind girl caught up in a web of terror and murder in the eerie Columbia thriller *Blind Terror*.

In Columbia's *Joe Egg*, emotional and domestic problems drive a young married couple into an existence which swings between wild fantasy and grim reality: the two youngsters are played by Alan Bates and Janet Suzman.

Paul Scofield in the title role in Peter Brook's Columbia film of the Shakespeare tragedy *King Lear*.

Professor Anthony Quinn lectures some of his students in Columbia's *R.P.M.*, a present-day story of complicated campus friction between blacks, whites, students, teachers, militants and the police.

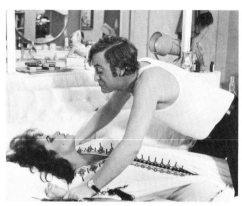

Fools Parade is a Columbia release telling a story of three convicts released in West Virginia in 1930 who are relentlessly tracked by their former warder, whose idea is to recover their cached $25,000 loot – and keep it for himself. James Stewart plays the trio's leader.

One of the many difficult situations in which Samantha Eggar becomes involved when she borrows her boss's car with the idea of a nice quiet holiday trip to the South of France but finds herself instead in a murderous puzzle in which she may be killed – or killer? in Columbia's *The Lady in the Car*.

Michael Caine and Elizabeth Taylor in Columbia's *X, Y and Zee*, a triangle story about the way that a marriage explodes when an outsider enters into the love–hate world of the husband and wife.

With the third "Ape" film completed, *Escape from the Planet of the Apes*, and another one in the pipe-line, it looks as if Fox may one day even rival the *Carry On* series!

Fox's *Celebration at Big Sur* is a documentary record of the Pop Festival to which come such stars as Joan Baez, to entertain one another as much as the onlookers!

Ex-racing driver Steve McQueen had no need for doubles for his scenes on the famous *Le Mans* track in the Fox (Cinema Center) film of that title, which is about a typical 24-hour race at *Le Mans*.

The ubiquitous Elliott Gould turns up again in Fox's *Little Murders*, a brutal satire about the violence which America allows to rage in her cities.

Walkabout is Fox's Australian film about a girl and a boy and a small aborigine boy and their adventures in the outback, when the white children's father kills himself and leaves them to fend for themselves. The trio are played by Jenny Agutter, Lucien John and David Gumpilil.

Jacqueline Bisset as the happy young wife who becomes enmeshed in a group of Satanists in Fox's *The Mephisto Waltz*.

Big John Wayne as *Big Jake* in the Fox Western of that title, in which he shares starring bracket with Maureen O'Hara. Formerly titled "The Million Dollar Kidnapping" it is a film about that, the kidnap victim being Big Jake's small grandson.

212

George C. Scott as a wealthy humanitarian who decides to withdraw from public life in the Universal–Rank film *They Might Be Giants*.

Director Jerry Schatzberg explains to stars Faye Dunaway and Harry Primus how he wants this scene from the Universal–Rank release *Puzzle of a Downfall Child*: the story of a girl who fails to cope with her sudden success as a model.

Elliott Gould and Jody Burrows as the young married couple whose marriage goes depressingly down the hill in Universal–Rank's *I Love My Wife*.

Geraldine Page and Elizabeth Hartman are among the stars opposite Clint Eastwood in Universal's *The Beguiled*, a story of the American Civil War.

Having passed their 21st mark, the Peter Rogers–Ralph Thomas team have been busy at Pinewood producing their 22nd *Carry On* lark, *Carry on at Your Convenience* in which most of the old familiar team of comics are engaged.

A brisk bedroom battle between – pretty, if fanged – vampiress Madeleine Collinson and the horrified young man – David Warbeck – who has mistaken her for her identical – though fangless – twin! It's in the new Hammer "horror" entitled suitably enough *Twins of Evil*.

The Peter Rogers film *All Coppers Are . . .* takes a look at Britain's modern police force.

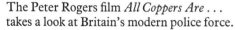

Eric Porter leads pretty if dishevelled Angharad Rees from the prison and the prostitutes in Hammer's Rank thriller *The Hands of the Ripper*.

Fox's *A Boy Named Charlie Brown* brings to the screen Charlie Brown, Snoopy and the Peanuts Gang – favourite American strip cartoon characters – in their first feature-length movie cartoon.

CINEMA CENTER FILMS "A BOY NAMED CHARLIE BROWN". RELEASED BY TWENTIETH CENTURY-FOX.

Jan Nielsen in the title role in Gala's
Swedish Cannes prize-winner *Harry Munter*
– the story of a sincere young man who finds
life just isn't what it ought to be.

Julian Mateos and Elisa Ramirez in Gala's
The Wanton of Spain, a version of a play
which dates from 1499 and which, although
with the same story, preceded "Romeo and
Juliet" by a hundred years.

Georg Rydesberg and Gunnel Lindblom in
Alf Sjöberg's film adaptation of the famous
Strindberg play *The Father* which will be
released in this country by Gala.

Looking remarkably like a real historical
photograph, a scene from Sam Spiegel's
lavish new Columbia film *Nicholas and
Alexandra*, the story of the last, ill-fated
Russian Royal couple murdered in the
Revolution. Playing the Czar, Michael
Jayston; the Czarina, Janet Suzman.

RELEASES OF THE YEAR IN DETAIL

1970-71

July 1st – June 30th

Note: In the following pages certain abbreviations have been made in order to save space. The technical abbreviations are as follows: (T) Technicolor; (C) CinemaScope; (Tech) Technirama; (Total) Totalscope; (M) Metrocolour; (D) Deluxe Colour; (Pan) Panavision. Company names you will find abbreviated as follows: (Anglo) Anglo-Amalgamated; (U.I.) Universal-International; (Lion) British Lion; (Fox) 20th Century-Fox; (U.A.) United Artists

The Adding Machine
Imaginative and entertaining screen adaptation of the Elmer Rice play about Mr. Zero in particular and the Human Fodder he represents in general. The dramatist sees his "hero" (who, after 25 years in one job, kills his boss when he's given the sack, is executed, goes to heaven and is outraged to his conventional suspenders when he finds out just the sort of place it is) as the perfect raw material for the dictator, the warmonger, and all others who need willing dupes! Brilliant acting by *Milo O'Shea* and *Phyllis Diller*, excellent performances by *Billie Whitelaw, Sydney Chaplin* and others in the cast: *Julian Glover, Raymond Huntley, Phil Brown, Libby Morris, Hugh McDermott, Paddie O'Neil, Carol Cleveland, Bruce Boa, John Brandon, Kenny Damon, Hal Galili, Tony Caunter, Bill Hutchinson, Helen Elliott, C. Denier Warren, Tommy Duggan, John Bloomfield, Helena Stevens, Alan Surtees, Christine Pryor, Cal McCord, Shirley Cooklin, Anthony Harwood, Bill Nagy, Nicholas Stuart, Gordon Sterne, Mike Reed, Lola Lloyd, George Margo, George Roderick, Janet Brown, Janie Baron, John Cook.* Dir, Pro & Written for the screen by Jerome Epstein. (Universal–Rank.) (T.) 99 mins. Cert. A.

The Adventures of Gerard
Adaptation of the Conan Doyle "Brigadier Gerard" stories; with *Peter McEnery* the swaggering, foolish swordsman finding more than his fair share of adventure, dodging between the French and English lines during the Spanish Campaign undertaken by Napoleon in 1808. Rest of cast: *Claudia Cardinale, Eli Wallach, Jack Hawkins, Mark Burns, Norman Rossington, John Neville, Paolo Stoppa, Ivan Desny, Leopoldo Trieste, Aude Loring.* Dir: Jerzy Skolimowski. Pro: Henry Lester & Gene Gutowski. Screenplay: H. A. L. Craig. (Sir Nigel Films–UA.) Rel: Dec. 20. (D.) 91 mins. Cert. A.

Again
Thriller about a young man home from abroad who isn't satisfied with the story that in his absence his sister has committed suicide, and with her friend starts out on a little private investigation which leads to several other corpses and a suspicion that all the deaths are connected with a certain piece of music! Cast: *Brett Halsey, Marilù Tolo, Romina Power.* Dir: Julio Buchs. Pro: Edmondo Amati. (E. J. Fancey.) Rel: Floating: first shown Jacey, Trafalgar Sq., Jan., 1971. (T & Techniscope.) 93 mins. Cert. X.

Airport
Smoothly expert, always efficient, latterly exciting large-scale "Grand Hotel"-type, starry film set in and about an American mid-West airport struggling against the worst blizzard the area has suffered in six years: some of the personal problems of the strugglers, too, including airport manager *Burt Lancaster* (whose wife announces she's fed up with his dedication to work and wants a divorce), his hated brother-in-law pilot *Dean Martin* (who learns he's put his stewardess in the family way), and nut-case *Van Heflin*, who takes on board the Rome plane a bomb, which goes off in mid-air, blowing a hole in the airplane, which then limps home – with everyone wondering if and how it can get down on the ground again; a really tense sequence to climax the show. Rest of cast: *Jean Seberg, Jacqueline Bisset, George Kennedy, Helen Hayes, Maureen Stapleton, Barry Nelson, Dana Wynter, Lloyd Nolan, Barbara Hale, Gary Collins, John Findlater, Jessie Royce Landis, Larry Gates, Peter Turgeon, Whit Bissell, Virginia Grey, Eileen Wesson, Paul Picerni, Robert Patten, Clark Howat, Lew Brown, Ilana Dowding, Lisa Garritson, Jim Nolan, Patty Poulsen, Ena Hartman, Malila Saint Duval, Sharon Harvey, Albert Reed, Jodean Russo, Nancy Ann Nelson, Dick Winslow, Lou Wagner, Janis Hansen, Mary Jackson, Shelly Novack, Chuck Daniel, Charles Brewer.* Dir & Written: George Seaton. Pro: Ross Hunter. Based on the novel by Arthur Hailey. (Ross Hunter/Universal–Rank.) Rel: Aug. 16. (T.) 136 mins. Cert. A.

AKA Cassius Clay
The AKA stands for "also known as". A documentary record of the life and career of the champ, Muhammad Ali (AKA Clay!), narrated and with interview by Richard Riley. (UA.) Rel: Floating: first shown at the New Victoria, March, 1971. Cert. U.

All About Women
Light-hearted romance about three girls and their daily life – and love! Cast: *Marie-Christine Auferil, Marlène Alexandre, Astrid Frank, Jean Perrin, Robert Piquet, Philippe Delmar.* Dir & Pro: Claude Pierson. (Richard Schulman Enterprises.) Rel: Floating: first shown at the Cameo-Royal, Jan., 1971. (E.) 83 mins. Cert. X.

All the Way Up
Straightforward adaptation of the David Turner stage comedy "Semi-Detached", an amusing portrait of a smart, wily, scheming little cockney insurance agent with visions of grandeur and the ruthless determination to transform them to reality, with the unscrupulous manipulation of his entire family. Grand performance by Warren Mitchell as the social climber. Rest of cast: *Pat Heywood, Elaine Taylor, Kenneth Cranham, Vanessa Howard, Richard Briers, Adrienne Posta, Bill Fraser, Terence Alexander, Maggie McGrath, Clifford Parrish, Lally Bowers, Frank Thornton, Valerie Leon, Robin Hunter, Mary Pratt, Ernest Hare, George Woodbridge, Arnold Diamond, Michael Robbins, Charles Rayford, Sheila Beckett, Geraldine Newman, Dennis Chinnery, Nina Francis, Paul Bacon, Terry Latham, Janet Montana.* Dir: James MacTaggart. Pro & Screenplay: Philip Mackie. (Granada–Anglo.) (T.) 97 mins. Cert. AA.

Alyse and Chloe
Sub-titled "The Lesbian Lovers", it's a quite tastefully treated story about a young woman lured from her lover into a liaison with another woman and the turmoil as each of the trio struggles against the others and themselves! Cast: *Katrin Jacobsen, Michèle Girardon, Karyn Balm, Christian Kerville.* Dir: René Gainville. Pro: Jean C. Roblin. Screenplay: Marie-Louise Villiers. (S.F.

216 Distributors.) Rel: Floating: first shown at Classic, Windmill, Jan., 1971. (E.) 82 mins. Cert. X.

Anatomy of Love – Anatomie des Liebesackts
Another of those German sex-education lessons; with a – rather pretty – couple demonstrating the arts and pleasures of love (to the quite amusingly suitable strains of Ravel's "Bolero"!) combined with diagrams and a rather startling, in part, lecture on the subject by a doctor. Cast: *Henriette Gonnermann, Günter Kieslich, Wolfgang Reinhardt.* Dir: Hermann Schnell. Pro: Sam Waynberg. Screenplay: H. Schnell. (Waynberg–Planet–S.F. List.) Rel: Floating: first shown at Cameo-Moulin, Jan., 1971. (E.) 90 mins. Cert. X (London).

And Soon the Darkness
Beautifully atmosphered, leisurely and occasionally repetitious thriller about two young nurses who go on a cycling holiday in Northern France, quarrel and part. Then the one left behind is murdered and the survivor tries to discover what has happened to her, helped or hindered by a bunch of suspicious characters. Cast: *Pamela Franklin, Michele Dotrice, Sandor Eles, John Nettleton, Clare Kelly, Hana-Maria Pravda, John Franklyn, Claude Bertrand, Jean Carmet.* Dir: Robert Fuest. Pro: Albert Fennell & Brian Clemens. Screenplay: B. Clemens & Terry Nation. (Warner–Pathé/Assoc. Brit.) Rel: Aug. 2. (T.) 100 mins. Cert. AA.

Andy Warhol and his Clan
German film about the now ubiquitous A.W.: building up a portrait by means of interviews with his friends and co-workers: and including extracts from some of the Warhol films. Dir: Bert Koetter. (Colour.) Rel: Floating: first shown at Paris Pullman, June, 1971. 46 mins.

Angels from Hell
Another in the small flood of films about young (American) rebels: this one about a soldier returned from Vietnam who quickly drifts into a crowd of motor-cycle hoodlums and with them fights other similar gangs and the cops: ironically dying in attacking the Establishment which in the war he had fought for! Cast: *Tom Stern, Arlene Martel, Ted Markland, Stephen Oliver, Paul Bertoya, James Murphy, Jack Starrett, Jay York, Pepper Martin, Bob Harris, Sandra Gayle, Suzy Walters, Luana Talltree, Susan Holloway, Judith Garwood, Susanne Sidney, Steve Rogers.* Dir: Bruce Kessler. Pro: Kurt Neumann. Screenplay: Jerome Wish. (Fanfare–MGM.) Rel: Oct. 4. (Perfect Color.) 86 mins. Cert. X.

Antonio das Mortes
Another strong film from Brazil's Glauber Rocha, about a bandit-killer who refuses the offer of a "degrading" mission to quell a peasant revolt and in consequence has to face up to the maniac boss, to political ambition, cultural scepticism and religious mysticism as he tries to act in the name of justice! Cast: *Mauricio do Valle, Odete Lara, Othon Bastos, Hugo Carvana, Joffre Soares, Lorival Pariz, Rosa*

Maria Penna. Dir: Glauber Rocha. Pro: Claude-Antoine Mapa & G. Rocha. (Connoisseur.) First shown at Times Cinema, Aug., 1970. (Colour.) 95 mins. Cert. X.

Anybody's
Swedish sex film about the erotic adventures of two women on holiday together, introducing a new Swedish sex star in *Marie Liljedahl.* Rest of cast: *Gio Petre, Francisco Rabal, Julian Mateos, Olivera Vuco, Bozidarka Frajt, Heinz Hopf, Erik Hell, Nevenka Filipovic.* Dir: Arne Mattsson. Pro: Lennart Berns. Screenplay: Ernest Hotch. (Miracle.) Rel: Floating. (E.) 100 mins. Cert. X.

The April Fools
Jack Lemmon as the unhappy Wall Street broker who finds promotion and the mixing with the Jet Set that it entails only makes him more unhappy. So when he meets his boss's lovely and equally unfulfilled wife (*Catherine Deneuve*) and they fall in love, they pop off to Paris and a new life leaving their respective spouses to carry on the social New York whirl. Rest of cast: *Peter Lawford, Jack Weston, Myrna Loy, Charles Boyer, Harvey Korman, Sally Kellerman, Melinda Dillon, Kenneth Mars, Janice Carroll, David Doyle, Gary Dubin, Susan Barrett, Dee Gardner, Tom Ahearne.* Dir: Stuart Rosenberg. Pro: Gordon Carroll. Screenplay: Hal Dresner. (Warner–Pathé.) (T & Pan.) 95 mins. Cert. A.

The Aristocats
Walt Disney feature cartoon about a family of well bred Parisian pussies and their adventures when Edgar, their doting owner's butler, decides they stand between him and his employer's fortune, and dumps them far away in the country. The voices of *Phil Harris, Eva Gabor, Sterling Holloway, Scatman Crothers, Paul Winchell, Lord Tim Hudson, Vito Scotti, Thurl Ravenscroft, Dean Clark, Liz English, Gary Dubin, Nancy Kulp, Pat Buttram, George Lindsey, Monica Evans, Carole Shelley, Charles Lane, Hermione Baddeley, Roddy Maude-Roxby, Bill Thompson.* Dir: Wolfgang Reitherman. Pro: W. Reitherman & Winston Hibler. Story by Larry Clemmons, Vance Gerry, Frank Thomas, Julius Svendsen, Ken Anderson, Eric Cleworth & Ralph Wright. (Walt Disney.) Rel: Dec. 27. (T.) 78 mins. Cert. U.

The Arrangement
Elia Kazan's own adaptation, direction and production of his novel of the same title, about a successful man, with a big job, lots of cash, a lovely wife and an exciting mistress, who suddenly realises the emptiness of it all, half-heartedly attempts suicide and then begins to sort things out! A fine start dwindling to a long and leisurely remainder. Cast: *Kirk Douglas, Faye Dunaway, Deborah Kerr, Richard Boone, Hume Cronyn, Michael Higgins, John Randolph Jones, Carol Rossen, Anne Hegira, William Hansen, Charles Drake, Harold Gould, E.J. Andre, Michael Murphy, Philip Bourneuf, Dianne Hull.* Dir, Pro & Written: Elia Kazan. (Athena–Warner–Pathé.) Rel: July 12. (T & Pan.) 126 mins. Cert. X.

Assault
First-class, straightforward, tense-atmosphered thriller about a sexual assault on a schoolgirl, followed by the murder of another one, with the sombre threat of more to follow; and the way in which the police tackle the problems, sorting the clues, sifting the suspects until the killer is finally and surprisingly (?) revealed. Not wholly acceptable in solution, but crisply paced and consistently enthralling. Nice performances by *Frank Finlay* as top cop on the case, *Suzy Kendall* as delectable bait in this trap: and a number of fresh, pretty and promising feminine faces in the background. Rest of cast: *James Laurenson, Lesley Anne Down, Freddie Jones, Tony Beckley, Dilys Hamlett, Anthony Ainley, James Cosmo, Patrick Jordan, Allan Cuthbertson, Anabel Littledale, Tom Chatto, Kit Taylor, Jan Butlin, William Hoyland, John Swindells, Jill Cary, David Essex, Valerie Shute, John Stone, Siobhan Quinlan, Marianne Stone, Janet Lynn.* Dir: Sidney Hayers. Pro: George H. Brown. Screenplay: John Kruse based on Kendal Young's book "The Ravine". (Peter Rogers–Rank.) Rel: March 7. (Colour.) 91 mins. Cert. X.

The Assistant
Half-hour featurette about a photographer's assistant with a colourful imagination who one day in his dark room brings the prints he is developing to life, to provide him with a series of romantic and thrilling adventures, shared by the glamorous models. Cast: *Richard Poore, Susan Drury, Tom Georgeson, Tessa Roberts.* Dir & Pro: Jim Dooley. Screenplay: John Pitt. (Armada–British Lion.) Rel: Feb. 14. (Colour.) 37 mins. Cert. AA.

Asterix the Gaul – Astérix le Gaulois
Feature colour cartoon adaptation of the famous French cartoon-strip about the small enclave in Brittany which, thanks to a magic, strength-giving potion, thumbs its nose at the mighty, all-conquering Romans. A comic cartoon which, like the original, is full of modern French political allusions (although some of them get lost in translation). (Dargaud Films–Connoisseur.) Rel: Floating: first shown at the ICA Cinema, April, 1971. (E.) 90 mins. Cert. U.

L'Aveu – The Confession
Another grim political film from the same team (director–star–cameraman) which made "Z", this time showing the opposite side of the coin in relating the story of a loyal and dedicated Czech communist who for some strange reason is physically and mentally tortured into admitting crimes against the State (of which he is innocent) and who is then made a centrepiece in a big show trial. A long, harrowing film made with brilliance and horrifying conviction: based on the true facts of the persecution and trial of ex-Resistance fighter, ex-Concentration Camp inmate Artur London, who went through all this experience and lived to tell the tale. Cast: *Yves Montand, Simone Signoret, Gabriele Ferzetti, Michel Vitold, Jean Bouise, Laszlo Szabo, Monique Chaumette, Guy Mairesse, Mark Eyraud, Gérard Darrieu, Gilles Segal, Charles Moulin, Nicole Vervil,*

Georges Aubert, André Cellier, Pierre Delaval, William Jacques, Henri Marteau, Michel Robin, Antoine Vitez. Dir: Costa-Gavras. Pro: Robt. Dorfmann & Bertrand Javal. Screenplay: Jorge Semprun, from the book by Lise and Artur London. (Warner.) First shown at Curzon, Oct., 1970. 139 mins. Cert. AA.

The Awful Story of the Nun of Monza
A story of 1608 (claimed to have been taken from the Vatican secret files) about a nun who is raped by the man she saves from the Spaniard's sword and then falls in love with the rapist, has a child by him and ends up condemned for her sins to be walled up alive in the Santa Valeria Convent in Milan. Cast: *Anne Heywood, Antonio Sabato, Hardy Kruger, Carla Gravina, Tino Carraro, Luigi Pistilli, Margherita Lozano, Anna Maria Alegiani, Giovanna Galletti, Caterina Boratto, Renzo Giovampietro.* Dir: Eriprando Visconti. Pro: Silvio Clementelli. Screenplay: E. Visconti, Giampiero Bona. (Miracle.) Rel: Floating: first shown at Cameo, Victoria, Jan., 1971. 101 mins. Cert. X.

The Baby Maker
The story of a marital experiment in which a young, childless couple persuade a young girl to come into their household and mate with the husband to produce the child they need to complete their marriage: and the obvious complications that interfere with the simple progression of the plan. Cast: *Barbara Hershey, Collin Wilcox-Horne, Sam Groom, Scott Glenn, Jeannie Berlin, Lily Valenty, Helena Kallianiotes, Jeff Siggins, Phyllis Coats, Madge Kennedy, Ray Hemphill, Paul Linke.* Dir (& Written): James Bridges. Pro: Richard Goldstone. (Robert Wise – National General.) Rel: June 6. (T.) 109 mins. Cert. AA.

Bamse
Swedish film about the teddy bear of the title and the girl to whom it belongs. When the toy is found among the belongings of a man killed in a car accident the man's son decides to trace the owner, and finds that it belongs to his late father's mistress – a discovery which leads to hatred for her, which changes to another kind of passion . . . and ultimate tragedy. Cast: *Ulla Jacobsson, Folke Sundquist, Grynet Molvig, Björn Thambert, Gio Petré.* Dir: Arne Mattsson. Pro: Ewert Granholm. (Miracle.) Rel: Floating: first shown Cameo, Victoria, Feb., 1971. (E.) 107 mins. Cert. X.

The Barefoot Executive
Comedy about a very clever chimp who has the ability to forecast the TV ratings and takes his young master to the top . . . in spite of all the crooks who are after his secret. Cast: *Kurt Russell, Joe Flynn, Harry Morgan, Wally Cox, Heather North, Alan Hewitt, Hayden Rorke, John Ritter, Jack Bender, Tom Anfinsen, George N. Neise, Ed Reimers, Morgan Farley, and 'Raffles'.* Dir: Robert Butler. Pro: Bill Anderson. (Disney.) Rel: April 11. (T.) 96 mins. Cert. U.

Battle of Algiers
French film that was long banned in its country of origin – in fact until 1970. A reasonably objective reconstruction of the struggle that led up to the granting of national independence. Cast: *Jean Martin, Yacef Saadi, Brahim Haggiag, Tommaso Neri, Fawzia El Kader, Michèle Kerbash, Mohamed Ben Kassen.* Dir: Gillo Pontecorvo. Pro: Antonio Musu and Yacef Saadi. Screenplay: Franco Solinas. (Rank.) Rel: Floating: first shown at The Other Cinema, March, 1971. 120 mins. Cert. X.

The Battle of Britain
Harry Saltzman's remarkable reconstruction of a stirring, heroic page of British history, made with some great air battle spectacle, balanced behind-the-scenes tension and general care for authenticity. A memorable movie; with plenty of stars in a large cast including *Laurence Olivier, Ralph Richardson, Kenneth More.* Rest of cast: *Harry Andrews, Michael Caine, Trevor Howard, Curt Jurgens, Ian McShane, Nigel Patrick, Christopher Plummer, Michael Redgrave, Robert Shaw, Patrick Wymark, Susannah York, Michael Bates, Isla Blair, John Bascomb, Tom Chatto, James Cosmo, Robert Flemyng, Barry Foster, Edward Fox, W. G. Foxley, David Griffin, Jack Gwillim, Myles Hoyle, Duncan Lamont, Sarah Lawson, Mark Malicz, Andre Maranne, Anthony Nicholls, Nicholas Pennell, Andrzey Scibor, Jean Wladon, Wilfried Van Aacken, Karl Otto Alberty, Alexander Allerson, Dietrich Frauboes, Alf Jungermann, Peter Hager, Wolf Harnish, Reinhard Horras, Helmut Kircher, Paul Neuhaus, Malte Petzel, Manfred Reddemann, Hein Riess, Rolf Stiefel.* Dir: Guy Hamilton. Pro: Harry Saltzman & S. Benjamin Fisz. Screenplay: James Kennaway & Wilfred Greatorex. (Saltzman–UA.) Rel: Oct. 25. (T & Pan.) 131 mins. Cert. U.

Bedroom Mazurka
Another Danish piece of comedy-erotica in the style of "Seventeen" and "Song of the Red Ruby" with the plump, bespectacled star of both, *Ole Søltoft* (as the young master at a boys' school who can become the new Head if he can be married by the time the position is to be filled), once again going through a course of sexual initiation and lip-smackingly enjoying it – to the rhythms of the mazurka! Such honest titillation, with such lovely girls, and presented, as it is, with a smile rather than a snigger, that it becomes fun. Rest of cast: *Axel Strøbye, Annie Birgit Garde, Karl Stegger, Birthe Tove, Anne Grete Nissen, Paul Hagen, Gunilla, Christoffer Bro, Jørn Bille, Carsten Brandt, Steen Frøhne, Freddie Andersen, Susanne Jagd.* Dir: John Hilbard. Screenplay: Bob Ramsing, based on a short story by C. E. Soya. (Palladium–Gala.) Rel: Floating: first shown at Classic, Piccadilly, Feb., 1971. (E.) 88 mins. Cert. X.

The Bed Sitting Room
A very black and sick comedy about life in the world after World War Three (which lasts 2 mins. 28 secs.): with *Rita Tushingham* as a 17-months-pregnant girl who lives on board an Inner Circle train with her parents, *Ralph Richardson* as a Lord who lives in fear

of turning into the apartment of the title . . . and so on. Based on the play by Spike Milligan and John Antrobus. Rest of cast: *Dudley Moore, Harry Secombe, Arthur Lowe, Roy Kinnear, Spike Milligan, Ronald Fraser, Jimmy Edwards, Michael Hordern, Peter Cook, Mona Washbourne, Richard Warwick, Frank Thornton, Dandy Nichols, Jack Shepherd, Marty Feldman, Henry Woolf, Rod Brody, Gordon Rollings.* Dir & Pro: Richard Lester. Screenplay: J. Antrobus. (UA.) Rel: Floating. (D.) 91 mins. Cert. X.

Beyond the Valley of the Dolls
One of 1971's most valid candidates for a permanent position in the celluloid chamber of horrors: a very funny deadpan send-up of porn, pop and corn in a slim story about a trio of downy little larks who sing their way to the celluloid city and there become involved in homosexuality, lesbianism, orgies, casual – nude – coupling and other amusements. Cast: *Dolly Read, Cynthia Myers, Marcia McBroom, John La Zar, Michael Blodgett, David Gurian, Edy Williams, Erica Gavin, Phyllis Davis, Harrison Page, Duncan McLeod, Jim Iglehart, Charles Napier, Henry Rowland* and *"The Strawberry Alarm Clock".* Dir & Pro: Russ Meyer. Screenplay: Roger Ebert. (Meyer–Fox.) Rel: Feb. 28. (Pan & D.) 106 mins. Cert. X.

Black Beauty
The story of a horse and its changing fortunes as it changes owners: from the Anna Sewell homily on the treatment of horses written in the 1870's. Cast: *Mark Lester, Walter Slezak, Peter Lee Lawrence, Uschi Glas, Patrick Mower, John Nettleton, Maria Rohm, Eddie Golden, Clive Geraghty, Johnny Hoey, Patrick Gardiner, Brian McGrath, Ronan Smith, John Franklyn, Margaret Lacey, Fernando Bilbao, Vicente Rola, José Niero, Eucilio Rodriguez, Daniel Martin, Luis Induni, Ricardo Palacios.* Dir: James Hill. Pro: Peter L. Andrews, Malcolm B. Heyworth. Screenplay: Wolf Mankowitz: based on the Anna Sewell novel. (Tigon-Chilton.) Rel: May 30. 106 mins. Cert. U.

The Blonde and the Black Pussycat
Reckoning on at least sharing the lovely Castle Portillon estate, the Count and the Colonel offer promises of riches to the local wenches for their favours, but then find that the mysterious Third Man, the valet, is the actual beneficiary! Cast: *Edwige Fenech, Angelica Ott, Barbara Capell, Ralf Wolter.* Dir: Josef Zachar. (S.F. Distributors.) First shown at Jacey, Strand, June, 1970. (E.) 82 mins. Cert. X.

Bloody Mama
The bloody gangster film which was for long refused any certificate by the censor; now trimmed to "X" proportions. A story of the horrible Ma (Kate) Barker and her brood of moronic sons, who rape and murder, and finally kidnap a millionaire – the crime which leads the police to surround their hideout and wipe them all out in a savage gun battle. *Shelley Winters'* performance in the title role is quite magnificent, giving the terrible woman pathos in addition to all else. Rest of cast: *Pat Hingle, Don Stroud, Diane Varsi, Bruce Dern, Clint Kimbrough, Robert de Niro, Robert*

Walden, *Alex Nicol, Michael Fox, Scatman Crothers, Stacy Harris, Pamela Dunlap.* Dir & Pro: Roger Corman. Screenplay: Robert Thom from a story by him and Don Peters. (American International/Anglo–EMI MGM.) Rel: June 27. (Colour.) 84 mins. Cert. X.

Blushing Charlie
Vilgot ('I Am Curious') Sjöman's film which, true to his pattern, includes a good deal of nudity (mainly male, frontal, in this case) and (Hoorah for Cuba) politics in a slim little story about a young man who takes a pregnant friend of a friend into his house (boat) and finds he likes a woman around the place so much he decides to ask her to marry him, but is beaten to the post by her old lover. Cast: *Bernt Lundquist, Solveig Ternstrøm, Lilian Johansson, Bertil Norström, Janet Potterson, Tomas Bolme, Inger Lilje-Joss, Christer Boustedt, Lasse Werner, Jösta Wolivaera, Jon Carlson, Olle Andersson.* Dir (and co-written): Vilgot Sjöman. (Miracle.) Rel.: Floating: first shown at Cameo, Victoria, March, 1971. (Colour.) 95 mins. Cert. X.

The Boatniks
Rather charming little Walt Disney farce concerning the sort of things that can happen to anyone who likes messing about with boats! Cast: *Robert Morse, Stefanie Powers, Phil Silvers, Norman Fell, Mickey Shaughnessy, Wally Cox, Don Ameche, Joey Forman, Vito Scotti, Tom Lowell, Bob Hastings, Sammy Jackson, Joe E. Ross, Judy Jordan, Al Lewis, Midori, Kelly Thordsen, Gil Lamb.* Dir: Norman Tokar. Pro: Ron Miller. Screenplay: Arthur Julian. (Disney.) Rel: July 26. (T.) 100 mins. Cert. U.

Bob and Carol and Ted and Alice
Contemporary American mores and morals come in for light satirical treatment when two married couples start out as best friends and move on from there! All very amusing. Cast: *Natalie Wood, Robert Culp, Elliott Gould, Dyan Cannon, Horst Ebersberg, Lee Bergere, Donald F. Muhich, Noble Lee Holderread, Jnr., K. T. Stevens, Celeste Yarnall, Greg Mullavey, André Philippe, Diane Berghoff, John Halloran, Susan Merin, Jeffrey Walker, Vicki Thal, Joyce Easton, Howard Dayton, Alida Ihle, John Brent, Garry Goodrow, Carol O'Leary, Constance Egan.* Dir: Paul Mazursky. Pro: Larry Tucker. Screenplay: Paul Mazursky, Larry Tucker. (M. J. Frankovich–Columbia.) Rel: Sept. 13. (T.) 105 mins. Cert. X.

The Body
Fascinating semi-documentary about our bodies and their environment, including a remarkable sequence filmed within a human being (a sort of Cook's tour of the intestines) and the birth of a baby, together with the dangers of pollution. A great many forbidding medical facts made fascinating by the way they are treated. Dir: Roy Battersby. Pro: Tony Garnett. Voices of *Vanessa Redgrave* and *Frank Finlay.* Commentary by *Adrian Mitchell.* Suggested by the Anthony Smith book with the film's title. (Kestrel–Anglo–EMI.) Rel: Jan. 24. (T.) 112 mins. Cert. X.

Borsalino
Quite outstanding French gangster film which, set in Marseilles in the 30's, relates the ruthless, assassination-stepped climb to the pinnacle of gangster power by two young crooks who, once there, eye each other for the final weeding out, but avoid it by the intervention of yet another climber... Superbly atmospheric, deadly but also in part amusing and, on occasion, broadly comic to the edge of farce. Acting honours to *Jean-Paul Belmondo* as a rather likeable villain. Rest of cast: *Alain Delon, Michel Bouquet, Catherine Rouvel, Françoise Christophe, Corinne Marchand, Julien Guiomar, Arnoldo Foa, Nicole Calfan, Laura Adani, Christian de Tillière, Mario David, Daniel Ivernel, Dennis Berry, André Bollet.* Dir: Jacques Deray. Pro: Alain Delon. Screenplay: Jean-Claude Carrière, Claude Sautet, Jacques Deray and Jean Cau. (Delon–Paramount.) (Colour.) 128 mins. Cert. AA.

The Boy – Shonen
Nagisa Oshima's brilliant film which, in telling the story of a small boy who takes over from his incapacitated mother the role of professional road accident victim (the father subsequently blackmailing the unfortunate motorist), also manages to examine human nature in depth. Cast: *Tetsue Abe, Fumio Watanabe, Akiko Koyama, Tsuyoshi Kinoshita.* Dir: Nagisa Oshima. Pro: M. Nakajima & T. Yamaguchi. Screenplay: Tsutomu Tamura. (Sozosha/Japan Art Theatre Guild–Academy.) First shown at Academy Cinema Two, June, 1970. (Colour.) 95 mins. Cert. A.

The Boys in the Band
Straightforward adaptation of the Mart Crowley stage play about a group of homosexuals who hold a party which starts with laughs and lightheartedness and degenerates into bitchy hurtings, hatred, pain and tears. You may find it moving, or loathsome, or amusing – whichever way you approach it. Cast: *Kenneth Nelson, Leonard Frey, Cliff Gorman, Reuben Greene, Robert La Tourneaux, Laurence Luckinbill, Frederick Combs, Keith Prentice, Peter White.* Dir: Wm. Friedkin. Pro: Mart Crowley. (Cinema Centre–Fox.) Rel: Nov. 29. 120 mins. Cert. X.

Bride of the Andes
Fascinating story (filmed entirely in a small Indian village high in the Andes) about a Japanese and his mail-order wife who together become deeply involved with the local Indians, among whom they have chosen to live, fighting the injustices and bad faith of the white settlers. Cast: *Sachiko Hidari, Koji Takahashi, Don Mateo, Ancermo Fukuda, Takeshi Hika.* Dir (& Screenplay): Susumu Hani. (Contemporary.) Rel: Floating: first shown at the Electric Theatre, W.11, April, 1971. (E.) 102 mins. Cert. A.

Bronco Bullfrog
He's the released Borstal Boy who helps one of his East End mates and his girlfriend when they run away because their parents don't approve of their poor little romance. Made in the East End, with amateurs, and painting a pretty sordid, sorry picture of the life there. Directed with a certain fluency which promises well for young director-writer Barney Platts-Mills. Cast: *Del Walker, Anne Gooding, Sam Shepherd, Roy Haywood, Freda Shepherd, Dick Philpott, Chris Shepherd, Stuart Stones, Geoff Wincott, J.Hughes, Snr., Mick Hart, Ken Field, Marguerite Hughes, E. E. Blundell, J. Hughes, Jnr., Trevor Oakley, Tina Syer.* Dir (& Written): Barney Platts-Mills. Pro: Andrew St. John. (British Lion.) Rel: Floating. 86 mins. Cert. AA.

Burn, Boy, Burn – Brucia, Ragazzo, Brucia
The sad seaside holiday that ends in tragedy as the wife, after an affair with a student, realises her husband will never understand her actions. Italian. Cast: *Françoise Prévost, Gianni Macchia, Michel Bardinet, Monica Strebel, Anna Pagano, Danika, Franca Sciutto, Miriam Alex, Maria Luisa Sala, Marco Veliante, Ettore Geri.* Dir: Fernando Di Leo. Pro: Tiziano Longo. Screenplay: Antonio Racioppi & Fernando Di Leo. (Miracle.) Rel: Floating. (E.) 86 mins. Cert. X.

The Buttercup Chain
Somewhat complicated and unsure story about four very immature young people and their relationships which starts on a light and fairytale note and weaves its way to a tragic and pathetic ending. Cast: *Hywel Bennett, Leigh Taylor-Young, Jane Asher, Sven-Bertil Taube, Clive Revill, Roy Dotrice, Michael Elphick, Jonathan Burn, Yutte Stensgaard, Susan Baker, Jennifer Baker.* Dir: Robt. Ellis Miller. Pro: John Whitney & Philip Waddilove. Screenplay: Peter Draper. (Columbia.) Rel: Nov. 1. (T & Pan.) 95 mins. Cert. X.

Cactus Flower
A delicious, bubbling, beautiful farce with witty lines, classical situations and superb performances: an I. A. L. Diamond screen adaptation of the Abe Burrows Broadway success which in turn was based on a French play by Barillet and Grédy. The story of a New York dentist who, in order not to be driven into marriage, tells his young mistress that he is already wed with a family. Once he decides to pretend he wants a divorce so he can marry the girl, the farcical complications begin to simmer to a boiling climax, involving his faithful nurse assistant, his friends and others. A wonderful trio of performances by *Walter Matthau, Goldie Hawn* and *Ingrid Bergman*; and nice ones by *Jack Weston* and *Rick Lenz.* Rest of cast: *Vito Scotti, Irene Hervey, Eve Bruce, Irwin Charone, Matthew Saks.* Dir: Gene Saks. Pro: M. J. Frankovich. Screenplay: I. A. L. Diamond. (Frankovich–Columbia.) Rel: July 5. (T.) 104 mins. Cert. A.

Carry on Loving
In their 20th "Carry On" the old team of comics under the expert guiding hands of Peter Rogers and Gerald Thomas get around to Sex – taking the blue-veined, chestnutty mickey out of the Marriage Bureaus! Well up to the usual British box-office bonanza standards. Cast: *Sidney James, Kenneth Williams, Charles Hawtrey, Joan Sims, Hattie Jacques, Terry Scott, Richard O'Callaghan, Bernard Bresslaw, Jacki*

Piper, *Imogen Hassall, Julian Holloway, Joan Hickson, Janet Mahoney, Bill Maynard, Amelia Bayntun, Harry Shacklock, Michael Grady, Valerie Shute, Derek Francis, Patsy Rowlands, Philip Stone, Patricia Franklin, Hilda Barry, Bart Allison, Ann Way, Dorothea Phillips, Gordon Richardson, Colin Vancao, Tom Clegg, Joe Cornelius, Anthony Sagar, Bill Pertwee, Alexandra Dane, Ronnie Brody, Sonny Farrar, Josie Bradly, Anna Karen, Lauri Lupino Lane, Gavin Reed, Len Lowe, Fred Griffiths, Kenny Lynch, Robert Russell.* Dir: *Gerald Thomas.* Pro: *Peter Rogers.* Screenplay: *Talbot Rothwell.* (Rogers–Rank.) Rel: Jan. 3. 88 mins. Cert. A.

Carry On Up the Jungle
Yet another chapter in the "Carry On" success story, with most of the old faithfuls engaged in a loosely (blue) knit story about the search for the rare Oozulum bird by Professor Inigo Tinkle, Bill Boosey, Upsidaisi, etc. Cast: *Frankie Howerd, Sidney James, Charles Hawtrey, Joan Sims, Terry Scott, Kenneth Connor, Bernard Bresslaw, Jacki Piper, Reuben Martin, Valerie Leon, Edwina Carroll.* Dir: Gerald Thomas. Pro: Peter Rogers. Screenplay: Talbot Rothwell. (Rogers–Rank.) Rel: Aug. 30. (Colour.) 89 mins. Cert. A.

Castle Keep
A somewhat odd mixture of beautiful photography, graceful sequences, incredible story and holocaust war scenes in an adaptation of William Eastlake's novel about a withdrawn U.S. Major and a jeep-load of cardboard characters, misfits all, who during the German breakthrough in the Ardennes take up defence positions in an old castle filled with treasure and defend it to the last man, and the last piece of flaming art. Cast: *Burt Lancaster, Patrick O'Neal, Jean-Pierre Aumont, Peter Falk, Astrid Heeren, Scott Wilson, Tony Bill, Al Freeman Jr., James Petterson, Bruce Dern, Michael Conrad, Caterina Boratto, Bisera, Elizabeth Tessier, Anne Marie Moskovenko, Marja Allanen, Eya Tuli, Elizabeth Darius, Karen Biangueron, Maria Danube.* Dir: Sydney Pollack. Pro: Martin Ransohoff. Screenplay: Daniel Tardash & David Rayfiel. (Ransohoff–Columbia.) (Pan & T.) 107 mins. Cert. X.

C.C. and Company
Another story about the young American motor-cycle hoodlum gangs: raping, thugging and robbing their way along the roads. Cast: *Joe Namath, Ann-Margret, William Smith, Jennifer Billingsley, Don Chastain, Teda Bracci, Mike Battle, Sid Haig, Greg Mullavey, Bruce Glover, Ted King, Gary Littlejohn, Frank Noel, Kiva Kelly, Jackie Rohr, Bob Keyworth, Wayne Cochran and the C.C. Riders.* Dir: Seymour Robbie. Pro: Allan Carr & Roger Smith. Screenplay: Roger Smith. (Joseph E. Levine–Avco Embassy.) Rel: June 20. (Colour.)

Change of Mind
And it is, too; the story of a brain transplant with the topical slant that it is a white man's brain which is put into a Negro, with all the to-be-anticipated complications, not necessarily all of them of a medical nature! And this is hung on the case of a white sheriff being accused of the murder of his coloured mistress. Cast: *Raymond St. Jacques, Susan Oliver, Janet MacLachlan, Leslie Nielsen, Donnelly Rhodes, David Bailey, Andre Womble, Clarisse Taylor, Jack Creley, Cosette Lee, Larry Reynolds, Hope Clarke, Rudy Challenger, Henry Ramer, Franz Russell, Joseph Shaw Sydney Brown, Tony Kamreither, Ron Hartmann, Murray Westgate, Guy Sanvido, Chuck Shamata, Dan MacDonald, Joseph Wynn, Charles Elder, Horace Bailey, Buddy Ferens, Don Crawford, Pat Collins, Sean Sullivan, Vivian Reis, Ellen Flood, Danny McIlravey, Keith Williams, Clarence Haynes.* Dir: Robert Stevens. Exec. Pro: Henry S. White. Screenplay: Seeleg Lester & Richard Wesson. (CIRO.) Rel: Floating. (E.) 99 mins. Cert. X.

Chariots of the Gods
Documentary about the unsolved mysteries of the past, based on the book by Erik von Deariken whose theory it is that the earth was at one time inhabited by people from other planets. Dir: Doctor Harald Reirl. Rel: Dec. 27. (MGM–EMI.)

Charlie, the Lonesome Cougar
Characteristic Disney animal movie. Cast: *Ron Brown, Brian Russell, Linda Wallace, Jim Wilson, Clifford Peterson, Lewis Sample, Edward C. Moller, Rex Allen* (narrator). Dir & Co-pro: Winston Hibler. Screenplay: Jack Speirs. (Disney.) Rel: Dec. 27. (T.) 75 mins. Cert. U.

The Cheyenne Social Club
Pleasant, new-style Western with strong comedy leanings: stetsoned specialists *James Stewart* and *Henry Fonda* forsaking horses for whores when the former finds that he has been left a successful brothel in Cheyenne. Rest of cast: *Shirley Jones, Sue Anne Langdon, Elaine Devry, Robert Middleton, Arch Johnson, Dabbs Greer, Jackie Russell, Jackie Joseph, Sharon De Bord, Richard Collier, Charles Tyner, Jean Willes, Robert J. Wilkie, Carl Reindel, J. Pat O'Malley, Jason Wingreen, John Dehner, Hal Baylor, Charlotte Stewart, Alberto Morin, Myron Healey, Warren Kemmerling, Dick Johnstone, Phil Mead, Hi Roberts, Ed Pennybacker, Red Morgan, Dean Smith, Bill Hicks, Bill Davis, Walt Davis, John Welty.* Dir & Pro: Gene Kelly. Screenplay: James Lee Barrett. (National General–Carthay Center.) Rel: Nov. 15. (T & Pan.) 102 mins. Cert. AA.

La Chinoise
Circa 1967 Jean-Luc Godard film about five students who form a Maoist cell in Paris and then talk a great deal about it. Cast: *Anne Wiazemsky, Jean-Pierre Léaud, Juliet Berto, Michel Sémeniako, Lex de Bruijn, Francis Jeanson.* Dir: Jean-Luc Godard. (Guéville–Fair Enterprises.) First shown at Times Cinema, Aug., 1970. (E.) 95 mins. Cert. AA.

Chisum
King of the Pecos, *John Wayne,* still in True Grit-ish mood, out-witting and out-gunning all types of Baddies as he determinedly struggles to keep law and order in this familiar, old-style Western which sees *Forrest Tucker* as a crooked businessman, *Geoffrey Deuel* as Billy the Kid and *Patric Knowles* as a true-blue British neighbour. Rest of cast: *Christopher George, Ben Johnson, Glenn Corbett, Bruce Cabot, Andrew Prine, Richard Jaeckel, Lynda Day, John Agar, Lloyd Battista, Robert Donner, Ray Teal, Edward Faulkner, Ron Soble, John Mitchum, Glenn Langan, Alan Baxter, Alberto Morin, William Bryant, Pedro Armendariz, Jr., Christopher Mitchum, Abraham Sofaer, Gregg Palmer, Pamela McMyler.* Dir: Andrew V. McLaglen. Pro: Andrew J. Fenady. Screenplay: A. J. Fenady. (Batjac–Warner.) Rel: Aug. 30. (T & Pan.) 110 mins. Cert. U.

Les Choses de la Vie – The Things of Life
Quite brilliant French film which takes a small, thin, routine story – about a man who has left his wife and family and now lives with a mistress and wonders if he should part from her – and makes it utterly absorbing by the attention to detail, the meticulous realism of every word and action and even gesture; highlighted by an astonishing car crash sequence which is faultless in its observation of every small reaction and incident. Beautifully acted. Cast: *Michel Piccoli, Romy Schneider, Lea Massari, Jean Bouise, Boby Lapointe, Hervé Sand, Henri Nassiet, Gérard Lartigau, Marcelle Arnold, Jean-Pierre Zola.* Dir: Claude Sautet. Pro: Raymond Danon. Screenplay: Paul Guimard, Jean-Loup Dabadie & Claude Sautet based on one of Guimard's novels. (Lira Films/Sonoco-Poly–Columbia.) Rel: Floating: first shown at the Cameo-Poly, Jan., 1971. (Colour.) 89 mins. Cert. AA.

The Christine Jorgensen Story
John Hansen playing both before and after the sex-change operation character upon which a rather needless romantic angle is hung. Rest of cast: *Quinn Redeker, John W. Himes, Ellen Clark, Rod McCary, Will Kuluva, Oscar Beregi, Lynn Harper, Trent Lehman, Pamelyn Ferdin, Bill Erwin, Joyce Meadows, Sondra Scott, Don Pierce, Elaine Joyce, Eddie Frank, Dee Carroll, Peter Bourne.* Dir: Irving Rapper. Pro: Edward Small. Screenplay: Robt. E. Kent & Ellis St. Joseph: based on the book by Christine Jorgensen. (Small–UA.) Rel: Floating. (D.) 89 mins. Cert. X.

Ciao, Federico!
Amusing documentary made by an American amateur during the shooting of Fellini's "Satyricon", giving a detailed sketch of the great Italian director and his flamboyant, theatrical flair. Dir & Photographed: Gideon Bachmann. Pro: Victor Herbert. (Connoisseur.) Rel: Floating: first shown at Academy Two, April, 1971. 60 mins. Cert. X.

The Circus
Chaplin's revival of his 1928 feature, to which he has now added a self-composed musical accompaniment and even a theme song, which he himself sings over the main and credit titles. A classic of silent screen comedy with one inspired sequence in which Charlie takes the place of the high-wire walker. Cast: *Charles Chaplin, Merna Kennedy, Betty Morrissey,*

220

Harry Crocker, Allan Garcia, Henry Bergman, Stanley J. Sanford, George Davis, John Rand, Steve Murphy, Doc Stone. Written, directed and produced: Charles Chaplin. 72 mins. Cert. U.

Colonel Wolodyjowski
Just about the most expensive, lavishly mounted and spectacular Polish film ever made: a superbly photographed epic tracing the career of a famous Polish commander during the wars against Turkey in the 17th century. Based on a Henryk ("Quo Vadis") Sienkiewicz novel, the film enlarges basic historic fact to portray a man who became a legend and a hero of Polish history. Cast: *Tadeusz Lomnicki, Mieczyslaw Pawlikowski, Hanna Bielicka, Jan Nowicki, Marek Perepeczko, Magdalena Zawadzka, Barbara Brylska, Irena Karel, Daniel Olbrychski, Mariusz Dmochowski.* Dir (& written with Jerzy Lutowski): Jerzy Hoffman. (Contemporary.) Rel: Floating. (Colour.) 155 mins. Cert. A.

Come Back Peter
Donovan Winter wrote, directed, produced and edited this made-on-location film about a swinging, permissive age lad's day-dream progress from bed to bed in Chelsea and around. Cast: *Erika Bergmann, Penny Riley, Christopher Matthews, Yolanda Turner, Maddy Smith, Valerie St. Helene, Annabel Levanton, Nicole Paget.* (Donwin–R.S.E.) Rel: Floating. (E.) 65 mins. Cert. X.

The Competitors
All-but-half-hour interest film about Show Jumping – all the behind-the-scenes preparations of horse and rider. Dir & Written: Joe Mendoza. Pro: John Spencer & Brian Little. (Midland Bank/Warner–Pathé.) Rel: Floating. (T.) 25 mins. Cert. U.

Cool it Carol!
A moral lesson in a not too well polished, titillatingly bare frame: the story of a butcher's boy and his girl-friend who come up from the country to London to make a fortune and find it in the shady hinterland of homosexuals, party orgies, prostitution – the lot! And then they go home; wiser, we hope! Cast: *Janet Lynn, Robin Askwith, Jess Conrad, Stubby Kaye, Peter Murray.* Dir & Pro: Pete Walker. (Miracle.) Rel: Floating. (E.) 101 mins. Cert. X.

Cotton Comes to Harlem
Filmed in New York, more especially in Harlem, this adaptation of the Chester Himes novel is about a couple of coloured 'tecs and their efforts to outwit two crooks who have dreamed up devious ways to separate some of the local residents from their hard-won savings. Cast: *Godfrey Cambridge, Raymond St. Jacques, Calvin Lockhart, Judy Pace, Redd Foxx, John Anderson, Emily Yancy, J. D. Cannon, Mabel Robinson, Dick Sabol, Theodore Wilson, Eugene Roche, Frederick O'Neal, Vinette Carroll, Gene Lindsey, Van Kirksey, Cleavon Little, Helen Martin, Turk Turpin, Tom Lane, Arnold Williams, Lou Jacobi, Leonardo Cimino.* Dir: Ossie Davis. Pro: Samuel Goldwyn Junr. Screenplay: Arnold Perl and Ossie Davis. (Goldwyn–UA.) Rel: June 13. (D.) 97 mins. Cert. X.

Count Yorga, Vampire
The 'orrid 'appenings that occur in the gloomy mansion of the Count Yorga, occult operator and lustful bloodsucker, as he impregnates his victims with his own dreadful disease. Cast: *Robert Quarry (the Count), Roger Perry, Michael Murphy, Michael Macready, Donna Anders, Judith Lang, Edward Walsh, Julie Conners, Paul Hansen, Sybil Scotford, Marsha Jordan, Deborah Darnell, Erica Macready.* Dir: Bob Kelljan. Pro: Michael Macready. Screenplay: Bob Kelljan. (American International/Anglo–MGM–EMI.) Rel: Dec. 6. (Colour.) 90 mins. Cert. X.

Countess Dracula
Ingrid Pitt as the old Countess who in a fit of temper and a chance blow discovers that the blood of young girls can wholly rejuvenate her, and how this obsession to retain her youth leads her to increasingly unspeakable crimes! Cast: *Nigel Green, Sandor Elès, Maurice Denham, Patience Collier, Peter Jeffrey, Lesley-Anne Down, Leon Lissek, Jessie Evans, Andrea Lawrence, Susan Brodrick, Ian Trigger, Nike Arrighi, Peter May, John Moore, Joan Haythorne, Marianne Stone, Charles Farrell, Sally Adcock, Anne Stallybrass, Paddy Ryan, Michael Cadman, Hulya Babus, Lesley Anderson, Biddy Hearne, Diana Sawday, Andrew Burleigh, Gary Rich, Ismed Hassan, Albert Wilkinson.* Dir: Peter Sasdy. Pro: Alexander Paal. Screenplay: Jeremy Paul. (Hammer–Rank.) Rel: Feb. 14. (Colour.) 93 mins. Cert. X.

Creatures the World Forgot
Stone Age action with plenty of pretty un-rocklike girls and lusty men. Cast: *Julie Ege, Brian O'Shaughnessy, Tony Bonner, Robert John, Marcia Fox, Rosalie Crutchley, Don Leonard, Beverley Blake, Doon Baide, Ken Hare, Sue Wilson, Derek Ward, Fred Swart, Josje Kiesouw, Hans Kiesouw, Gerard Bonthuis, Frank Hayden, Leo Payne, Rosita Moulin, Tamsin Millard, Christine Hudson, Heinke Thater, Cheryl Stewardson, Trudy Inns, Samantha Bates, Debbie Aubrey-Smith, Joan Boshier, Audrey Allen, Vera P. Crosdale, Mildred Johnston, Lilian M. Nowag, Jose Rozendo, Jose Manuel, Mark Russell, Dick Swain, Alwyn van der Merwe, Manuel Neto, Mike Dickman.* Dir: Don Chaffey. Pro (& Screenplay): Michael Carreras. (Hammer–Columbia.) Rel: April 18. (T.) 95 mins. Cert. X.

Cry of the Banshee
Elisabeth Bergner as a wicked witch out to get revenge on hated Lord, *Vincent Price,* by means of her Sidhe, who loves killing and gets in plenty of practice before the gory tale is ended and the thing goes off, without body or soul, to roam outer space! Rest of cast: *Essy Persson, Hugh Griffith, Hilary Dwyer, Sally Geeson, Patrick Mower, Pamela Farbrother, Marshall Jones, Carl Rigg, Michael Elphick, Stephen Chase, Andrew McCulloch, Robert Hutton, Godfrey James, Terry Martin, Richard Everett, Quin O'Hara, Jan Rossini, Peter Forest, Joyce Mandre, Gertan Klauber.* Dir & Pro: Gordon Hessler. Screenplay: Tim Kelly & Christopher Wicking. (Anglo–MGM/EMI.) Rel: Dec. 6. 87 mins. Cert. X.

Dad's Army
Reasonably successful adaptation to the large screen of the popular small screen comedy series: with all the familiar faces larking around in a story of the local Home Guard as they try out their own particular – and peculiar – horror weapon, a home-made rocket which homes on its despatchers! Cast: *Arthur Lowe, John le Mesurier, Clive Dunn, John Laurie, James Beck, Arnold Ridley, Ian Lavender, Liz Fraser, Bernard Archard, Derek Newark, Bill Pertwee, Frank Williams, Edward Sinclair, Anthony Sagar, Pat Coombs, Roger Maxwell, Paul Dawkins, Sam Kydd, Michael Knowles, Fred Griffiths, John Baskcomb, George Roubicek, Scott Fredericks, Ingo Mogendorf, Franz van Norde, John Henderson, Harriet Rhys, Dervis Ward, Robert Raglan, John D. Collins, Alan Haines, Desmond Cullen-Jones, Frank Godfrey, Freddie White, David Fennell, George Hancock, Colin Bean, Freddie Wiles, Leslie Noyes, Hugh Hastings, Bernard Severn.* Dir: Norman Cohen. Pro: John R. Sloan. Screenplay: Jimmy Perry & David Croft. (Norcon–Columbia.) Rel: April 4. (T.) 95 mins. Cert. U.

Darker Than Amber
Rod Taylor as paperback hero Travis McGee, an amateur detective of the thick-ear school who, having rescued pretty little prostitute Vangie (*Suzy Kendall*) from her exploiter bosses and fallen in love with her, grimly sets out to sort them out – for good – when having recaptured her they kill her! Rest of cast: *Theodore Bikel, Jane Russell, James Booth, William Smith, Robert Philips.* Dir: Robert Clouse. Pro: Walter Selzter & Jack Reeves. Screenplay: Ed Waters. (Cinema Center-Fox.) Rel: June 13. (Colour.) 97 mins. Cert. X.

Day of Rest
The aimless Sunday of a suburban family; a comedy of life. Cast: *Giselle Townclear, Avis Bunnage, Roy Holder, Lee Montague, Jo Gladwin, Doris Hare, Rosalind Atkinson.* Dir: Jim Clark. Pro: Donald Rankin. Screenplay: Bill Naughton. (Signal Films–Columbia.) Rel: Sept. 13. (T.) 25 mins. Cert. A.

Death by Hanging
The first Nagisa Oshima film which, shown out of competition at the Cannes Film Festival, brought him to European notice, but shown in England after the two critically acclaimed successors: "Diary of a Shinjuku Thief" and "The Boy". An initially documentary style which switches into fiction and fantasy and even humour as it tells the story of an intelligent young man, a Korean, who rapes and murders two young girls and then has to pay the price, and Oshima is concerned about that price and its effect on all concerned. Cast: *Yun-Do Yun, Kei Sato, Fumio Watanabe, Toshiro Ishido, Masao Adachi, Mutsuhiro Toura, Hosei Komatsu, Masao Matsuda, Akiko Koyama, Nagisa Oshima.* Dir: Nagisa Oshima. Pro: Masayuki Nakajima, Takuji Yamaguchi & N. Oshima. Screenplay: Tsutomo Tamura, Mamoru Sasaki, Michinori Fukao & Nagisa Oshima. (Sozosha–Connoisseur.) Rel: Floating: first shown at Academy Three, Feb., 1971. 117 mins. Cert. X.

Deep End
Fascinating Jerzy Skolimowski film (he co-scripted Polanski's "Knife in the Water" and Wajda's "Innocent Sorcerers" with which films it bears some striking resemblances) about a 15-year-old boy who, in his first job as a public baths attendant, falls in love with the older, more sophisticated girl who runs the Ladies side of the business: and how this touching passion leads him to accidental murder. A comedy which turns to tragedy at the end, and has beautifully observed portraits of the two central characters. Cast: *Jane Asher, John Moulder-Brown, Diana Dors, Karl Vogler, Christopher Sandford, Louise Martini, Erica Beer, Anita Lochner*. Dir: Jerzy Skolimowski. Exec. Pro: Judd Bernard. Screenplay: Jerzy Skolimowski, Boleslaw Sulik & J. Gruza. (Maran/Kettledrum/Bararia Atelier–Connoisseur.) Rel: Floating: first shown at Academy, March, 1970. (Colour.) 88 mins. Cert. X.

Dirty Dingus Magee
Western comedy about a small-time crook, *Frank Sinatra*, his dimwit victim, *George Kennedy*, and the trouble that their duel leads to, embracing the local whorehouse, the US Cavalry, Injuns . . . but it never, unfortunately, gets off the ground. Rest of cast: *Anne Jackson, Lois Nettleton, Jack Elam, Michele Carey, John Dehner, Henry Jones, Harry Carey, Paul Fix, Donald Barry, Mike Wagner, Terry Wilson, David Burk, David Cass, Tom Fadden, Mae Old Coyote, Lillian Hogan, Florence Real Bird, Ina Bad Bear, Marya Christen, Mina Martinez, Sheila Foster, Irene Kelly, Diane Sayer, Jean London, Gayle Rogers, Timothy Blake, Lisa Todd, Maray Ayres, Carol Andreson*. Dir & Pro: Burt Kennedy. Screenplay: Tom and Frank Waldman & Joseph Heller, based on the David Markson book, "The Ballad of Dingus Magee". (MGM/EMI.) (Pan & Metrocolor.) 91 mins. Cert. AA.

Doctor in Trouble
Further "medical" fun, largely set in ships at sea, where *Leslie Phillips* has stowed away when he finds out that the girl he plans to marry is having a cruise on the same ship as his hated rival. Rest of cast: *Harry Secombe, James Robertson Justice, Angela Scoular, Irene Handl, Simon Dee, Robert Morley, Freddie Jones, Joan Sims, John Le Mesurier, Graham Stark, Janet Mahoney, Graham Chapman, Jacki Piper, Fred Emney, Yuri Borienko, Gerald Sim, Yutte Stensgaard, Jimmy Thompson, Sylvana Henriques, Marcia Fox, Tom Kempinski, Anthony Sharp, Marianne Stone, John Bluthal*. Dir: Ralph Thomas. Pro: Betty E. Box. Screenplay: Jack Davies. (Box/Thomas–Rank.) Rel: Sept. 27. (Colour.) 90 mins. Cert. AA.

Don't Just Stand There!
Complicated comedy about smuggling watches dipped in *crème de menthe*, mistaken identity, crooked writers, crooked crooks . . . and that's only just the start. Cast: *Robert Wagner, Mary Tyler Moore, Glynis Johns, Harvey Korman, Barbara Rhoades, Vincent Beck, Joseph Perry, Stuart Margolin, Emile*

Genest. Dir: Ron Winston. Pro: Stan Margulies. Screenplay: Charles Williams, based on his own novel "The Wrong Venus". (Rank.) Rel: Sept. 13. (T.) 99 mins. Cert. A.

Don't Look Back
Documentary about pop star *Bob Dylan's* tour of Britain in 1965. With *Bob Dylan, Joan Baez, Bob Neuwirth, Alan Price*. Dir: D. A. Pennebaker. Pro: Albert Crossman, John Cort & Leacock Pennebaker Inc. Rel: Floating. 95 mins. Cert. X.

The Dunwich Horror
The odd happenings on Miskatonic campus, where a young man called Wilbur, son of a man hanged as a demon, studies secret occult books, lures pretty student Sandra Dee into his sexual rites and generally raises Old Nick, finally confronting a professor in a battle between Good and Evil. Cast: *Dean Stockwell, Ed Begley, Lloyd Bochner, Donna Baccala, Joanna Moore Jordan, Talia Coppola, Barboura Morris, Mike Fox, Jason Wingreen, Michael Haynes, Sam Jaffe*. Dir: Daniel Haller. Pro: J. H. Nicholson & S. Z. Arkoff. Screenplay: Curtis Lee Hanson, Henry Rosenbaum, Ronald Silkosky. (American International–Warner-Pathé.) Rel: July 19. (Movielab Colour.) 86 mins. Cert. X.

Elbow Play
German sex comedy about the arts of seduction and, in particular, the success of serving tea to milady in the nude! Cast: *Susanne von Sass, Joav Jasinski, Jochen Busse, Hannelore Cremer, Henry van Lyck, Margot Trooger, Konrad Georg, Marika von Mindszenthy, Curt Bock*. Dir: Wolfgang Becker. Pro: Klaus Dudenhöfer. Screenplay: Willibald Eser. (Miracle.) Rel: Floating. (E.) 83 mins. Cert. X.

El Condor
The struggle between General Chavez, within the fortress of the title, and chain-gang escapee Luke, and crooked Jaroo, and their little band of Apaches, to gain the golden fortune which the former holds and the latter seeks: and it's a bloody and bitter struggle which ends on an ironical note with the survivor gaining the girl and gaining the gold and realising that while he can take the former the latter is not portable! Cast: *Jim Brown, Lee Van Cleef, Patrick O'Neal, Mariana Hill, Iron Eyes Cody, Imogen Hassall, Elisha Cook, Jnr., Gustavo Rojo, Florencio Amarilla, Julio Peña, Angel Del Pozo, Patricio Santiago, John Clark, Raul Mendoza Castro, Rafael Albaicin, George Ross, Ricardo Palacios, Charles Stalnaker, Carlos Bravo, Dan Van Husen, Peter Lenahan, Art Larkin, Per Barclay*. Dir: John Guillermin. Pro: André de Toth. Screenplay: Larry Cohen & Steven Carabatsos. (National General–Carthay Center.) Rel: Sept. 6. (T.) 102 mins. Cert. AA.

L'Enfant Sauvage – The Wild Boy
Remarkable Truffaut film in which in a semi-documentary manner and in almost clinical detail he tells the based-on-truth story of a small boy who in the 18th century was discovered completely wild in the

woods, was captured, abused and finally taken in hand by a good and patient doctor who tamed and gradually taught him to be human. In spite of the cool, factual treatment, a moving and always fascinating film. A most impressive performance by *Jean-Pierre Cargol*, a nicely underplayed one by *Truffaut* himself as the doctor. Rest of cast: *Jean Saste, Françoise Seigner, Paul Villé, Claude Miler, Annie Miler*. Dir: François Truffaut. Pro: Marcel Barbent. Screenplay: F. Truffaut & Jean Gruault adapted from "Mémoire et Rapport sur Victor de L'Aveyron" by Jean Itard (1806). (UA.) Rel: Floating. 85 mins. Cert. U.

The Engagement
Comedy about a young man whose young lady, having chosen an expensive engagement ring, leaves him with a taxi and 5d to pay for it – thereafter he spends his time driving from place to place trying to raise the money for the ever increasing taxi fare, with mounting panic. Cast: *David Warner, George Innes, Michael Bates, Juliet Harmer, Paul Curran, Barbara Couper, Gillian Raine, Norman Rossington, Peter Copley, Angus MacKay, Jeffrey Morris, Julian Holloway, Roy Evans, Keith Smith, Geoffrey Palmer, Ray Mort, Diane Aubrey, Vicky Hodge, Harriet Harper, Gillian Cave, Nell Brennan, Karen Ford, Harriet Rhys*. Dir: Paul Joyce. Pro: David Barber. Screenplay: Tom Stoppard. (Memorial/Anglo–EMI.) Rel: Aug. 23. 44 mins. Cert. U.

Erotissimo
Larky, satirical, crazy Franco–Italian comedy which takes the mickey out of the current craze for using erotica in every form of advertising; presented through a thin story about a worried wife trying to arouse her busy businessman husband to the attraction of her charms while he is wholly concerned with the tax inspector who has descended on his firm and is investigating his affairs. A sly comment not only on erotica but on the French character and universal marital attitudes. But oh, so flashily edited! Cast: *Annie Girardot, Jean Yanne, Francis Blanche, Dominique Maurin, Erna Schurer, Didi Perego, Jacques Higelin, Venantino Venantini*. Dir: Gérard Pirès. Screenplay: Nicole de Buron. (Contemporary.) Rel: Floating: first shown at Paris-Pullman, Jan., 1971. (Colour.) 100 mins. Cert. X.

The Executioner
Another highly complicated Russian *v.* American and British spies melo, with *George Peppard* as the agent who, when his suspicions about a colleague are refuted by a committee of his superiors, obstinately kills the man, tosses him out of a plane over the Channel – and then finds out he was wrong – or was he? Rest of cast: *Joan Collins, Judy Geeson, Oscar Homolka, Charles Gray, Nigel Patrick, Keith Michell, George Baker, Alexander Scourby, Peter Bull, Ernest Clark, Peter Dyneley, Gisela Dali*. Dir: Sam Wanamaker. Pro: Chas. H. Schneer. Screenplay: Jack Pulman, based on the Gordon McDonell book. (Schneer–Columbia.) Rel: Sept. 20. (Pan & T.) 111 mins. Cert. AA.

222 **Explosion**
Slanted story about two unstable young Americans
unable to take the strain of modern life who use this as
an excuse to explode into violence and brutal murder.
Cast: *Don Stroud, Gordon Thomson, Michele Chicoine,
Cecil Linder, Robin Ward, Ted Stidder, Murray
Matheson, Ann Sears, Sherry Mitchell, Olga Kaya,
Harry Saunders, Richard Conte.* Dir: Jules Bricken.
Pro: Julian Roffman. Screenplay: Alene & Jules
Bricken. (Rank.) Rel: Floating. 98 mins. Cert. X.

The Extraordinary Seaman
A strange story of World War Two, and the sinking
of a captured Japanese battleship by a mysterious
small British ship not listed at the Admiralty and
captained by a strange, in fact, extraordinary, skipper
in snow-white uniform who perpetually sips his
Scotches . . . *David Niven.* Rest of cast: *Faye Dunaway,
Alan Alda, Mickey Rooney, Jack Carter, Juano
Hernandez, Manu Tupou, Barry Kelley, Leonard O.
Smith, Richard Guizon, John Cochran, Jerry Fujikawa.*
Dir: John Frankenheimer. Pro: Edward Lewis.
Screenplay: Phillip Rock & Hal Dresner, based on the
book by the former. (Frankenheimer–Lewis/MGM.)
Rel: Dec. 27. (Pan & Metrocolor.) 80 mins. Cert. A.

Eyewitness
Interesting thriller which never quite achieves the
success one could hope for it: about a small boy whose
lies mitigate seriously against him when, having seen a
visiting statesman assassinated, and being the only
surviving witness of the crime, he flies before the
killer trying to convince his elders – initially completely
unsuccessfully – of his danger. A good performance
from *Lionel Jeffries* as the lad's military uncle. Rest of
cast: *Mark Lester, Susan George, Tony Bonner,
Jeremy Kemp, Peter Vaughan, Peter Bowles, Betty
Marsden, Antony Stambouliah, John Allison, Joseph
Furst, Robert Russell, Jonathan Burn, Christopher
Robbie, Jeremy Young, Tom Eytle, David Lodge,
Maxine Kalli.* Dir: John Hough. Pro: Paul
Maslansky. Screenplay: Ronald Harwood from the
Mark Hebden novel of the same title as the film.
(Irving Allen/MGM–EMI.) Rel: Oct. 11. 91 mins.
Cert. A.

Female Sexuality
Another in the German "medical" sex films series:
this one presenting three cases of feminine problems,
including pregnancy, commented upon and
introduced by Dr. Oswalt Kolle. Cast: *Heidrun
Kussin, Sonja Lindorf, Kathrin Kretschmer.* Dir:
Alexis Neve. Pro: Karin Wecker-Jacobsen.
(Crispin.) Rel: Floating. (Colour.) 93 mins. Cert. X.

Fidel
Interesting, overlong but well-balanced documentary
about Castro, his travels with his cabinet, about the
country, his speeches, his meetings with his people: all
interweaved with newsreel shots of the revolution and
the events that followed. Made by Saul Landau.
(The Other Cinema.) Rel: Floating. 96 mins. Cert. U.

Figures in a Landscape
A fine example of the true art of the film from Joseph
Losey, who takes the ambiguous story of two escaped
prisoners (from where? from whom?) struggling against
jungle, swamp and mountain in order to get to the
safety that the elder one says they'll find above the
everlasting snow line, away from the persistently
pestering, hovering, prying, harassing helicopter, and
makes it into magnificent cinema: wonderfully
photographed against glorious backgrounds. Cast:
*Robert Shaw, Malcolm McDowell, Henry Woolf,
Christopher Malcolm, Andrew Bradford, Warwick
Sims, Roger Lloyd Pack, Robert East, Tariq Younus.*
Dir: Joseph Losey. Pro: John Kohn. Screenplay:
Robert Shaw. (Cinema Center–Fox.) Rel: June 13.
(T & Pan.) 110 mins. Cert. AA.

For a Few Bullets More
Made-in-Europe Western in which a trio of more-
than-shady characters struggle against each other for
the possession of a million stolen dollars in gold and
end up many bodies later prepared to share it between
them. Cast: *George Hilton, Edd Byrnes, Gilbert
Roland, Kareen O'Hara, Pedro Sanchez, Ivano
Staccioli, Gerard Herter, José Torres.* Dir: Enzo G.
Castellari. Pro: Edmondo Amati. Screenplay:
Giovanni Simonelli & E. G. Castellari. (Admondo
Amati–Gala.) Rel: Dec. 27. (T & Techniscope.)
100 mins. Cert. A.

Fragment of Fear
Extremely interesting, most ably directed, finely
atmosphered suspense thriller about a young
ex-junkie whose aunt is murdered at Pompeii and
whose worried investigation of the crime, in view of
apparent police disinterest, leads to threats and a
series of frightening incidents which follow him back
to the South Coast and Kensington and lead to . . .
well, that's the rub: the final shriekingly exciting
climax is followed by an ambiguous ending which is
either brilliant or ludicrous according to the way you
see it. Cast: *David Hemmings, Gayle Hunnicutt, Flora
Robson, Wilfrid Hyde-White, Daniel Massey, Roland
Culver, Adolfo Celi, Mona Washbourne, John Rae,
Zakes Mokae, Angelo Infanti, Hilda Barry,
Georgina Moon, Petra Markham, Lois Hyett, Mary
Wimbush, Glyn Edwards, Derek Newark, Arthur Lowe,
Yootha Joyce, Patricia Hayes.* Dir: Richard C.
Sarafian. Pro: John R. Sloan. Screenplay: Paul Dehn.
(Columbia.) Rel: Nov. 8. (T.) 95 mins. Cert. AA.

Fräulein Doktor
Suzy Kendall as a very busy lady spy in World War
One, who having organised the destruction of a
British warship, returns to Germany to be
honoured, subsequently becoming involved in the first
German counter-attack using poison gas. Victories all
the way along the line – until she is defeated by her
one weakness – drugs! Cast: *Kenneth More, Capucine,
James Booth, Alexander Knox, Nigel Green, Roberto
Bisacco, Malcolm Ingram, Giancarlo Giannini, Mario
Novelli, Kenneth Poitevin, Bernard de Vries, Ralph
Nossek, Michael Elphick, Olivera, Andreina Paul, Silvia
Monti, Virginia Bell, Colin Tapley, Gerard Herter,*

*Walter Williams, John Atkinson, Neale Stainton, John
Webb, Joan Geary, Aca Stojkovic, Mavid Popovic,
Janez Vrhovec, Bata Paskaljevic, Zoran Longinovic,
Dusan Bulajic, Miki Micovic, Dusan Djuric.* Dir:
Alberto Lattuada. Pro: Dino de Laurentiis.
Screenplay: Duilio Coletti, Stanley Mann, H. A. L.
Craig, Vittoriano Petrilli, A. Lattuada. (De
Laurentiis–Paramount.) Rel: Floating. (T.) 101 mins.
Cert. AA.

The Gallery Murders
An American writer on holiday in Italy accidentally
sees a murder, is himself suspected of being the killer
and becomes involved in a horrible series of mad
knifings which threaten him and his girl-friend. Cast:
*Tony Musante, Suzy Kendall, Eva Renzi, Umberto
Raho, Enrico Maria Salerno, Mario Adorf.* Dir (&
Written): Dario Argento. Pro: Salvatore Argento.
(Eagle.) Rel: Floating: first shown at Cameo Royal,
March, 1971. 94 mins. Cert. X.

The Games
The story of four competitors in the Olympic Games
Marathon: the reasons they run and what they
achieve. Cast: *Michael Crawford, Stanley Baker,
Ryan O'Neal, Charles Aznavour, Jeremy Kemp,
Elaine Taylor, Athol Compton, Fritz Wepper, Kent
Smith, Sam Elliott, Reg Lye, Mona Washbourne,
Don Newsome, Emmy Werner, Harvey Hall, June Jago,
Karel Stepanek, Gwendolyn Watts, John Alkin, Dale
Ishimoto, Rafer Johnson, Ron Pickering, Adrian
Metcalfe, Alexander Werner.* Dir: Michael Winner:
Pro: Lester Linsk. Screenplay: Erich Segal.
(Winner–Linsk–Fox.) Rel: Aug. 9. (D & Pan.)
96 mins. Cert. U.

Games That Lovers Play
Sex comedy about the Madames of two London
bawdy houses who compete against each other in
order to find out which has the most desirable damsel
on her books! A struggle which after various episodes
ends, it is agreed, as a draw, with honours even,
between Fanny Hill (*Joanna Lumley*) and
Constance Chatterley (*Penny Brahms*). Rest of cast:
*Richard Wattis, Jeremy Lloyd, Diane Hart, Nan
Munro, John Gatrell, Charles Cullum, Graham
Armitage, New Temperance Seven.* Dir & Screenplay:
Malcolm Leigh. Pro: Negus-Fancey & Judith Smith.
(Border Films.) Rel: March 14. 91 mins. Cert. X.

The Gay Deceivers
Permissive-period story about two young Americans
who in order to dodge the draft pretend to be homo-
sexuals – and then have to keep up appearances!
Cast: *Kevin Coughlin, Larry Casey, Brooke Bundy,
Jo Ann Harris, Michael Greer, Sebastian Brook, Jack
Starrett, Richard Webb, Eloise Hardt, Jeanne Baird,
Marishka, Mike Kopscha, Joe Tornatori, Robert Reese,
Christopher Riordan, Doug Hume, Dave Osterhout,
Marilyn Wirt, Ron Gans, Rachel Romen, Tom Grubbs,
Louise Williams, Randee Lynne, Meridith Williams,
Harry Sidoni, Lenore Stevens, Trigg Kelly, Tony Epper.*
Dir: Bruce Kessler. Pro: Joe Solomon. Screenplay:
Jerome Wish. (Grand National.) Rel: Floating.
(Colour.) 91 mins. Cert. X.

A Gentle Creature
Robert Bresson's interesting, if cold and withdrawn, adaptation of a Dostoievsky story about a pawnbroker who marries a young girl and, apparently, drives her to suicide. Cast: *Dominique Sanda, Guy Frangin, Jane Lobre*. Dir & Screenplay: Robt. Bresson. Pro: Mag Bodard. (Marianne Parc Academy–Connoisseur.) First shown at the Academy Cinema, Oct., 1970. 88 mins. Cert. AA.

Get Carter
Smooth, tremendously professional, brutal, horribly fascinating British gangster piece about a London racketeer who goes back to his home town, Newcastle, to ferret out the reasons for the sudden tragic death of his elder, "straight" brother: and when he finds it is murder sets out methodically to take his grim revenge on all concerned, leaving a trail of mangled men and women in his wake. An outstanding performance as the hooded-eyed, cool killer by *Michael Caine*. Rest of cast: *Britt Ekland, John Osborne, Ian Hendry, Bryan Mosley, Geraldine Moffatt, Dorothy White, Alun Armstrong, Glynn Edwards, Tony Beckley, George Sewell, Rosemarie Dunham, Bernard Hepton, Petra Markham, Terence Rigby, Godfrey Quigley, John Bindon*. Dir (& Screenplay): Mike Hodges. Pro: Michael Klinger. (Klinger–MGM.) Rel: May 2. (Metrocolor.) 112 mins. Cert. X.

Getting Straight
Hirsute new star *Elliott Gould* as the ex-student, back at his Alma Mater for a teaching degree, who becomes involved in student unrest: and though he's "for" them, the film, ambiguously it is to be admitted, appears committed "agin 'em", suggesting that the young people are really, aware or not, merely supporting nihilism! Rest of cast: *Candice Bergen, Robert F. Lyons, Jeff Corey, Max Julien, Cecil Kellaway, Jon Lormer, Leonard Stone, William Bramley, Jeannie Berlin, John Rubinstein, Richard Anders, Brenda Sykes, Jenny Sullivan, Gregory Sierra, Billie Bird, Harrison Ford, Elizabeth Lane, Hilarie Thompson, Irene Tedrow, Joanna Serpe, Scott Perry*. Dir & Pro: Richard Rush. Screenplay: Robert Kaufman based on the Ken Kolb novel. (Columbia.) Rel: Jan. 31. (Colour.) 125 mins. Cert. X.

Girls for Pleasure
Jean-Claude Roy's screen adaptation of the Dominique Dallayrac book "Dossier Prostitution", which examines the problem by giving cases of various kinds to show how and why it happens and the dangers it brings. Cast: *Jean-Phillippe Ancelle, Line Arnel, Adaly Bayle, Valerie Boisgel, Beatrice Gardon, Adrien Cayla, Michel Charrel, Michel Dacquin, Marc Dudicourt, France Durin, Jackie Foucault, Christian Forges, Noelle Hussenot, Liana Marelli, Edith Ploquin, Nadir Samir, Katia Tchenko*. Dir & script: Jean-Claude Roy. Pro: René Thevenet. (OCF Tanagra–Kenneth Rive Gala.) Rel: Floating: first shown at Classic, Piccadilly, Feb., 1971. (E.) 90 mins. Cert. X.

Goodbye Gemini
Technically polished, intermittently amusing, often horrifying story about a very nasty set of characters, including the pair of identical twins whose ambiguous but tremendously intimate relationship, during London adventures that take them right into the vice area, eventually leads to double murder and suicide. A very unpleasant story about some horrible people, including pimps, deviates, blackmailers, etc. Cast: *Judy Geeson, Martin Potter, Michael Redgrave, Alexis Kanner, Mike Pratt, Marion Diamond, Freddie Jones, Peter Jeffrey, Terry Scully, Daphne Heard, Laurence Hardy, Joseph Furst, Brian Wilde, Ricky Renee, Barry Scott, Hilda Barry, Jack Connell*. Dir: Alan Gibson. Pro: Peter Snell. Screenplay: Edmund Ward, based on the Jenni Hall novel "Ask Agamemnon". (Shaftel–CIRO.) Rel: Sept. 6. (E.) 89 mins. Cert. X.

Le Grand Amour
Another of *Pierre Etaix's* brilliant comedies: pure cinema. The story of a man more or less trapped into a good marriage who suddenly finds himself terribly in love with his secretary, then sees reason and returns, more or less happily, into his marital rut. Full of ideas (not fully explored in all cases), visual gags and witty tricks. Rest of cast: *Annie Fratellini, Nicole Calfan, Ketty France, Louis Mais, Alain Janey, Jacqueline Rouillard*. Dir: Pierre Etaix. Screenplay: Etaix & Jean-Claude Carrière. (Curzon.) First shown, Curzon, Dec., 1970. (E.) 86 mins. Cert. U.

Grazie Zia
Rather odd little Italian contribution which obviously intends to be taken seriously, about a psychiatric cripple, a nasty young man, and the lovely doctor aunt who becomes obsessed with him and his erotic games until she decides the best thing for both of them is a kindly killing. Cast: *Lisa Gastoni, Lou Castel, Gabriele Ferzetti, Luisa de Santis, Massino Sarghielli, Nicoletta Rizzi, Anita Dreyer*. Dir & Written – with Sergio Bazzini & Pier Luigi Murgia – from his own story: Salvatore Samperi. (Avco Embassy.) First shown at Paris Pullman, Kensington, Aug., 1970. 92 mins. Cert. X.

The Great Bank Robbery
Comedy Western with just about everybody – including a not-so-Reverend *Zero Mostel* – trying to rob the Friendly (that's the name of the place, not the inhabitants) bank and *Clint Walker* as the Texas Ranger trying to foil them. Rest of cast: *Kim Novak, Claude Akins, Akim Tamiroff, Larry Storch, John Anderson, Sam Jaffe, Mako, Elisha Cook, Ruth Warrick, John Fiedler, John Larch, Peter Whitney, Norman Alden*. Dir: Hy Averback. Pro: Malcolm Stuart. Screenplay: Wm. Peter Blatty, based on the novel by Frank O'Rourke. (Warner.) Rel: Oct. 25. (Pan & T.) 95 mins. Cert. U.

The Great White Hope
Screen adaptation of the big Broadway stage success based on the story of the rise – and fall – of the great American coloured boxer Jack Johnson. More or less routine fight story but with racial angles: and the surprising suggestion that Johnson was deliberately toppled from his throne by boxing promoters and U.S. agents, using the champion's love for a white woman. Cast: *James Earl Jones, Jane Alexander, Lou Gilbert, Joel Fluellen, Chester Morris, Robert Webber, Marlene Warfield, R. G. Armstrong, Hal Holbrook, Beah Richards, Moses Gunn, Lloyd Gough, George Ebeling, Larry Pennell, Roy E. Glenn Senr., Bill Walker, Marcel Dalio, Rodolfo Acosta, Virginia Capers, Rockne Tarkington, Oscar Beregi, Karl Otto Alberty, Jim Beattie, Scatman Crothers, Manuel Padilla Junr., Basil Dignam*. Dir: Martin Ritt. Pro: Lawrence Turman. Screenplay: Howard Sackler – based on his own stage play. (Turman-Fox.) Rel: May 23. 103 mins. Cert. AA.

Greetings
The title is an allusion to the wording on a U.S. conscription paper, and the film deals with the efforts of a young American to dodge the draft by pretending to be homosexual, a physical wreck or anything else likely to work. Meanwhile his two friends chase the girls, in one case computer-chosen! Cast: *Jonathan Warden, Robert De Niro, Gerritt Graham, Megan McCormick, Ashley Oliver, Cynthia Peltz, Ruth Alda, Mona Feit, Carol Patton, Allen Garfield, Sara-Jo Edlin, Roz Kelly, Ray Tuttle, Tisa Chiang*. Dir: Brian De Palma. Pro: Charles Hirsch. Screenplay: B. De Palma. (Eagle.) Rel: Floating. (Colour.) 85 mins. Cert. X.

Groupie Girl
Somewhat sensational fictional story built on a background of the sad little fans of the Pop Groups who follow their heroes around from place to place, "collecting" (actually sleeping with) them: this G.G. in particular has a very hard and humiliating time of it! Cast: *Esme Johns, Billy Boyle, Richard Shaw, Neil Hallett, Charles Finch, Eliza Terry, Tom Docherty, Simon King, Trevor Adams, Ken Hutchison, Donald Sumpter, Bobby Parr, Bill Jarvis, Sion Probert, Emmett Henessy, Paul Bacon, Lynda Priest, Sue Carstairs, Ruth Harrison, Archie Wilson, Cherokee, Walter Swash, Flanagan, James Beck, Jimmie Edwards, Lynton Guest, Paul Woloff, Paul Pryde*. Dir: Derek Ford. Pro: Stanley Long. Screenplay: Derek Ford & Suzanne Mercer. (Salon–Eagle.) Rel: Floating. (E.) 87 mins. Cert. X.

Guess What We Learned in School Today
Comedy about sexual education in America: in particular at Three Rivers, where a lot of the inhabitants don't need it and a lot certainly do. Cast: *Richard Carballo, Devin Goldenberg, Zachary Haines, Jane MacLeod, Yvonne McCall, Rosella Olson, Diane Moore*. Dir: John G. Avildsen. Pro: David Gil. Screenplay: Eugene Price. (Cannon Releasing Corp.) Rel: Floating first shown at Cinecenta, March, 1971. Cert. X.

Guess Who's Coming for Breakfast
German film of the Guy de Maupassant novel "The Nieces of Madame Colonel", a story of loose morals and passionate amours. Cast: *Tamara Baroni, Heidrun van Hoven, Kai Fischer, Britt Lindberg,*

224 Claus Tinney, Heiner Hitz, Peter Capra, Steven Tedd. Dir: Michael Thomas. Pro: Erwin C. Dietrich. Screenplay: Claus Martin. (E. J. Fancey.) First shown at Jacey, Trafalgar Square, Oct., 1970. (Colour.) 90 mins. Cert. X.

Guess Who's Sleeping With Us Tonight
German film about a series of sexual romps between a mother, her three nubile daughters, an adventurer and the butler! Cast: *Ursula von Manescul, Marianne Lebau, Andrea Rau, Petra Schroeder, Heidrun Kussin, Frank Glaubrecht, Peter Wesp, Wildried Herbst, Harry Riebauer.* Dir: Alexis Neve. (Arca–Winston/Butcher's.) Rel: Floating: first shown Cinephone, Feb., 1970. 80 mins. Cert. X.

Hands Off Gretel!
Modernised version of the fairy story with the updated witch doing her erotic best to seduce Hansel and win him from the rather old-fashioned thinking Gretel, who, after the witch has had her way with him in the back seat of her Rolls, eventually gets him back for keeps by some shrewd feminine strategy. Cast: *Barbara Klingered, Francy Fair, Dagobert Waerlt, Herbert Fux, Karl Dall, Rainer Basedown, Erika Karnbach.* Dir: F. J. Gottlieb. Pro: Hans Jürgen Pohland. (New Realm.) Rel: Floating: first shown at Cinephone, March, 1971. (Colour.) 71 mins. Cert. X.

Hang Your Hat on the Wind
Long/short (or short/long!) Walt Disney film about an Indian boy, the escaped horse he finds and rescues and covets, and what happens when his decision to return the animal to its owner is spoilt by a couple of thieves who take it from him. A nice, charming little moral tale. With *Ric Natoli,* as the boy, and *Judson Pratt* the Holy Father. Rest of cast: *Angel Tompkins, Edward Faulkner, Pete Logan, Bill Cornford, Monica Ramirez, Carlos Rivas, Alex Tinne.* Dir & Pro: Larry Lansburgh. Screenplay: Paul West. (Walt Disney.) Rel: July 26. (T.) 48 mins. Cert. U.

Hell Boats
Melodrama set against a background of the war in 1942 and the desperate struggles of a certain Lt. Cmdr. to break the German blockade of Malta with his motor torpedo boats, christened as the craft of the film's title. Cast: *James Franciscus, Elizabeth Shepherd, Ronald Allen, Reuven Bar-Yotam, Inigo Jackson, Mark Hawkins, Drewe Henley, Magda Konopka, Takis Emmanuel, Philip Madoc, Sean Barrett, Andreas Malandrinos.* Dir: Paul Wendkos. Pro: Lewis J. Rachmil. Screenplay: Anthony Spinner, Donald & Derek Ford, based on a story by S. S. Schweitzer. (Oakmont–UA.) Rel: Nov. 22. (T.) 95 mins. Cert. A.

Hello, Dolly!
One of the brightest, liveliest, most spectacular and generally entertaining movie musicals in a long time: based on the stage play about Jewish life by Thornton Wilder called "The Matchmaker". With *Barbra Streisand* as the widow who fixes weddings (and just about everything else) but has a heck of a time fixing it so that wealthy, skinflint merchant *Walter Matthau* will ask her to be his wife. Rest of cast: *Michael Crawford, Louis Armstrong, Marianne McAndrew, E.J. Peaker, Danny Lockin, Joyce Ames, Tommy Tune, Judy Knaiz, David Hurst, Fritz Feld, Richard Collier, J. Pat O'Malley.* Dir: Gene Kelly. Pro & Written: Ernest Lehman, based on the Michael Stewart/Jerry Herman stage musical which in turn was based on Thornton Wilder's "The Matchmaker". (Chenault Prods. Inc.–Fox.) Rel: Jan. 24. (D.) 148 mins. Cert. U. (Listed in the "In-betweens" feature of last year's *Review*.)

Hello–Goodbye
Michael Crawford as the British car salesman–mechanic who, while doing a spot of business in the South of France, meets and falls in love with the pretty girl in the broken-down Rolls – and so becomes involved with the loose-living Baroness and the car-loving Baron, her patient hubbie. Rest of cast: *Curt Jurgens, Geneviève Gilles, Ira Furstenberg, Mike Marshall, Didier Haudepin, Ann Bell, Vivien Pickles, Lon Satton, Agathe Natanson.* Dir: Jean Negulesco. Pro: André Hakim. Screenplay: Roger Marshall. (Fox.) Rel: Nov. 29. (D.) 101 mins. Cert. AA.

Hell's Belles
Another story about the young motor-cycle hoodlums: in this case the pursuit by one youngster of another who has stolen his bike – a chase on which he is accompanied by the latter's former girl-friend. Cast: *Jeremy Slate, Adam Roarke, Jocelyn Lane, Angelique Pettyjohn, Michael Walker, Astrid Warner, William Lucking, Eddie Hice, Dick Bullock, Jerry Randall, Jerry Brutsche, Kristian van Buren, Elaine Gefner.* Dir & Pro: Maury Dexter. Screenplay: James Gordon White & R. G. McMullen. (American International–MGM–EMI.) Rel: Feb. 14. (Colour.) 95 mins. Cert. X.

Heterosexual
One for the collector of cinematic curios, about an up-dated de Sade character called Juliette who runs, walks, twists and convolutes her way through the gamut of sexual experience: and this hot little piece is played by *Maria Pia Conti.* Rest of cast: *Lea Nanni, Christine Delit, Angela De Leo.* Dir: Warren Kiefer. Pro: Ninki Maslansky. (Anthony Balch.) Rel: Floating. 78 mins. Cert. X.

Highway Pickup
Julien Duvivier crime thriller about a young woman whose greed leads to her killing her husband, blackmailing his best friend and otherwise causing havoc before she herself is killed by one of the men she is trying to use. Cast: *Robert Hossein, Jean Sorel, Catherine Rouvel, George Wilson, Lucien Raimbourg, Sophie Grimaldi, Nicole Berger, Armand Mestral, J.-J. Delbo, Jacques Bertrand, Robert Dalban, Jean Lefevre.* Dir: Julien Duvivier. Pro: Robert & Raymond Hakim. Screenplay: Julien Duvivier & René Barjavel, based on the James Hadley Chase story. (Gala.) Rel: Floating: first shown at Continentale, Jan., 1971. 95 mins. Cert. AA.

Hoffman
Peter Sellers plays it quite straight as the rather sad, middle-aged businessman who falls madly in love with one of the girls in his typing pool and, using a blackmail threat over her not-too-straight boy-friend, persuades her to spend a week with him at his flat . . . and it all works like a fairy-tale! Rest of cast: *Sinead Cusack, Jeremy Bulloch, Ruth Dunning.* Dir: Alvin Rakoff. Pro: Ben Arbeid. Screenplay: Ernest Gebler. (Warner–Pathé.) Rel: Aug. 9. (T.) 113 mins. Cert. X.

A Hole Lot of Trouble
Short comedy about a gang digging up the road, and the complications caused by their hole! Cast: *Arthur Lowe, Victor Maddern, Tim Barrett, Bill Maynard, Ken Parry.* (Monarch–Crispin.) Rel: Jan. 31. (E.) 27 mins. Cert. A.

Hook, Line and Sinker
Jerry Lewis comedy – he plays the dupe of his wife and a doctor who dream up a plan to get rid of him and live the rest of their lives happily together. But once in the know, Jerry soon puts a stop to their little larks. Rest of cast: *Peter Lawford, Anne Francis, Pedro Gonzalez Gonzalez, Jimmy Miller, Jennifer Edwards, Eleanor Audley, Henry Corden, Sylvia Lewis, Phillip Pine, Felipe Turich, Kathleen Freeman.* Dir: George Marshall. Pro: Jerry Lewis. Screenplay: Rod Amateau. (Columbia.) Rel: Jan. 31. (T.) 92 mins. Cert. U.

Hornets' Nest
World War Two story set in Italy, where the survivors of a German village massacre, a group of youngsters, a pretty German doctor they hi-jack and a wounded parachuted American officer together with a motley, and often divided, crew manage, after various adventures, to blow up the dam which was the American's original mission. Cast: *Rock Hudson, Sylva Koscina, Sergio Fantoni, Jacques Sernas, Giacomo Rossi Stuart, Tom Felleghi, Andrea Bosic, Bondy Esterhazy, Gerard Herter, Hardy Stuart, Max Turilli, Raphael Santos, Viti Caronia, Jacques Stany, Bruno Marco Gobbi, Alain Shammas, Amos Davoli, Alessandro Jogan, Jean Valmont, Giancarlo Prete, Mino Doro, Wehrner Hasselmann, Rod Dana, John Lemma, Rick Petersen, Mark Colleano, John Fordyce, Mauro Gravina, Daniel Keller, Daniel Dempsey, Joseph Cassuto, Fabrizio Tempio, Maurizio Tempio, Luisa Giacinti, Anna Giacinti, Vincenzo Danaro.* Dir: Phil Karlson. Pro: Stanley S. Canter. Screenplay: S. S. Schweitzer. (Canter–UA.) Rel: Feb. 7. (D.) 109 mins. Cert. AA.

The Horror of Frankenstein
Another enjoyably grisly Hammer Horror! About the late bad Baron's son (*Ralph Bates*) who decides to follow in his dad's footsteps and soon has enough bits and pieces, thanks to grave robber *Dennis Price*, to make a monster: all that he needs to complete the job is a brain . . . and that is soon obtained thanks to a handy little murder . . . but like father, like son, and soon the monster gets away and out on the rampage. . . Rest of cast: *Kate O'Mara, Graham James, Veronica*

Carlson, Bernard Archard, Joan Rice, David Prowse. Dir, Pro & Written (the last with Jeremy Burnham): Jimmy Sangster. (Hammer–EMI–MGM.) Rel: Nov. 8. (T.) 95 mins. Cert. X.

House of Dark Shadows
American chiller-diller about a mysterious stranger who arrives at the sombre, dark old house in the Maine countryside, claims he is a British cousin of the Collins family who own the mansion, moves in, restores the house – and then begin a series of strange, macabre deaths, all of which have the Vampire's marks upon them! Cast: *Jonathan Frid, Grayson Hall, Kathryn Leigh Scott, Roger Davis, Nancy Barrett, John Karlen, Thayer David, Louis Edmonds, Donald Brice, David Henesy, Dennis Patrick, Lisa Richards, Jerry Lacy, Barbara Cason, Paul Michael, Humbert Astredo, Terry Crawford, Michael Stroka, Joan Bennett.* Dir & Pro: Dan Curtis. Screenplay: Sam Hall & Gordon Russell. (MGM–EMI.) Rel: Feb. 7. (Metrocolor.) 97 mins. Cert. X.

House of Pleasure
Another chapter in the sensual story of Sexy Susan: in this one she meets the Little Corporal Napoleon himself and is able to offer him a most useful service! Cast: *Terry Torday, Margaret Lee, Claudio Brook, Jacques Herlin.* Dir: François Legrand. Pro: Jacques Herlin. (Miracle.) Rel: Floating: first shown at Jacey, Leicester Sq., Feb., 1971. (E.) 81 mins. Cert. X.

The House That Dripped Blood
A sort of thriller "Quartet" of Poe-like horror stories about a house in which each lessee in turn disappears . . . a combination of Grand Guignol, psychological thriller and tongue-in-cheek satire. Cast: (a) *John Bennett, John Bryans, John Malcolm.* (b) *Denholm Elliott, Joanna Dunham, Tom Adams, Robert Lang.* (c) *Peter Cushing, Joss Ackland, Wolfe Morris.* (d) *Christopher Lee, Nyree Dawn Porter, Chloe Franks.* (e) *Jon Pertwee, Ingrid Pitt.* Dir: Peter Duffell. Pro: Max J. Rosenberg & Milton Subotsky. Screenplay: Robert Bloch. (Amicus–CIRO.) Rel: Feb. 21. (E.) 102 mins. Cert. X.

How Do I Love Thee?
A comedy which starts off with a miracle at Lourdes in reverse, *Jackie Gleason* as Stan getting struck down as he enters the healing waters. Luckily it isn't permanent and with conscience eased (it's all psychological!) he exuberantly recovers. Rest of cast: *Maureen O'Hara, Shelley Winters, Rosemary Forsyth, Rick Lenz, Maurice Marsac, Don Beddoe, Jack Nagle, J. Edward McKinley.* Dir: Michael Gordon. Pro: Everett Freeman & Robert Enders. Screenplay: E. Freeman & Karl Tunberg, from the Peter De Vries novel "Let Me Count the Ways". (Freemen: Enders–CIRO.) Rel: May 9. (Colour.) 109 mins. Cert. AA.

I Had My Brother's Wife
A story of the struggle for water and women, the great desirables, in a poor peasant tribe in the Middle East. Cast: *Ulvi Dogan, Julia Kotch, Errol Tash.* Dir: Metin. Pro: Ulvi Dogan. (New Realm.) Rel:

Floating: first shown at Classic, Windmill, Jan., 1971. 77 mins. Cert. X.

I Start Counting
Pleasantly unpretentious, warmly understanding story of a girl growing up (against the everyday background of a typical Council Estate) and suddenly, and terrifyingly, finding out the hard facts of life when she comes upon her adored elder step-brother in bed with his girl-friend and soon afterwards becomes the central figure in a hitherto shadowy series of sex murders in her district. A lovely performance by 16-year-old *Jenny Agutter* in the leading role. Rest of cast: *Bryan Marshall, Clare Sutcliffe, Simon Ward, Gregory Phillips, Lana Morris, Billy Russell, Madge Ryan, Michael Feast, Fay Compton, Lally Bowers, Charles Lloyd Pack, Lewis Fiander, Gordon Richardson.* Dir & Pro: David Greene. Screenplay: Richard Harris, based on the Audrey Erskine Lindop novel. (UA.) Rel: Dec. 13. (D.) 105 mins. Cert. AA.

I Walk the Line
John Frankenheimer's film adaptation of the Madison Jones novel "The Exile"; a retelling against a background of modern, deepest Tennessee of the classic story of the violent passion of a middle-aged man for a lovely young girl: in this case the bored local sheriff and the daughter of an illicit whisky-distiller. Doomed from the start, the romance ends tragically of course. Cast: *Gregory Peck, Tuesday Weld, Estelle Parsons, Ralph Meeker, Lonny Chapman, Charles Durning, Jeff Dalton, Freddie McCloud, Jane Rose, J. C. Evans, Margaret Morris, Bill Littleton, Leo Yates, Dodo Denney.* Dir: John Frankenheimer. Pro: Harold H. Cohen. Screenplay: Alvin Sargent. (John Frankenheimer/Edward Lewis–Columbia.) Rel: May 9. (Pan. & Colour.) 98 mins. Cert. AA.

If It's Tuesday, This Must be Belgium
Comedy based on the quickie American package tour of Europe – shepherded by a guide with an international line-up of dollies. Cast: *Suzanne Pleshette, Ian McShane, Mildred Natwick, Murray Hamilton, Sandy Baron, Michael Constantine, Norman Fell.* Dir: Mel Stuart. Pro: David L. Wolper. (Stan Margulies–UA.) Rel: Floating. (Colour.) 99 mins. Cert. U.

I'm an Elephant, Madame
Technically gimmicky, surrealistic, Peter Zadek West German film which is concerned with all protests in general and that by the 1968 Bremen students in particular. A sort of jigsaw puzzle, the pieces of which are thrown at the audience to assemble how they may, and which is aimed rather obviously at its country of origin, with its peculiar traditions and implications. Cast: *Wolfgang Schneider, Günther Lüders, Tankred Dorst, Heinz Baumann, Peter Palitzsch, Robert Dietl, Werner Dahms, Ernst Rottluff, Margot Trooger, Maja Eigen, Rolf Becker, Ingria Resch, Christiane Philipp, George Michael Fischer.* Dir: Peter Zadek. Screenplay: P. Zadek, Robert Müller & Wolfgang Menge, based on the Thomas Valentin novel. (Iduna/Academy–Connoisseur.) Rel: Floating: first shown at Academy Two, March, 1971. (E.) 100 mins. Cert. X.

In Search of Gregory
Julie Christie as the girl who returns to her father's home, and her recluse brother's possessiveness, to conduct a romantic quest of her dad's house guest – the mysterious Gregory of the title – played by *Michael Sarrazin.* Rest of cast: *John Hurt, Adolfo Celi, Paola Pitagora, Roland Culver, Tony Selby, Jimmy Lynn, Violetta Chiarini, Gabriella Giorgelli, Luisa de Santis, Ernesto Pagano, Roderick Smith, Gordon Gostelow.* Dir: Peter Wood. Pro: Joseph Janni and Daniele Senatore. Screenplay: Tonino Guerra & Lucille Laks. (Vic–Vera Spa/Rank.) (T.) 90 mins. Cert. X.

Interviews with My Lai Veterans
Joseph Strick's "Oscar"-winning (1970) documentary. (Contemporary.) Rel: Floating: first shown at Round House, May, 1971. (Colour.) 22 mins. Cert. A.

It All Goes to Show
Small comedy centred on *Arthur Lowe's* assignment to brighten up Brightsea Bay's Summer Show, an assignment which leads to a series of outrageously blue performances which delight the audiences as they offend the local clergy and others of the town's old guard. Rest of cast: *Bill Maynard, Tim Barrett, Sheila Keith, Valerie Van Ost.* Dir & Pro: Francis Searle. (Crispin.) Rel: Sept. 27. 27 mins. Cert. U.

It's the Only Way To Go
Short, black comedy performed in mime about an old man who dies from excitement while watching a young girl undress! Cast: *Dave Kerry, Tony Sympson, Cathy Howard, Janet Burnell, John Rutland, June Palmer, Janet Webb, Paddy Ryan, Garry Marsh, Totti Truman Taylor, Lionel Ngakane, Cardew Robinson, Johnny Vyvyan, Roger Avon, Neil Wilson, Andrew Dallimeyer, Arthur Lovegrove, Annie Leake, Keith Smith, Jim Bishop, George Curtis, Graham Tonbridge, Charlotte Sullivan, Tony Lang.* Dir: Ray Austin. Pro: Ralph Solomons. Script: Sid Green & Dick Hills (Polytel–Hallelujah/Gala.) Rel: Aug. 9. (E.) 28 mins. Cert. U.

It's Tough to be a Bird
Brilliant, wonderfully funny Walt Disney cartoon about our feathered friends. Rel: July 26.

Jane Eyre
Careful, effective and sympathetic new adaptation of the Charlotte Brontë classic: the tragic story of the poor, plain little lass who falls in love with her rich and handsome employer and eventually returns to end her life with him after both have suffered all the travails typical of Victorian melodrama. Cast: *George C. Scott, Susannah York, Ian Bannen, Jack Hawkins, Nyree Dawn Porter, Rachel Kempson, Kenneth Griffith, Peter Copley, Michele Dotrice, Kara Wilson, Sarah Gibson, Jean Marsh, Rosalyn Landor, Sharon Rose, Clive Morton, Fanny Rowe, Hugh Latimer, Nan Munro, Peter Blythe, Carl Bernard, Jeremy Child, Angharad Rees, Sue Lawe, Louise Pajo, Sheila Brownrigg, Helen Goss, Barbara Young, Helen Lindsay, Lockwood West, Stella Tanner, Shirley Steedman, Patrick Jordan.* Dir: Delbert Mann.

226 Pro: Frederick Brogger. Screenplay: Jack Pulman. (Omnibus/Sagittarius–British Lion.) Rel: April 4. 110 mins. Cert. A.

Jemima and Johnny
A simple story about two youngsters, one white, one black, and their day out together in London, on the bomb sites, in the streets: made on location with a mixed amateur and professional cast. Cast: *Nicolette Robinson, Patrick Hatfield, Thomas Baptiste, Brian Phelan, Myrtle Robinson, Dorothy Bromley*. Dir & Screenplay: Lionel Kgalcane. Pro: Robert Angell. (Derrick Knight–Monarch.) Rel: Floating. 30 mins. Cert. U.

Joan
Documentary about *Joan Baez*, her songs, her concert tours and her reactions to her political activist husband being sent to jail. With *Joan Baez* and *David Harris*. Dir: James Coyne, Robert Jones, Christopher Knight. Pro: Robert Silverthorne. (New Film Co.–Fair Enterprises.) Rel: Floating. 95 mins. Cert. U.

Joaquin Murieta
Ricardo Montalban, Roosevelt Grier and *Slim Pickens*, in the turbulent California of the 1840s, become involved in the Golden Madonna, stolen from the peons, and through this are also involved in some very rough stuff indeed. Rest of cast: *Jim McMullan, Earl Holliman, Ina Balin, Miriam Colon, Robert J. Wilke, Anthony Caruso, Armando Silvestre, Charles Horvath, Alan Pinson, Ben Archibek, Lina Marin, Victor Eberg, Barbara Turner, Ivan Scott, Tamara Girina, Miguel Fernandez, Juan Garcia, Jose Galvez, Francisco Cordova, Eldon Burke, Eddra Gale, Juan Edwards*. Dir: Earl Bellamy. Pro: David Silver. Screenplay: Jack Guss. (Fox.) Rel: Aug. 9. (D.) 83 mins. Cert. U.

Julius Caesar
Stuart Burge, director of this latest example of adapting the bard to cinema, sacrifices the poetry of the lines – or at least a lot of it – in order to get vigorous and naturalistic performances and to keep the whole thing moving at a cracking rate. Cast: *Charlton Heston, Jason Robards, John Gielgud, Richard Johnson, Robert Vaughn, Richard Chamberlain, Diana Rigg, Jill Bennett, Christopher Lee, Alan Browning, Norman Bowler, Andrew Crawford, David Dodimead, Peter Eyre, Edwin Finn, Derek Godfrey, Michael Gough, Paul Hardwick, Laurence Harrington, Thomas Heathcote, Ewan Hooper, Robert Keegan, Preston Lockwood, John Moffatt, André Morell, David Neal, Steven Pacey, Ron Pember, John Tate, Damien Thomas, Ken Hutchinson, Michael Keating, Derek Hardwicke, Michael Wynne, David Leland, Ronald McGill, Linbert Spencer, Trevor Adams, Robin Chadwick, Christopher Cazenove, Roy Stewart, Liz Geghardt*. Dir: Stuart Burge. Pro: Peter Snell. Adapted for the screen: Robert Furnival. (Commonwealth United.) 117 mins.

Keith Potger and The New Seekers
Half-hour interest film spotlighting the new group that ex-Seeker *Keith* has founded to carry on the successful tradition of the old, now disbanded Australian group. (Butcher's.) Rel: Nov. 15. (T.) 31 mins. Cert. U.

Kes
Wholly delightful little film, a minor classic of the screen, which with sincerity and humour and not a touch of sentimentality, tells the story of a small Barnsley schoolboy, with a brutal young miner brother and a tarty, pre-occupied mother, who finds a new interest in life when he catches and trains a kestrel. A film full of rich and unforgettable character studies: and a football match which one wants to cut out and keep for oneself as a gem of comic moviemaking. Cast: *David Bradley, Freddie Fletcher, Lynne Perrie, Colin Welland, Brian Glover, Bob Bowes*. Dir: Ken Loach. Pro: Tony Garnett. Screenplay: Barry Hines, Ken Loach & Tony Garnett, adapted from the first's book "Kestrel for a Knave". (Kestrel–Woodfall–UA.) Rel: July 26. (T.) 113 mins. Cert. U.

The Kremlin Letter
Technically first-class, always gripping international spy thriller, a condensation and stripping down to story essentials of the Noel Behn book about a letter written by an indiscreet US diplomat promising American help to any Russian adventure against China's atomic plant. The horrified State Dept. want to get it back, the Russians want to keep it, China would like to look at it: and nobody knows where it is. That's why *Patrick O'Neal, Richard Boone* and other ruthless types are recruited to outwit the Russians, by fair means or foul, to recover the document. Rest of cast: *Bibi Andersson, Nigel Green, Dean Jagger, Lila Kedrova, Michael MacLiammoir, Barbara Parkins, Ronald Radd, George Sanders, Raf Vallone, Max Von Sydow, Orson Welles, Sandor Eles, Niall MacGinnis, Anthony Chinn, Guy Deghy, John Huston, Fulvia Ketoff, Vonetta McGee, Marc Lawrence, Cyril Shaps, Christopher Sanford, Hana-Maria Pravda, George Pravda, Ludmilla Dudarova, Dimitri Tamarov, Pehr-Olof Siren, Daniel Smid, Victor Beaumont, Steve Zacharias*. Dir & co-Screenplay with Gladys Hill: John Huston. Pro: Carter De Haven & Sam Wiesenthal. (Huston–Fox.) Rel: July 5. (D & Pan.) 121 mins. Cert. X.

The Landlord
Amusing comedy about a rich and restless socialite young man who buys a tenement house in a black ghetto district and, to prove his new and obscure theory, proceeds to convert it into a sort of "psychedelic cathedral" but is tamed and turned by his black tenants. And beneath the fun there are all sorts of racial and political implications – if you care to sort them out. Cast: *Beau Bridges, Pearl Bailey, Diana Sands, Louis Gossett, Douglas Grant, Melvin Stewart, Lee Grant, Walter Brooke, Susan Anspach, Bob Klein, Will McKenzie, Gretchen Walther, Stanley Green, Marki Bey*. Dir: Hal Ashby. Pro: Norman Jewison. Screenplay: Bill Gunn, based on the Kristin Hunter novel. (Mirisch–UA.) Rel: June 13. (D.) 110 mins. Cert. X.

The Language of Love
Just about the most outspoken and visually explicit sex education movie yet: apparently utterly sincere discussion between a number of medical and scientific experts – *Inge* and *Sten Hegeler, Maj-Brith Bergstrom* and *Sture Cullhed* – with some pretty startling illustrations of everything from feminine masturbation to detailed, clinical examination of lovemaking, often in startling close-up. Dir: Torgny Wickman. (Darville Organisation.) Rel: Floating: first shown at Jacey, Trafalgar Sq., and Jacey-Tatler, Feb., 1971. (Colour.) 107 mins. Cert. X (London).

The Last Adventure
A daredevil pilot (*Alain Delon*), a wild sculptress (*Joanna Shimkus*), and a Grand Prix racing driver (*Lino Ventura*) as a trio hunting for treasure which is supposedly in a sunken airplane: a search complicated by the fact that both men love the woman and there are plenty of others after the loot and not too careful about the way they get it! Based on the José Giovanni story. Rest of cast: *Serge Reggiani, Hans Meyer, Thérèse Quentin, Guy Delorme, Jean Darie, Jean Trognon, Odile Poisson, Irène Tunc, Paul Crauchet*. Dir: Robert Enrico. Pro: René Pignères & Gérard Beytout. (Rank.) Rel: Sept. 13. 102 mins. Cert. U.

The Last Warrior
The tragi-comedy of a hard-drinking but not unintelligent Red Indian (*Anthony Quinn*) who, tired of his people's poverty and their bad living conditions, starts a new Indian uprising which culminates in the hi-jacking of a train and the taking over the nearest town – all legally justified by a series of dusty old treaties dug out by the tribe's lawyer. A series of somewhat uneasy comedy situations built upon a serious social theme. Rest of cast: *Claude Akins, Tony Bill, Victor Jory, Don Collier, Victor French, Rodolfo Acosta, Anthony Caruso, Shelly Winters, Susana Miranda, William Mims, Rudy Diaz, Pedro Regas, J. Edward McKinley, Robert Cleaves, John War Eagle*. Dir: Carol Reed. Pro: Jerry Adler. Screenplay: Clair Huffaker, based on the author's book "Nobody Loves a Drunken Indian". (Warner.) Rel: Floating. (Pan & T.) 106 mins. Cert. AA.

Lawman
British-made Western about a stern, cool lawman who one day is confronted with the problem of taking seven convicted men from a hostile town to meet the justice which he is determined they shall face. Cast: *Burt Lancaster, Robert Ryan, Lee J. Cobb, Sheree North, Joseph Wiseman, Robert Duvall, Albert Salmi, J. D. Cannon, John McGiver, Richard Jordan, John Beck, Ralph Waite, William Watson, Charles Tyner, John Hillerman, Robert Emhardt, Richard Bull, Hugh McDermott, Lou Frizzell, Walter Brooke, Bill Brimley*. Dir & Pro: Michael Winner. Screenplay: Gerald Wilson. (Scimitar–UA.) Rel: May 2. (T.) 99 mins. Cert. AA.

Leo the Last
Beautifully, brilliantly dressed (and technically full of magnificent, Fellini-like fireworks), rather mundane little moral fable about a foreign gentleman of great inheritance who, recovering from ennui, spies from his great old house into the slum dwellings surrounding him and the ponces, prostitutes and other unsavoury

characters (mostly black, but some white) who live there. And then Leo decides to interfere, with always unfortunate but finally with pyrotechnic consequences! Cast: *Marcello Mastroianni, Billie Whitelaw, Calvin Lockhart, Glenna Forster Jones, Graham Crowden, Gwen Ffrangcon Davies, David De Keyser, Vladek Sheybal, Keefe West, Kenneth J. Warren, Patsy Smart, Ram John Holder, Thomas Buson, Tina Solomon, Brinsley Forde, Robert Redman, Malcolm Redman, Robert Kennedy, Phyllis McMahon, Princess Patience, Bernard Boston, Roy Stewart, Lucita Lijertwood, Ishaq Bux, Doris Clark.* Dir: John Boorman. Pro: Irwin Winkler & Robert Chartoff. Screenplay: Wm. Stair & John Boorman. (Chartoff/Winkler–UA.) (D.) 104 mins. Cert. X.

The Liberation of L. B. Jones
Careful, thoughtful film about a high-principled attorney in Tennessee who finds himself caught up in a nasty racial prejudice mess when a Negro undertaker is murdered by two cops, one of whom is having an affair with the Negro's fascinating wife. Cast: *Lee J. Cobb, Anthony Zerbe, Roscoe Lee Browne, Lola Falana, Lee Majors, Barbara Hershey, Yaphet Kotto, Arch Johnson, Chill Wills, Zara Cully, Fayard Nicholas, Joe Attles, Lauren Jones, Dub Taylor, Brenda Sykes, Larry D. Mann, Ray Teal, Eve McVeagh, Sonora McKeller, Robert Van Meter, Jack Grinnage, John S. Jackson.* Dir: William Wyler. Pro: Ronald Lubin. Screenplay: Stirling Silliphant & Jesse Hill Ford, based on a novel by the latter. (Wyler–Lubin/Columbia.) Rel: Dec. 6. (T.) 102 mins. Cert. AA.

Loot
Film version of the late Joe Orton's sick black comedy about a couple of loathsome louts who rob a bank and then decide to hide the money in the coffin of the newly deceased mother of one of them and, when the money won't fit in, take out the corpse and from then on play a sort of hide-and-seek game with the corpse, the cops and the cash! Leavened a little by the performances of, especially, *Richard Attenborough, Lee Remick* and *Milo O'Shea.* Rest of cast: *Hywel Bennett, Roy Holder, Dick Emery, Joe Lynch, John Cater, Aubrey Woods, Enid Lowe, Andonia Katsaros, Harold Innocent, Kevin Brennan, Jean Marlow, Robert Raglan, Hal Galili, Douglas Ridley, Adrian Correger, Edwin Finn.* Dir: Silvio Narizzano. Pro: Arthur Lewis. Screenplay: Ray Galton & Alan Simpson. (Lewis–British Lion.) Rel: March 7. 101 mins. Cert. X.

The Losers
Vietnam war episode about a quintet of Hell's Angel-type motor-cycle menaces who for some reason are recruited by the army and sent on a mission to rescue an American politician held prisoner by the Chinese in Cambodia – and the "Ten Little Nigger Boys" style of progress the five make towards success. Cast: *William Smith, Bernie Hamilton, Adam Roarke, Houston Savage, Gene Cornelius, Paul Koslo, John Garwood, Ana Korita, Lillian Margarejo, Paraluman, Paul Nuckles, Ronnie Ross, Armando Lucero, Fran Dinh Hy, Vic Diaz, Allan Caillou, Paquito Salcedo, Von Deming, Hernan Robles, Jack*

Starrett, Monica Phillips. Dir: Jack Starrett. Pro: Joe Solomon. Screenplay: Alan Caillou. (Fanfare–Anglo–EMI.) Rel: Jan. 17. (E.) 91 mins. Cert. X.

Love and Anger
Four-layer Italian portmanteau picture, with a quartet of incidents told by four directors all concerned in one way or another with problems of today. 1: Indifference: the only man to come to the aid of a dying woman is a criminal and he has to use violence to get her attended to in the hospital! 2: Agony: the meditations of an old man dying, a cardinal of the Church. 3: Love: a troubled lovemaking between two young people over whom looms the threat of racial prejudice. 4: The Sequence of the Paper Flower: how God opens the eyes of a happy young man walking in Rome. Dir: Bertolucci, Pasolini, Godard, Lizzani. Pro: Carlo Lizzani. Screenplays: Lizzani, Bertolucci, Pasolini, Godard. (Miracle.) Rel: first shown at Cameo, Victoria, March, 1971. 78 mins. Cert. X.

The Love Circle – Metti, una Sera a Cena
A strange, involved story about the adventures of one woman and three men and the sort of sexual musical chairs game they play: the husband, the wife, and her two lovers, working it all out to a reasonable compromise solution for all of them. Cast: *Jean-Louis Trintignant, Lino Capolicchio, Tony Musante, Florinda Bolkan, Annie Girardot.* Dir & Written: Giuseppe Patroni Griffi. Pro: Marina Cicogna & Giovanni Bertolucci. (Cinecenta.) First shown at the Cinecenta, July, 1970. (T.) 108 mins. Cert. X.

Love Me, Baby, Love Me
The wild romance of a married woman who falls in love with a younger man who turns out to be a blackmailer who photographs women making love to him in his flat. Italian. Cast: *Anna Moffo, Gianni Macchia, Jean Claudia, Alice Brandet, Caterine Boratto, Pupo de Luca, Beryl Cunningham, Bedy Moratti, Claudi Large, Jacques Merlin, Tamara Boroni, Aldo Farina, Marcello Michelangeli, Elina de Witt, Edda Ferronas, Marina Borgo, Orlando Borella, Sandro Morli.* Dir: Michele Lupo. Pro: Piero Lazzari. Screenplay: Leone-Antonio Viola. (Empire Films, Rome & Jacques Roitfeld, Paris – E. J. Fancey.) Rel: Floating. (T & Techniscope.) 101 mins. Cert. X.

Love of Life – Artur Rubinstein: L'Amour de la Vie
The story of the life, career and outlook of the great pianist, with plenty of his music. Dir: François Reichenbach & S. G. Patris. Pro: F. Reichenbach & Bernard Gavoty. Israel Philharmonic Orch. & Orchestre de Paris. (Midem–Rank.) Rel: Floating. (Colour.) 92 mins. Cert. U.

Love Variations
Film ("does not seek to entertain, only to inform") about the ways which can be used to make love: the positions in which satisfaction can best be achieved, etc., etc. Dir: Terry Gould. Pro: David Grant. (Oppidan Films.) Rel: Floating. 80 mins. Cert. X.

Lovers and Other Strangers
Amusing adaptation of the stage comedy by Joseph Bologna and Renee Taylor which in relating the story of the wedding of two normal, rather charming youngsters (who unknown to their families have been living together for more than a year), takes a somewhat deeper look at the marital relationships of the two families involved and there mixes understanding and sadness with the laughs. Cast: *Gig Young, Bonnie Bedelia, Beatrice Arthur, Michael Brandon, Richard Castellano, Robert Dishy, Harry Guardino, Marian Hailey, Joseph Hindy, Anne Jackson, Diane Keaton, Cloris Leachman, Anne Meara, Anthony Holland, Bob Kaliban, Amy Stiller, Charlotte Jones, Morton Marshall.* Dir: Cy Howard. Pro: David Susskind. Screenplay: Renee Taylor, Joseph Bologna and David Zelag Goodman, based on the first two's stage play. (Susskind/ABC–CIRO.) Rel: Floating. 104 mins. Cert. AA.

Loving
Perceptive portrait of American suburbia: the ambitious executive drinking just that too much at his business lunches, insecure, sex-seeking; the distressed housewife, who sees the gulf that is widening towards divorce; the loose-living, predatory wife "over the road"; the friends and neighbours. Well acted and ably directed. Cast: *George Segal, Eva Marie Saint, Sterling Hayden, Keenan Wynn, Nancie Phillips, Janis Young, David Doyle, Paul Sparer, Andrew Duncan, Sherry Lansing, Roland Winters.* Dir: Irvin Kershner. Pro: Don Devlin (also credited with the screenplay, from a novel by J. M. Ryan). (Columbia.) Rel: Nov. 8. (Colour.) 89 mins. Cert. X.

Lust for a Vampire
One of the gorgeous Hammer Horrors: *Michael Johnson* as a young English writer whose search for material leads him – posing as a teacher – into the school for young ladies which is housed in the macabre castle of Karnstein, where he finds that some of the pretty young things have hidden fangs and odd tastes...! Rest of cast: *Barbara Jefford, Suzanna Leigh, Yutte Stensgaard, Mike Raven, Helen Christie, David Healy, Michael Brennan, Pippa Steele, Luan Peters, Christopher Cunningham, Judy Matheson, Caryl Little, Jack Melford, Eric Chitty, Christopher Neame, Harvey Hall, Erica Beale, Jackie Leapman, Melita Clarke, Patricia Warner, Christine Smith, Vivienne Chandler, Sue Longhurst, Melinda Churcher.* Dir: Jimmy Sangster. Pro: Harry Fine & Michael Style. Screenplay: Tudor Gates. (Hammer–EMI.) Rel: Jan. 17. 95 mins. Cert. X.

Machine Gun McCain – Gli Intoccabili
An Italian-made gangster melodrama set in America where the Mafia are involved in a plot to rob a Las Vegas hotel, a plot which ends with the thieves perishing in a hail of lead. Cast: *John Cassavetes, Britt Ekland, Peter Falk, Gabriele Ferzetti, Salvo Randone, Pierluigi Aprà, Gena Rowlands, Florinda Bolkan, Margherita Guzzinati, Stephen Zacharias, Luigi Pistilli, Jim Morrison, Claudio Biava, Tony Kendall, Ermanno Consolazione, Annabella*

228 *Andreoli, Val Avery, Dennis Sallas, Jack Ackerman, Billy Lee.* Dir: Giuliano Montaldo. Pro: Marco Vicario & Bruno Cicogna. Screenplay: Mino Roli & Giuliano Montaldo. (Columbia.) Rel: July 3. 96 mins Cert. X.

Macho Callahan
Western about a very illogical love affair set against a turbulent background of 1864: with *David Janssen* as the brutalised Confederate trooper on the run. Rest of cast: *Jean Seberg, Lee J. Cobb, James Booth, Pedro Armendariz Junr., David Carradine, Anne Revere, Richard Anderson, Matt Clarke, Diane Ladd, Richard Evans, Bo Hopkins, Jim Gammon, Ron Sobel, Diana Iverson, Curt Conway, Robert Dowdell, Robert Morgan.* Dir: Bernard Kowalski. Pro: Martin C. Schute & B. Kowalski. Screenplay: Cliff Gould. (J. Levine–Avco Embassy.) Rel: June 20. (Colour.)

The Madwoman of Chaillot
Bryan Forbes's film of the ironic and witty Jean Giradot play about a group of high-placed crooks who think there is oil under Paris and are prepared to destroy the city to get at it; a fantastic plan thwarted by the delicious Madwoman, who uses their greed to lure them to a dingy doom. Deftly directed, wonderfully acted by a great cast headed by the superb *Katharine Hepburn* in the title role, and exquisitely photographed in stunning colour effects by Claude Renoir and Burnett Guffey. Rest of cast: *Charles Boyer, Claude Dauphin, Edith Evans, John Gavin, Paul Henreid, Oscar Homolka, Margaret Leighton, Giulietta Masina, Nanette Newman, Richard Chamberlain, Yul Brynner, Donald Pleasence, Danny Kaye, Fernand Gravet, Gordon Heath, Gerald Sim.* Dir: Bryan Forbes. Pro: Ely Landau. Screenplay: Edward Anhalt, based on a Jean Giradot play. (Landau/Forbes–Warner-Pathé.) (T.) 137 mins. Cert. U.

Mafia Mob
Italian-made American gangster thriller set in Chicago during the prohibition era and trying hard to look – and sound – authentic. Cast: *Jeffrey Hunter, Margaret Lee, William Bogart, Gogó Rojo, Anna Maria Pierangeli, Eduardo Fajardo, Beni Deus, Miguel del Castillo.* Dir: Javeir Setó. (Border Films.) Rel: Floating. (E.) 93 mins. Cert. X.

The Magus
Michael Caine as the British schoolteacher whose appointment to a school on a lonely Greek island draws him to the rich recluse who lives there and into a maelstrom of strange, confusing and frightening mystery. Rest of cast: *Anthony Quinn, Candice Bergen, Anna Karina.* Dir: Guy Green. Pro: John Kohn & Jud Kinberg. Screenplay: John Fowles, based on his own novel. (Fox.) (Colour, Pan.) 116 mins. Cert. X.

A Man Called Horse
Very – literally – painfully authentic story of an English milord who in the early 19th century went hunting in the Dakotas, was captured by the Sioux, used by them as a beast of burden, but who by blood, sweat and tears and endless courage climbed back into the Indians' estimation and, after a bloody initiation ceremony, was accepted as a warrior of the tribe and a suitable husband for the lovely Running Deer. With *Richard Harris* as the stoical Englishman. Rest of cast: *Dame Judith Anderson, Jean Gascon, Manu Tupou, Corinna Tsopei, Dub Taylor, William Jordan, James Gammon, Edward Little Sky, Lina Marin, Tamara Garina, Michael Baseleon, Manuel Padilla, Iron Eyes Cody, Richard Fools Bull, Ben Eagleman, Terry Leonard.* Dir: Elliot Silverstein. Pro: Sandy Howard. Screenplay: Jack DeWitt, from the original story by Dorothy M. Johnson. (Cinema Center.) Rel: Sept. 27. (T.) 114 mins. Cert. AA.

A Man Called Sledge
James Garner as the wanted bandit involved with some other undesirable characters in plots and counter-plots to seal the half-million in gold that each week is turned out by the mines near the town of 3W's. Rest of cast: *Dennis Weaver, Claude Akins, John Marley, Laura Antonelli, Paola Barbara, Mario Valgoi, Lorenzo Piani, Franco Giornelli, Bruno Corazzari, Altiero Di Giovanni, Wade Preston, Laura Betti, Lorenzo Fineschi, Tony Young, Didi Perego, Ken Clark, Remo de Angelis.* Dir: Vic Morrow. Co-pro: Harry Bloom. Screenplay: Vic Morrow & Frank Kowalsky. (Dino de Laurentiis–Columbia.) Rel: Sept. 20. (T & Techniscope.) 92 mins. Cert. AA.

A Man for Emmanuelle
The story of a girl, depressed by world violence, who goes from lover to lover, all in one afternoon, to seek some sort of permanent solace, only to be disillusioned by their superficial attitude; the theme of the difference between male and female approach to physical love being enlivened by plenty of nude wrestling and romping and long, cool, wandering looks at the naked female form divine. Cast: *Erika Blanc, Adolfo Celi, Milla Sannoino, Sandro Korso, Ben Salvador, Paolo Ferrari, Lia Rho Barbieri.* Dir: Cesare Canevari. Screenplay: Cesare Canevari, Guiseppe Mangione. (S.F. Distributors.) Rel: Floating. (E.) 94 mins. Cert. X.

Man of Violence
He's Moon, a smart, unscrupulous operator working for both sides (one a North country tycoon, the other a protection racketeer) in a struggle to gain the gold – £30,000,000 of it – originally pinched from a revolting (!) Arab sheikdom! Cast: *Michael Latimer, Luan Peters, Derek Aylward, Maurice Kaufmann, Derek Francis, Kenneth Hendel, George Belbin, Sidney Conabere, Erika Raffael, Virginia Wetherell, Steve Emerson, Peter Thornton, Michael Balfour, Andreas Melandrinos, Patrick Jordan, Jessica Spencer, Sheila Babbage, John Keston, Mark Allington.* Dir & Pro: Pete Walker, who also shares screenplay credit with Brian Comport. (Miracle.) Rel: Floating. (E.) 107 mins. Cert. X.

Man on a Staircase
Half-hour suspense thriller about a lonely little man who lives on the sixth floor of a Victorian house and is one night confronted by a massive villain who tries to throttle him. When in the struggle he accidentally kills the intruder he subsequently tries to get the body down past the other five flats without being seen, a horrible journey that ends in final disaster. Cast: *John Cazabon, Frank Maher, Peter Dawson, Megan Hooley, Pru Dawson.* Dir & Pro: Roy Cannon. (Crispin.) Rel: Floating. 27 mins. Cert. A.

The Man Who Had Power Over Women
Reasonably entertaining story of the problems of a pop star manager, whose troubles include the death of one of his unpleasant young client's girl-friends after a cheap abortion, falling in love with his partner's wife and so on. Cast: *Rod Taylor, Carol White, James Booth, Penelope Horner, Charles Korvin, Alexandra Stewart, Keith Barron, Clive Francis, Marie-France Boyer, Magali Noël, Geraldine Moffat, Wendy Hamilton, Ellis Dale, Sara Booth, Matthew Booth.* Dir: John Krish. Pro: Judd Bernard. Screenplay: Alan Scott & Chris Bryant. (J. Levine–Avco Embassy.) Rel: Nov. 15. (Colour.) 90 mins. Cert. X.

The Man Who Haunted Himself
Off-duty "Saint" *Roger Moore* in a conventional but entertaining, if somewhat spun-out, thriller about a businessman who, after a near-fatal car accident, begins to suspect that he has a double – and grows certain when this odd being starts to complicate his life for him in a big way. Rest of cast: *Hildegard Neil, Alastair Mackenzie, Hugh Mackenzie, Kevork Malikyan, Thorley Walters, Anton Rodgers, Olga Georges-Picot, Freddie Jones, John Welsh, Edward Chapman, Laurence Hardy, Charles Lloyd Pack, Gerald Sim, Ruth Trouncer, Aubrey Richards, Anthony Nicholls, John Carson, John Dawson, Terence Sewards.* Dir: Basil Dearden. Pro: Michael Relph. Screenplay: Basil Dearden, Michael Relph. (Assoc. British–Warner-Pathé.) Rel: Aug. 16. (T.) 94 mins. Cert. A.

A Married Couple
Experimental "Actuality Drama" in which *Allan King* took his cameras and crew into the home of 42-year-old Canadian advertising man *Billy Edwards*, 30-year-old wife and 3-year-old son (not to mention the dog) and proceeded to record their life as it veered towards marital break-up after seven years of life together. For seventy hours they observed, pried and recorded and then edited it all down to 97 often quarrelsome minutes, from which emerge no sensational revelations. A quite interesting experiment if less than a wholly successful one – cinematically. Dir & Pro: Allan King. (Contemporary.) First shown at the Paris-Pullman, Jan., 1971. (Colour.) 97 mins. Cert. X.

Marry Me! Marry Me! – Mazel Tov ou le Mariage
Rather charming little Jewish marital comedy set against a background of Paris (where two young people and his furrier parents live) and Antwerp (where her rich diamond merchant parents reside) and

concerning the aftermath of the couple's decision (she already happily pregnant) to get married. Ending with an untidy, overlong but interesting sequence about the ritual of a Jewish marriage. Something of a one-man band: star *Claude Berri* also wrote, directed and produced! Rest of cast: *Elizabeth Wiener, Régine, Luisa Colpeyn, Grégoire Aslan, Prudence Harrington, Betsy Blair, Gabriel Jabbour, Estera Galion.* Dir, Pro & Screenplay: Claude Berri. (Gala.) Rel: Floating; First shown at the Berkeley, Nov., 1970. (D.) 90 mins. Cert. A.

M*A*S*H
Anarchic, crazy, sick black comedy set in a field hospital a few miles from the never-seen Korean front, where a group of young doctors and nurses live, certainly love (carnally) and joke among the mangled, bloody bodies they patch, stitch, saw and otherwise operate upon in that all the stomach-turning g(l)ory of Technicolor. Some deft performances including those of *Donald Sutherland, Elliott Gould, Tom Skerritt, Sally Kellerman* and *Jo Ann* – wait for it! – *Pflug.* Rest of cast: *Robert Duvall, Rene Auberjonois, Roger Bowen, Gary Burghoff, David Arkin, Fred Williamson, Michael Murphy, Kim Atwood, Tim Brown, Indus Arthur, John Schuck, Ken Prymus, Dawne Damon, Carl Gottlieb, Tamara Horrocks, G. Wood, Bobby Troup, Bud Cort, Danny Goldman, Corey Fischer.* Dir: Robert Altman. Pro: Ingo Preminger. Screenplay: Ring Lardner, Jnr. (Aspen–Fox.) Rel: July 12. (Pan & D.) 116 mins. Cert. X.

Massacre Harbour
The efforts of a Special Service group to get into one of Rommel's North African ports, save the 5,000 Allied Prisoners who are helping to operate it, and then destroy it. Cast: *Christopher George, Gary Raymond, Larry Casey, Justin Tarr, Claudine Longet, Stanley Adams, Will Kuluva, John Anderson, Harry Lander.* Dir: John Peyser. Pro: Fred Lemoine. Screenplay: Richard Landau. (UA.) Rel: July 19. (T.) 80 mins. Cert. U.

Master of the Islands
Another film based on material in the vast James A. Michener novel about the history of Hawaii – the actual title of the book and the first film, shown in 1967. This second one is particularly concerned with the desperate fight for life by the Chinese and Japanese inhabitants of the islands and, once again, the power that the white missionaries held. Cast: *Charlton Heston, Geraldine Chaplin, John Phillip Law, Tina Chen, Alec McCowen, Mako, Don Knight, Miko Mayama, Virginia Ann Lee, Naomi Stevens, Harry Townes, Khigh Dhiegh, Keye Luke, James Gregory, Lyle Bettger, Mary Munday, George Paulsin.* Dir: Tom Gries. Pro: Walter Mirisch. Screenplay: James R. Webb. (Mirisch–UA.) Rel: Nov. 22. (Pan & D.) 132 mins. Cert. A.

The McKenzie Break
A new angle on the "escape" thriller – this time the scene is a British PoW camp in Scotland and it is the German inmates who plan the escape . . . hoping to

be taken off by a rendezvousing U-boat. But Captain *Brian Keith* has other ideas, counter-planning to get sub *and* escapees! Rest of cast: *Helmut Griem, Ian Hendry, Jack Watson, Patrick O'Connell, Horst Janson, Alexander Allerson, John Abineri, Constantin de Goguel, Tom Kempinski, Eric Allan, Caroline Mortimer, Mary Larkin, Gregg Palmer, Michael Sheard, Ingo Mogendorf, Franz Van Norde, Desmond Perry, Jim Mooney, Vernon Hayden, Maura Kelly, Noel Purcell, Paul Murphy, Frank Hayeen, Paddy Robinson, Robert Somerset, Des Keogh, Barry Cassin, Denis Latimer, Conor Evans, Stephen Good, Brendan Mathews, Emmet Bergin, John Kavanagh, Joe Pilkington, David Kelly, Mark Mulholland, Martin Dempsey, Alec Doran.* Dir: Lamont Johnson. Pro: Arthur Gardner & Jules Levy. Screenplay: William Norton. (Levy–Gardner–Laven/UA.) Rel: May 16. (D.) 106 mins. Cert. AA.

The McMasters . . . Tougher than the West Itself!
A Western with colour-bar implications: the struggle of returning, black, warrior *Brock Peters*, offered a partnership in his ranch by kindly white foster-father *Burl Ives*, to establish himself in spite of all the efforts of the black-hating neighbours to run him off the place. Rest of cast: *David Carradine, Nancy Kwan, Jack Palance, Dane Clark, John Carradine, L. Q. Jones, R. G. Armstrong, Frank Raiter, Alan Vint, Marian Brash, Neil Davis, Paul Eichenberg, Richard Alden, Lonnie Samuel, Albert Hochmeister, David Strong, Dumas Slade, Joan Howard, William Kiernan, José Moranio, Leo Dillen Schneider, Richard Martinez, Joseph Duran, Bill Alexander, Frank Nanoia, David Welty.* Dir: Alf Kjellin. Pro: David Sachson. Screenplay: Harold Jacob Smith. (De Grunwald. London Film Dist.) Rel: May 16. (Colour.) 90 mins. Cert. X.

The Mind of Mr. Soames
Odd but quite fascinating story of a man who has the mind of a child, and what happens when he manages to break away from the constant scientific surveillance with which he is surrounded. Cast: *Terence Stamp, Robert Vaughn, Nigel Davenport, Donal Donnelly, Christian Roberts, Vickery Turner, Scott Forbes, Judy Parfitt, Norman Jones, Dan Jackson, Joe McPartland, Pamela Moiseiwitch, Eric Brooks.* Dir: Alan Cooke. Pro: Max J. Rosenberg & Milton Subotsky. Screenplay: John Hale & Edward Simpson from the novel by Charles Eric Main. (Columbia.) Rel: Dec. 6. 98 mins. Cert. AA.

Mr. Jerico
Jaunty "Avenger" *Patrick MacNee* as a con man who, in trying to replace a criminal's famous jewel with a fake, finds himself with the fake and Rosso, the crook, with the real one – and that is the heart of this lightly-treading, amusing comedy-thriller. Rest of cast: *Connie Stevens, Herbert Lom, Marty Allen, Leonardo Pieroni, Bruce Boa, Joanne Dainton, Paul Darrow, Jasmina Hilton, Peter Yapp.* Dir: Sidney Hayers. Pro: Julian Wintle. Screenplay: Philip Levene. (Rank.) Rel: Aug. 30. (Colour.) 85 mins. Cert. U.

Mr. Kinky
The story of a mountain-top hermit lured back to the lush life, first by the TV cameras, then by a tart and finally by a good girl, with whom, as his wife, he opens a successful restaurant. Cast: *Vittorio Gassman, Ann-Margret.* Dir: Dino Risi. Pro: Mario Cecchi Gori. Screenplay: Ettore Scola, Ruggero Maccari. (Border Films.) Rel: Floating. (T.) 94 mins. Cert. A.

Mondo Sex
This is a follow-up to Luciano Martino's film "The Queer . . . The Erotic" and surveys the various changes that have taken place between the morals of the past and those that exist today. With a spoken commentary by *Edmund Purdom.* Dir: Sergio Martino. Pro: Luciano Martino. (Border.) Rel: Floating. 90 mins. Cert. X.

Monte Walsh
Western with *Lee Marvin* and *Jack Palance* as a couple of old-time cowboys who in the late 1880s realise with reluctance that their world, the easy-going frontier world, is going as surely as the new-fangled motor car is coming. And the final, strange showdown is at the same time an epilogue and a memorial to the violent, lawless past. Rest of cast: *Jeanne Moreau, Mitch Ryan, Jim Davis, Bear Hudkins (John), Ray Guth, John McKee, Michael Conrad, Tom Heaton, G. D. Spradlin, Ted Gehring, Bo Hopkins, Matt Clark, Billy Bush, Allyn Ann McLerie, John McLiam, Leroy Johnson, Eric Christmas, Charles Tyner, Dick Farnsworth, Fred Waugh, Jack Colvin, Wm. Graeff, Jnr., John Carter, Guy Wilkerson, Roy Bancroft.* Dir: William A. Fraker. Pro: Hal Landers & Bobby Roberts. Screenplay: Lukas Heller & David Z. Goodman. (Cinema Center–Fox.) Rel: Jan. 31. (Pan & T.) 108 mins. Cert. A.

Monterey Pop
The original Pop Festival film, made at Monterey in 1967 and such a success it inspired the many other similar movies that followed. Made by D. A. Pennebaker. (Fair Enterprises.) Rel: Floating. 79 mins.

Moonlighting Wives
Sad little tale of the ambitious housewife who builds up a big business in prostitution under cover of a secretarial service but eventually finds her dreams of power and cash come tumbling down! Cast: *Diane Vivienne, Joan Nash, John Aristedes, Fatima.* Dir: Joe Sarno. (Amanda.) Rel: Floating. (Colour.) 85 mins. Cert. X.

The Moonshine War
The story of a flare-up in 1932 – the gangster era – in the long and still flickering war between the Southern moonshiners (or illegal still sluers) and the government agents struggling to eradicate the trade in homemade whisky. Cast: *Patrick McGoohan, Richard Widmark, Alan Alda, Will Geer, Joe Williams, Lee Hazlewood, Melodie Johnson, Suzanne Lenor.* Dir: Richard Quine. Pro: Martin Ransohoff. Screenplay: Elmore Leonard – from his own novel.

(Ransohoff–MGM/Filmways.) Rel: Nov. 22. (Pan & Metrocolor.) 100 mins. Cert. AA.

Mosquito Squadron

The story of a desperate mission by the group of planes of the title to smash the French château which the Germans are using for the production of their new V3 and V4 weapons: and the several personal human stories in the periphery of this main one. Cast: *David McCallum, Suzanne Neve, David Buck, David Dundas, Dinsdale Landen, Charles Gray, Michael Anthony, Vladek Sheybal, Gordon Sterne, Robert Urquhart, Brian Grellis, George Layton, John Landry, Derek Steen, Bryan Marshall, Michael Latimer.* Dir: Boris Sagal. Pro: Lewis J. Rachmil. Screenplay: Donald S. Sanford & Joyce Perry. (Oakmont–UA.) Rel: Jan. 17. (D.) 90 mins. Cert. U.

Mumsy, Nanny, Sonny and Girly

Modestly made, highly effective, and completely incredible little black thriller about a "happy family" who live in a crumbling mansion, pick up guests as "playfellows" and then when they tire of them, "send them to heaven!" And yet in spite of all the implications – and Nanny's head boiling and bubbling on the stove – it never gets really tasteless or less than amusing. Very well acted by *Michael Bryant* (new friend), *Ursula Howells* (Mumsy), *Patricia Heywood* (Nanny), *Vanessa Howard* (Girly), *Howard Trevor* (Sonny), *Robert Swann, Imogen Hassall, Michael Ripper, Hugh Armstrong.* Dir: Freddie Francis. Pro: Ronald J. Kahn. Screenplay: Brian Comport, based on the play by Maisie Mosco. (Fitzroy–CIRO.) Rel: Sept. 6. 102 mins. Cert. X.

Murphy's War

Murphy is a mad Irishman, in the truest and perhaps finest sense, sole survivor of a U-boat attack on a British Merchantman during the final weeks of the war, an attack in which the Germans ruthlessly machine-gun the men swimming from the sinking ship. Thereafter Murphy has his own obsessional war: to sink the sub, which he attempts first with a patched-up seaplane and then with a dredger. Wonderfully entertaining, finely acted, consistently and tremendously exciting. Cast: *Peter O'Toole, Sian Phillips, Philippe Noiret, Horst Janson, John Hallam, Ingo Mogendorf.* Dir: Peter Yates. Pro: Michael Deeley. Screenplay: Stirling Silliphant. (Dimitri de Grunwald–London Screen Distributors.) Rel: March 28. (Pan & E.) 106 mins. Cert. A.

Music

Documentary on the subject: all kinds of music, from pop to piano, for all purposes. Dir: Michael Tuchner. Pro: James Archibald. (James Archibald Productions–Anglo/Warner–Pathé.) Rel: July 12. (E.) 43 mins. Cert. U.

My Bed is Not for Sleeping

The unfortunate adventures of a fashion photographer, whose boss is murdered, becomes the lover of a married woman whose husband kills her and cleverly fastens the crime on the photographer. German. Cast: *Ira Furstenberg, Gérard Blain, Serge Marquand, Christa Linder, Ricky Cooper, Volker Heim, Paul Hubschmid, Eva Renzi, Errol Garner.* Dir: Klaus Lemke. (FIOR–E. J. Fancey.) First shown at Jacey, Trafalgar Square, Oct., 1970. (Colour.) 91 mins. Cert. X.

My Lover, My Son

Turgid little piece about a too-loving, sensual young mother who sees – in red flashes – her lover in her son and is less than giving to her self-made, rough but oh-so-rich hubbie. And it finishes up with inter-family – physical – strife and murder most foul. Cast: *Romy Schneider, Donald Houston, Dennis Waterman, Patricia Brake, Peter Sallis, William Dexter, Alexandra Bastedo, Mark Hawkins, Maggie Wright, Janet Brown, Tom Chatto, Michael Forrest, Peter Gilmore, Rosalie Horner, Arthur Howard, Chrissie Shrimpton, David Warbeck, Robert Wilde.* Dir: John Newland. Pro: Wilbur Stark. Screenplay: Wm. Marchant & Jenni Hall. (Metrocolor.) Rel: Nov. 22. 95 mins. Cert. X.

My Side of the Mountain

Extremely simple, quite pleasing story about a 13-year-old boy who leaves his Montreal home and journeys into the wildest mountain country to prove he can live off the land and exist by himself, and the months he spends in his hollow-tree home with his pet racoon and a falcon until the winter and greater understanding make him decide to return home. Cast: *Teddy Eccles, Theodore Bikel, Tudi Wiggins, Frank Perry, Peggi Loder, Gina Dick, Karen Pearson, Danny McIlravey, Cosette Lee, Larry Reynolds, Tom Harvey, Paul Herbert, Ralph Endersby, George Allan, Patrick Pervion.* Dir: James B. Clark. Pro: Robt. B. Radnitz. Screenplay: Ted Sherdeman, Jane Klove, Joanna Crawford: based on the Jean George novel. (Radnitz–Paramount.) Rel: Floating. (T & Pan.) 101 mins. Cert. U.

My Swedish Meatball

About two Swedish couples on holiday in Normandy who play a game of erotic musical chairs with each other, with the men finding out that instead of them playing with the women, the women are in fact and always have been playing with them! Cast: *Margarete von Trotta, Jürgen Draeger, Horst Janson, Brigitte Harrer, Eva-Ingeborg Scholz, Joachim Schneider, H. von Schaab.* Dir: Gustav Ehmck. Screenplay: Günther Seuren. (E. J. Fancey.) Rel: Floating. (Colour.) 78 mins. Cert. X.

Myra Breckinridge

Very – in fact beyond – it story of a sex change, with lots of vulgar jokes and four-letter words, all put together in a jazzy fashion with interspersed snippets from old films – a contrast that hardly reflects credit to progress! Cast: *Mae West, John Huston, Raquel Welch, Rex Reed, Farrah Fawcett, Roger C. Carmel, Roger Herren, George Furth, Calvin Lockhart, Jim Backus, John Carradine, Andy Devine, Grady Sutton, Robert Lieb, Skip Ward, Kathleen Freeman, B. S. Pully, Buck Kartalian, Monty Landis, Tom Selleck, Peter Ireland, Nelson Sardelli.* Dir: Michael Sarne. Pro: Robert Fryer. Screenplay: Michael Sarne, David Giler & Gore Vidal, based on the book by Gore Vidal. (Fox.) Rel: Feb. 28. (Pan & D.) 91 mins. Cert. X

Naked England

Vittorio De Sisti-directed documentary about the Permissive Period in this country and, more especially, in London, where drugs, sex of all sorts, perversions and The Lot have become a way of lewd life! Commentary spoken by *Edmund Purdom.* (Miracle.) Rel: Floating. (E.) 87 mins. Cert. X.

The Naked Kiss

Samuel Fuller's story about a Korean war hero whose triumphant return to his home town is followed by his gradual exposure as corrupt. Cast: *Constance Towers, Anthony Eisley, Michael Dante, Virginia Grey, Patsy Kelly, Betty Bronson, Marie Devereux, Karen Conrad.* Dir: Samuel Fuller. (Amanda.) Rel: Floating. 93 mins. Cert. X (London).

The Navy is a Ship

Documentary (narrated by *Anthony Quayle*) about the changes in the work, responsibility and tools of the Royal Navy. Dir: Peter Bayliss. Pro: Stanley Long. Screenplay: Peter Bayliss. (Salon–Eagle Films.) Rel: Floating. (Colour.) 36 mins. Cert. U.

Ned Kelly

A sort of cartoon strip version of the story of the notorious Australian bushranger Ned Kelly, with *Mick Jagger* revealing nothing in the title role! Rest of cast: *Allen Bickford, Geoff Gilmour, Mark McManus, Serge Lazareff, Peter Sumner, Ken Shorter, James Elliott, Clarissa Kaye, Diane Craig, Susan Lloyd, Alexi Long, Bruce Barry, Janne Wesley, Ken Goodlet, Nigel Lovell, Martyn Sanderson, Robert Bruning, John Laws, Liam Reynolds, Lindsay Smith, John Gray, Reg Gorman, John Hopkins, Peter Whittle, Anne Harvey, Bill Charlton, Graham Keating, Ben Blakeney, Bill Hunter, Frank Thring, Alexander Cann, Gerry Duggan, John Dease, Andrew Sanders, Patsy Dance, Erika Crowne, Tony Bazell, Jessica Noad, Colin Tilley, Tim Van Rellim, Patrick McCarville, Kamahl, Ronald Golding, Gordon McDougall, Clifford Neate, Brian Niland, Doreen Warburton, Gary Fisher, Karin Altman, David Copping, Penny Stehli, Francis Yin, Shirley May Donald, Mary Marshall, Claire Balmford, Kurt Beimel, Moshe Kedem, Keith Peterson, Terry Erwin, Harry Kelly, Jack Allan.* Dir: Tony Richardson. Pro: Neil Hartley. Screenplay: Tony Richardson & Ian Jones. (Woodfall–UA.) Rel: July 19. (T.) 103 mins. Cert. A.

Negatives

About a young man and wife living over an antique shop, owned by the former's father, who is in hospital dying of cancer, and their fantasies as they dress in old clothes and make love: a relationship split open when a German woman arrives on the scene as a lodger. Cast: *Peter McEnery, Diane Cilento, Glenda Jackson.* Dir: Peter Medak. Pro: Judd Bernard. Screenplay: Peter Everett, Roger Lowry. (Crispin/Kettledrum Narizzano.) Rel: Floating. 98 mins. Cert. X.

Night after Night after Night
The tracking down of a psychopath rapist and killer of women: and how the wrong man is nearly . . . so nearly . . . but not quite made to pay for the crimes committed by the last suspect one might expect. Or would one? Cast: *Jack May, Justine Lord, Gilbert Wynne, Linda Marlowe, Terry Scully, Donald Sumpter, Peter Forbes-Robertson, Jacqueline Clerk, Jack Smethurst, Philip Caton, Simon Lack, Michael Nightingale, Carol Haddon, April Harlow.* Dir: Lewis J. Force. Pro: James Mellor. Screenplay: Dail Ambler. (Butcher's.) Rel: Floating. (E.) 87 mins. Cert. X.

The Oblong Box
Another of Poe's famous horror stories brought to the screen; a flesh-creeping tale about two brothers, one with a horribly disfigured face, and false burial, and grisly revenge: and starring those twin kings of grislydom, *Vincent Price* and *Christopher Lee.* Rest of cast: *Alastair Williamson, Hilary Dwyer, Sally Geeson, Michael Balfour, Hira Talfrey, Peter Arne, Rupert Davies, Carl Rigg, James Miller, Maxwell Shaw, John Wentworth, Harry Baird, Ivor Dean, Paul Ferris, Godfrey James, Betty Woolfe.* Dir & Pro: Gordon Hessler. Screenplay: Lawrence Huntingdon. (American International–Warner-Pathé.) Rel: July 19. 91 mins. Cert. X.

Obsessions
A Van Gogh painting drops from the wall . . . and through the small hole revealed are seen a man and a woman making love . . . then the man injects the girl to make her unconscious . . . and so starts this English-speaking Dutch/German thriller. Cast: *Dieter Geissler, Alexandra Stewart, Tom Van Beek, Fons Rademakers, Marijke Boonstra, Vibeke Lokkeberg, Donald Jones, Hasmig Terveen, Michael Krebs, Elisabeth Verslygs, Adrian Brine, Sarah Heyblom, Ingeborg Uijt den Bogaard, Viktoria Naelin, Rista Schuyt, Margareta Orrje.* Dir: Pim de la Parra. Pro: Wim Verstappen. Screenplay: Pim de la Parra, Martin Scorsese, Wim Verstappen. (Scorpio–Border Films.) First shown at the Cameo Victoria, Oct., 1970. 90 mins. Cert. X.

One Brief Summer
Old-fashioned, top-drawer romantic drama about a middle-aged banker who falls in love with and marries a girl younger than and a friend of his horrified daughter, whose possessive love for him leads her to help along the inevitable disaster which follows the marriage. And a lovely background of English summer, of big houses, Rolls and E-Types and all they stand for. Cast: *Felicity Gibson, Clifford Evans, Jennifer Hilary, Jan Holden, Peter Egan, Fanny Carby, Richard Vernon, Helen Lindsay, Basil Moss, David Leland, Brian Wilde, Lockwood West, Neville Marten, Keith Smith, Susan Harvey, Carolyn Seymour, Robert Wilde, Virginia Balfour, Moira Foot, Pauline Challoner.* Dir: John Mackenzie. Pro: Guido Coen. Screenplay: Wendy Marshall, from a story by Harry Tierney & Guido Coen. (Twickenham Film Assoc.–Fox.) Rel: March 14. (E.) 86 mins. Cert. AA.

One Fine Day
Another small masterpiece by Ermanno Olmi – of "Il Posto" and "The Engagement" fame – in which once again he shows his interest if not obsession with observing man at work, and how that work directs his life, conditions his being. The story of an assistant M.D. of a Milanese advertising agency, efficient, dedicated and ambitious, who takes over from his boss when the latter has to rest after a heart attack: and how his accidental killing of a man in a road accident brings him his particular moment of truth. By using real people, not actors, a mixture of old and new styles, washed colour, Olmi achieves a sense of reality not often obtained or seen on the screen. Cast: *Brunetto del Vita, Maria Crosignani, Vitaliano Damioli, Lidia Fuortes, Raffaele Modugno, Giovanna Ceresa.* Dir, Written & Edited: Ermanno Olmi. (Ital Noleggio–Academy/Connoisseur.) Rel: Floating: first shown at Academy Two, Feb., 1971. (Colour.) 102 mins. Cert. A.

One More Time
A kind of sequel to "Salt and Pepper", with *Sammy Davis Junior* and *Peter Lawford* again the co-stars involved in a complicated comedy which includes *Lawford* playing his brother as well as himself, revengeful beauties, Interpol spies, gangsters and a jewel-thieving racket. Rest of cast: *Maggie Wright, Leslie Sands, John Wood, Sydney Arnold, Edward Evans, Percy Herbert, Bill Maynard, Dudley Sutton, Glyn Owen, Lucille Soong, Esther Anderson, Anthony Nicholls, Allan Cuthbertson, Cyril Luckham, Moultrie Kelsall, Julian D'Albie, Gladys Spencer, Joanna Wake, Juliette Bora, Florence George, Amber Dean Smith, Lorraine Hall, Carmel Stratton, Thelma Neal.* Dir: Jerry Lewis. Pro: Milton Ebbins. Screenplay: Michael Pertwee. (Chrislaw/Trace–Mark–UA.) Rel: Dec. 20. (D.) 93 mins. Cert. A.

One on Top of the Other
Intricate Italian murder thriller with characters pretending to be other characters and everyone scrabbling to gain the mysterious million dollars insurance money. Cast: *Marisa Mell, Jean Sorel, Elsa Martinelli, Alberto de Mendoza, John Ireland, Jean Sobieski, Faith Domergue.* Dir: Lucio Fulci. Pro: Edmondo Amati. Screenplay: Lucio Fulci, Roberto Giamvili & José Luis Martinez Molla. (Amati–Border Films.) Rel: March 14. (T & Scope.) 103 mins. Cert. X.

OSS 117 Murder for Sale
Minor, Bondish adventure with *John Gavin* the heroic agent infiltrated into a professional murder mob and duly splitting it from tough major top to pretty medical bottom. Franco-Italian origin. Rest of cast: *Margaret Lee, Curt Jurgens, Luciana Paluzzi, Robert Hossein, Guido Alberti, George Eastman, Piero Lulli, Rosalba Nari, Ryan Baldwin, Sayna Seyn, Romario Moschin, Emilio Messina.* Dir: J.-P. Desagnat & R. Cerrato. Pro: Marcello Danon. (Rank.) Rel: Sept. 27. (T.) 91 mins. Cert. A.

The Out-Of-Towners
Extremely amusing farce about a couple of out-of-town innocents who fly to New York so that hubbie can attend the interview which will gain him the big job in the big city – and then within the space of a few hectic, painful hours suffer just about every danger, indignity and disaster that could normally be experienced in years. A superbly timed performance by *Jack Lemmon* as George and an equally apt one by *Sandy Dennis* as his wife, Gwen. Rest of cast: *Ann Prentiss, Mary Norman, Robert Nichols, John Brown, Ron Carey, Paul Jubara, Hash Howard, Jon Korkes, Bob Walden, Anthony Holland, Phil Burns, Jack Crowder, Billy Dee Williams, Luis Arroyo, Milt Kamen, Carlos Montalban, Ann Meara.* Dir: Arthur Hiller. Pro: Paul Nathan. Screenplay: Neil Simon. (Jalem–Paramount.) (Movielab Colour.) 97 mins. Cert. U.

A Passion
Continuation of the Ingmar Bergman bleak philosophical saga; once again set on a lonely, windswept, cold and inhospitable island off the Swedish mainland where some of his favourite players (*Max Von Sydow, Liv Ullmann, Bibi Andersson,* together with newcomer *Erland Josephson*) dance the agonised Bergman measure, illustrating the thesis that Hell is The Other, The Self, and Life itself. Slow, sombre, and extremely powerful in its uncinematic, symbolic manner. Rest of cast: *Erik Hell, Sigge Fürst, Svea Holst.* Dir & Screenplay: Ingmar Bergman. Pro: Lars-Owe Carlberg. (Svensk Filmindustri–UA.) (D.) 100 mins. Cert. AA.

Patton: Lust for Glory
Excellently made, if to British moviegoers a shade controversial, biographical movie about that extrovert American General of the title, associated with the cry "Blood and Guts", who with his pearl-handled revolvers and conviction of reincarnation swaggered his troops to a series of undoubtedly brilliant victories during World War Two. With *George C. Scott* giving a tremendously impressive performance in the title role. Rest of cast: *Karl Malden, Stephen Young, Michael Strong, Cary Loftin, Albert Dumortier, Frank Latimore, Morgan Paull, Karl Michael Vogler, Bill Hickman, Patrick J. Zurica, James Edwards, Lawrence Dobkin, David Bauer, John Barrie, Richard Muench, Siegfried Rauch, Michael Bates, Paul Stevens, Gerald Flood, Jack Gwillim, Edward Binns, Peter Barkworth, Lionel Murton, David Healy, Sandy Kevin, Douglas Wilmer, John Doucette, Tim Considine, Abraxas Aaran, Clint Ritchie, Alan MacNaughtan.* Dir: Franklin J. Schaffner. Pro: Frank McCarthy. Screenplay: Francis Ford Coppola & Edmund H. North. (Fox.) Rel: Jan. 10. (Colour.) 171 mins. Cert. A.

The People Next Door
The problems of a superficially respectable, middle-class New Yorker family whose whole existence is suddenly split asunder when they discover that their young daughter is a depraved drug-addict. Cast: *Eli Wallach, Julie Harris, Deborah Winters, Stephen*

232

McHattie, Hal Holbrook, Cloris Leachman, Don Scardino, Rue McClanahan, Nehemiah Persoff, Mike Kellin, Sandy Alexander, Anthony Call, Mathew Cowles, Joseph Leon, Bruce Scott, Anita Dangler. Dir: David Greene. Pro: Herbert Brodkin. Screenplay: J. P. Miller. (J. Levine–Avco Embassy.) Rel: June 20. (Colour.)

Percy
Coarse comedy about a penis transplant, with *Hywel Bennett* as the recipient of another man's member – going around to find out about the man through the women who knew him! Rest of cast: *Denholm Elliott, Elke Sommer, Britt Ekland, Cyd Hayman, Janet Key, Tracey Crisp, Antonia Ellis, Tracy Reed, Patrick Mower, Pauline Delany, Adrienne Posta, Julia Foster, Sheila Steafel, Arthur English, Angus Mackay, Rita Webb, Charles Hodgson, Sue Lloyd, Denise Coffey.* Dir: Ralph Thomas. Pro: Betty E. Box. Screenplay: Hugh Leonard. (Anglo–EMI.) Rel: March 21. (T.) 103 mins. Cert. X.

Perfect Friday
Neatly worked out, very workmanlike comedy-thriller about an assistant bank manager (that's *Stanley Baker*) persuaded by an overdrawn but otherwise very acceptable client (*Ursula Andress*) to join in with her upper-crust husband (*David Warner*) to rob the former's bank: and what happens when they've got the loot. Rest of cast: *Garfield Morgan, Georgina Simpson, Barbara Ogilvie, Derek Cox, Patrick Jordan, Howard Lang, T. P. McKenna, Malcolm Johns, Patience Collier, Brian Peck, Johnny Briggs, Joan Benham, Eric Longworth, Carleton Hobbs, Audrey Noble, David Waller, Julian Orchard, Fred Griffiths, Hugh Halliday.* Dir: Peter Hall. Pro: Jack Smith. Screenplay: Anthony Greville-Bell, C. Scott Forbes. (Dimitri de Grunwald.) Rel: April 18. 95 mins. Cert. AA.

Performance
An interesting film marking the debut of two new directors, Donald Cammell and Nicolas Roeg, the former responsible for the sometimes uncertain but often exciting baroque treatment of the story about the confrontation of two highly contrasting worlds; brought about when petty gangster *James Fox* (one of his finest performances) allows his personal feelings to overcome his discretion and so kills his victim, from which moment he is on the run from his erstwhile boss (who has no wish to become involved in this kind of crime) and his minions and the cops. This is where he finds refuge with a retired Pop star living in disordered Notting Hill seclusion. There, hating each other and the worlds they stand for, comes the final confrontation, the flowering of violence by which both of them have lived. Not an easy film to like or to understand; a blemished film, but an excitingly intellectual effort of more than passing importance. Rest of cast: *Mick Jagger, Anita Pallenberg, Michele Breton, Ann Sidney, John Bindon, Stanley Meadows, Allan Cuthbertson, Antony Morton, Johnny Shannon, Anthony Valentine, Ken Colley, John Sterland, Laraine Wickens.* Dir: Donald Cammell (who also wrote the screenplay) &

Nicolas Roeg. Pro: Sanford Lieberson. (Goodtimes–Warner.) Rel: Floating. 102 mins. Cert. X.

Picture Mommy Dead
Grim little chiller about a young girl who becomes a key figure in plot and counter plot between three adults, one of them her father, to discover the whereabouts of the child's murdered mother's jewels, a situation which culminates in murder, madness and conflagration. Cast: *Don Ameche, Martha Hyer, Zsa Zsa Gabor, Susan Gordon, Maxwell Reed, Wendell Corey, Signe Hasso, Anna Lees.* Dir & Pro: Bert I. Gordon. Screenplay: Robt. Sherman. (Levine/Avco–Embassy.) Rel: Nov. 15. (Colour.) 82 mins. Cert. X.

Pookie
Quite charming and pleasantly "old-fashioned" story about an eccentric sort of young girl (she sees practically everyone else as a "weirdo" —something which she is herself!) who latches on to a shy young man on the bus that carries them both to new schools, cements the friendship at the first weekend and thereafter leads to shy advances, to love and sex – all done with consummate taste and delightful humour – and then reluctantly lets him go. With *Liza Minnelli* as "Pookie" looking, talking and acting in a startlingly similar way to her late mother when Judy Garland was around her age. *Wendell Burton* gives a perfect performance as the boy. Rest of cast: *Tim McIntire, Elizabeth Harrower, Austin Green, Sandra Faison, Chris Bugbee, Jawn McKinely.* Dir & Pro: Alan J. Pakula. Screenplay: Alvin Sargent. (Paramount.) (Colour.) 107 mins. Cert. X.

Portraits of Women
Jörn Donner film which tells a story about a maker of pornographic films who returns to his native Finland to make another but in his efforts to win a trio of females loses the whole when, after various complications, he finishes it! Cast: *Ritva Vespä, Kirsti Wallasvaara, Marianne Holmström, Jörn Donner, Henrik Granö.* Dir (& Screenplay): J. Donner. Pro: Arno Carlstedt. (FJ–Filmi/Jörn Donner–Target International.) Rel: Floating: first shown at the Cameo Royal, March, 1971. 87 mins. Cert. X.

The Private Life of Sherlock Holmes
Billy Wilder's amusing and yet traditional addition to the Holmes stories: this one supposedly kept secret until fifty years after the great sleuth's death and now for the first time revealed: the case in which a lovely woman made a fool of the detective and all but defeated him although in the end she failed, after touching his heart. A beautifully worked out suspense-detection story which involves six vanished circus midgets, the Loch Ness monster, a procession of Trappist Monks, death from poison gas, an aviary of canaries, Sherlock's diplomat brother, Queen Victoria . . . all tied neatly into a tidy bow at the end. With *Robert Stephens* as Holmes, *Colin Blakely* as Watson. Rest of cast: *Irene Handl, Stanley Holloway, Christopher Lee, Geneviève Page, Clive Revill, Tamara Toumanova, Catherine Lacey, Mollie Maureen, Peter*

Madden, Robert Cawdron, Michael Elwyn, Michael Balfour, Frank Thornton, James Copeland, Alex McCrindle, Kenneth Benda, Graham Armitage, Eric Francis, John Garrie, Godfrey James, Ina De La Haye, Ismet Hassan, Charlie Young Atom, Teddy Kiss Atom, Willie Shearer, Daphne Riggs, John Gatrell, Martin Carroll, John Scott, Philip Anthony, Phillip Ross, Annette Kerr. Dir, Pro & Written (the last with I. A. L. Diamond): Billy Wilder. (Mirisch–UA.) Rel: Jan. 17. (Pan & D.) 125 mins. Cert. A.

Putney Swope
A wild but occasionally amusing underground movie which takes a series of uneven swipes at various facets of the Establishment. Cast: *Arnold Johnson, Antonio Fargas, Laura Greene, Eric Krupnik, Pepi Hermine, Ruth Hermine, Larry Wolfe.* Dir & Written: Robert Downey. (Contemporary.) Rel: Floating. First shown at the Paris-Pullman, Oct., 1970. 85 mins. Cert. X.

A Question of Honour – Una Questione d'Onore
Italian film about a Sicilian blood feud and the hired killer who finds that in order to clear his bride of a charge of infidelity, and himself to keep the code which says he must kill the lover (who only he and she knows doesn't exist), he has to admit to a murder of which he is innocent! A knotty problem which gets knottier and knottier as it reaches its climax. Cast: *Ugo Tognazzi, Nicoletta Machiavelli, Bernard Blier, Franco Fabrizi, Lucien Raimbourg, Tecla Scarano, Leopoldo Trieste, Sandro Merli, Franco Bucceri, Franco Gulà, Armando Malpede.* Dir: Luigi Zampa. (Mega of Rome–Orphée de Paris–Border Films.) Rel: Floating: first shown at Cameo, Victoria, Jan., 1971. (T.) 110 mins. Cert. A.

The Raging Moon
Bryan Forbes's (screenplay and direction) tender, sympathetic but never sentimental adaptation to screen terms of the Peter Marshall story about two cripples, a doctor's daughter and a rough, Northern ex-footballer, both of whom have lost the use of their legs, who meet and fall in love in a home for the paralysed: and how, when this love has given the lad a new interest in life, the girl dies. Not as depressing as it sounds, for Forbes has given it humour as much as pathos. Superbly acted by every member of a cast that includes *Nanette Newman* as the girl and *Malcolm McDowell* as the young man. Rest of cast: *Georgia Brown, Bernard Lee, Gerald Sim, Michael Flanders, Margery Mason, Barry Jackson, Geoffrey Whitehead, Christopher Chittell, Jack Woolgar, Norman Bird, Constance Chapman, Michael Lees, Geoffrey Bayldon, Patsy Smart, Theresa Watson, Sylvia Coleridge, Brook Williams, Richard Moore, George Hilsdon, Nellie Hanham, Aimee Delamain, Rachel Herbert, Rosalyn Elvin, Judith Paris, Anne Dyson, Norman Tyrrell, Jenny Logan, Elsie Wagstaffe, Mary Baxter, Cathy Collins, Petra Markham, Jacqueline Maude, Winifride Shelley, John Savident, Michael Nightingale, Wilfred Boyle, Jackie Afrique, Paul Darrow, Marianne Stone, Catherine Crewe, Jack Bux, Lee Carter, Sarah Forbes, Emma Forbes.* Dir (& Screenplay): Bryan Forbes. Pro: Bruce Cohn Curtis. (MGM–EMI.) Rel: Floating. (T.) 111 mins. Cert. AA.

The Railway Children
Actor Lionel Jeffries's labour of love: his first effort as scriptwriter and director: an adaptation of the favourite Victorian children's story by E. Nesbit. All about a happy trio of youngsters whose family problems are solved by their sojourn in a cottage close to a Yorkshire railway cutting, where they make friends with the local porter and the grand old travelling gent and everyone else with whom they come in contact. Warm, cosy family piece with a nice pinafored, frilly, formal period atmosphere. Cast: *Jenny Agutter, Sally Thomsett, Gary Warren* (the children), *Dinah Sheridan, Bernard Cribbins, William Mervyn, Iain Cuthbertson, Peter Bromilow, Ann Lancaster, Gordon Whiting, Beatrix MacKey, Eddie Davies, David Lodge, Christopher Witty, Brenda Cowling, Paddy Ward, Erik Chitty, Sally Janes, Dominic Allen*. Dir & Screenplay: Lionel Jeffries. Pro: Robert Lynn. (EMI–MGM.) Rel: Dec. 27. (Colour.) 108 mins. Cert. U.

Ravaged – La Rose Écorchée
Chiller-thriller about a painter who, when his model-wife is ravaged by fire, blackmails a professor (who has invented a new, secret method of skin-grafting) into treating her: and as this method demands the skin of a live woman you can imagine the situations which arise, especially when one of the skinned victims, subsequently killed, has a sister with an enquiring sort of mind. Cast: *Philippe Lemaire, Anny Duperey, Howard Vernon, Elisabeth Teissier, Olivia Robin, Michèle Perello, Valérie Boisgel, Gérard Huart, Johnny Cacao*. Dir & Screenplay: Claude Mulot. Pro: Édgar Oppenheimer. (S.F. Distributors.) First shown at Jacey, Strand, June, 1970. (E.) 88 mins. Cert. X.

Reggae
Interest feature about Jamaican music and centred on the 1970 Caribbean Music Festival at Wembley. Dir & Pro: Horace Ove. (Contemporary.) Rel: Floating: first shown at ICA, Feb., 1971.

The Reivers
Beautifully atmospheric, thin-storied movie set in the wonderfully recreated Memphis of 1905, where come an 11-year-old boy and his older friend after an adventurous journey of 80 miles in a borrowed yellow Winton Flyer car, and where, when the lad finds his pal is staying at a brothel rather than the hotel he pretends, his boyish illusions begin to crumble. A wonderful celluloid capture of the sense of discovery that belongs exclusively to adolescence. Cast: *Steve McQueen, Sharon Farrell, Will Geer, Michael Constantine, Rupert Crosse, Mitch Vogel, Lonny Chapman, Juano Hernandez, Clifton James, Ruth White, Dub Taylor, Allyn Ann McLerie, Diane Shalet, Diane Ladd, Ellen Geer, Pat Randall, Charles Tyner, Vinette Carroll, Gloria Calomee, Sara Taft, Lindy Davis, Raymond Guth, Shug Fisher, Logan Ramsey, Jon Shank, Ella Mae Brown, Florence St. Peter, John McLiam, Lou Frizzell, Roy Barcroft*. Dir: Mark Rydell. Pro: Irving Ravetch. Screenplay: Irving Ravetch & Harriet Frank, Jnr. (Warner–Pathé.) Rel: Nov. 1. (Pan & T.) 111 mins. Cert. AA.

Rider on the Rain
René Clément (French but English speaking) thriller about a woman raped who in defence of further assault kills the rapist and throws the body in the sea – and then finds her secret is shared by the mysterious American who follows her, questioning, questing... Cast: *Marlène Jobert, Charles Bronson, Annie Cordy, Jill Ireland, Gabriele Tinti, Jean Gaven, Marc Mazza, Corinne Marchand, Jean Piat, Marika Green, Ellen Bahl*. Dir: René Clément. Pro: Serge Silberman. Screenplay: Sébastien Japrisot. (Levine–Avco Embassy.) Re: June 20. (Colour.) 119 mins. Cert. AA.

Rio Lobo
Routine, entertaining Western with an expert team (director Howard Hawks, star *J. Wayne*) at the helm: with *Wayne* as the Union Army Colonel guarding a gold train, who is defeated by the machinations of a couple of his traitorous soldiers, whom after the war he seeks out determined to even the score with them. And it is a search which leads him into plenty of lead-punctuated action before he walks off winner. Rest of cast: *Jorge Rivero, Jennifer O'Neil, Jack Elam, Christopher Mitchum, Victor French, Susana Dosamantes, David Huddleston, Mike Henry, Bill Williams, Jim Davis, Sherry Lansing, Dean Smith, Robert Donner, George Plimpton, Edward Faulkner, Peter Jason*. Dir & Pro: Howard Hawks. Screenplay: Burton Wohl & Leigh Brackett from the former's story. (Cinema Center–Fox.) Rel: Jan. 10. (T.) 114 mins. Cert. U.

The Rite
Ingmar Bergman's fined-down, oddly different (in its implications) film about three wandering, world-famous thespians who are brought before a magistrate on a charge of obscenity. Examined by him they are revealed as unhappy, untidy and frightened people; yet together in their act they produce such magic of art that they defeat and kill their persecutor by it! A very deep and significant message. Superbly acted by a cast of four: *Ingrid Thulin, Gunnar Björnstrand, Anders Ek, Erik Hell*. Dir & Written: Ingmar Bergman. (Persona/Darvill–Academy.) Rel: Floating: first shown at the Academy Two, April, 1971. 74 mins. Cert. X.

riverrun
John ("Funnyman") Korty's quite fascinating, visually poetic and altogether highly personal film about an old sea captain back from the sea (retired) who immediately comes into conflict with the young sheep farmer who has made his daughter pregnant, a friction which increases as they all wait for the child to be born until it climaxes into violence and leads, at least indirectly, to the death of the old man. *John McLiam* brilliant in the main role. Rest of cast: *Louise Ober, Mark Jenkins, Josephine Nichols, Joseph Nichols, Joseph Miksak, Stefanie Priest, George Hellyer, Jnr., Esther Sutherland, Laura Kwong, Orion de Winter, Paula Preston, Wilhelm Joerres, Sheila Emmett, Roy Parks, Robert Bertrand*. Dir & Screenplay: John Korty. Pro: Stephen Schmidt. (Columbia.) Rel: Floating; first shown at Paris-Pullman, July, 1970. (Colour.) 89 mins. Cert. X.

Run, Virgin, Run
German sex comedy about the village of Bumshausen, which wins the national award for the highest birthrate. Investigating the reasons, the Minister is told that it is an invigorating local wind, whereas in fact it is the local brawny blacksmith's appetite and endeavours which is the explanation. Cast: *Joav Jasinki, Helga Tölle, Michaela Martin, Alexander Allerson, Christina Kuon, Ilona Grubl*. Dir: Hans Billian. (S.F. Films.) First shown at Jacey, Leicester Sq., Sept., 1970. (E.) 84 mins. Cert. X.

Sabata
Mexican border (Italian) Western with *Lee Van Cleef* the cool gunman who outwits, out-shoots and gradually wipes out the rich villain's private army of hired assassins and collects some $65,000 for doing it. Rest of cast: *William Berger, Franco Ressell, Linda Veras, Pedro Sanchez, Gianni Rizzo, Anthony Gradwell, Nick Jordan, Robert Hundar, Spanny Convery, Marco Zuanelli, Gino Marturano, Joseph Mathews, Franco Ukmar, Bruno Ukmar, R. Lodi, Allan Collins, Vittorio Andre, Romano Puppo, Andrea Aureli, Franco Marletta, John Bartha, Charles Tamblyn*. Dir: Frank Kramer (Gianfranco Parolini). Pro: Alberto Grimaldi. Screenplay: Gianfranco Parolini & Renato Izzo. (Grimaldi–UA.) Rel: May 16. (T & Techniscope.) 106 mins. Cert. AA.

Salt of the Earth
A documentary with professional as well as amateur players, made for the Independent Productions Corporation and the International Union of Mine, Mill and Smelter Workers! Professional Cast: *Rosaura Revueltas, Will Geer, David Wolfe, Mervin Williams, David Sarvis*. Non-Professional cast: *Juan Chacon, and the people of locale 890 as themselves*. Dir: H. J. Biberman. Screenplay: Michael Wilson. (Contemporary.) Rel: Floating: first shown at Paris Pullman, March, 1970. 94 mins. Cert. A.

Sanjuro
Dazzling, dotty and very funny Kurosawa melodrama set in the past and telling the story of the untidy but magnificent Samurai – *Toshiro Mifune* – who comes to the rescue of a group of honest but rather silly young men trying to save their State from a take-over by crooked politicians. Tremendously entertaining in its comically stylised manner. Rest of cast: *Tatsuya Nakadai, Masao Shimizu, Yunosuke Ito, Takako Irie, Reiko Dan, Yuzo Kayama, Takashi Shimura, Kamatari Fujiwara, Keiju Kobayashi, Akihiko Hirata, Kunie Tanaka, Hiroshi Tachikawa, Tatsuhiko Hari, Tatsuyoshi Ehara, Kenzo Matsui, Yoshio Tsuchiya, Akira Kubo*. Dir: Akira Kurosawa. Pro: Ryuzo Kikushima & Tomoyuki Tanaka. Screenplay: Ryuzo Kikushima, Hideo Oguni & Akira Kurosawa. (Orb.) First shown at Academy Three, Nov., 1970. (Tohoscope.) 95 mins. Cert. A.

234

The Satanists
Italian documentary about the way that wizardry, black and white magic and other occult studies live on, and indeed grow, in the modern computerised world. Dir: *Luigi Scattini.* Commentary by *Edmund Purdom.* (Miracle.) Rel: Floating. (E.) 86 mins. Cert. X.

Say Hello to Yesterday
Mixed way-out and way-back comedy about a stockbroker's wife from Cobham who, taking a day out in London, is pestered and provoked by a young maniac who eventually seduces her in a borrowed bed. None of it ever rings true, apart from a lovely, tender and compelling performance by *Jean Simmons,* as the wayward (for just a day) wife. Rest of cast: *Leonard Whiting, Evelyn Laye, John Lee, Jack Woolgar, Constance Chapman, Gwen Nelson, Richard Pescud, Laraine Humphrys, Ben Aris, Nora Nicholson, Carla Challoner, Jimmy Gardner.* Dir: *Alvin Rakoff.* Pro: *Josef Shaftel.* Screenplay: A. Rakoff & Peter King, from a story by A. Rakoff & Ray Mathew. (CIRO.) Tel: Feb. 21. (E.) 92 mins. Cert. AA.

Scars of Dracula
Further Hammer Horror chapter in the long and ever-(blood-)sucking life of the evil Count, who survives everything including death! Cast: *Christopher Lee, Dennis Waterman, Jenny Hanley, Christopher Matthews, Patrick Troughton, Michael Gwynn, Wendy Hamilton, Anoushka Hempel, Delia Lindsay, Bob Todd, Toke Townley, David Lealand, Richard Durden, Morris Bush, Margot Boht, Clive Barrie.* Dir: Roy Ward Baker. Pro: Aida Young. Screenplay: John Elder. (Hammer–EMI–MGM.) Rel: Nov. 8. (T.) 96 mins. Cert. X.

Secret French Prostitution Report
A screen adaptation of the Dominique Dallayrac book "Dossier Prostitution": examining the whole situation and the problems of prostitution with a series of cases showing the relationship between seller and purchaser and the wide-ranging career of one particular lady of leisure who runs the whole gamut of her trade from street-walking to luxury call-girl. Cast: *Jean-Phillippe Ancelle, Line Arnel, Adaly Bayle, Valerie Boisgel, Beatrice Gardon, Adrien Cayla, Michel Charrel, Michel Dacquin, Marc Dudicourt, France Durin, Jackie Foucault, Christian Forges, Noelle Hussenot, Liana Marelli, Edith Ploquin, Nadir Samir, Katia Tchenko.* Dir & Screenplay: Jean-Claude Roy. Pro: René Thevenet. (OCF Tangara–Gala.) Rel: Floating. 90 mins. Cert. X.

The Secret of Santa Vittoria
Rather jolly, musical comedyish adaptation of a story based, 'tis said, on fact, about the way that the people of a small Northern Italian town when Mussolini fell and the Germans took over, managed in spite of all their "allies" could do, to fool them, and keep hidden the million bottles of wine which represented their greatest asset and which the Germans wanted to take. With *Anthony Quinn* in the tailor-made role of the not-quite-so-simple local mayor and *Hardy Kruger* giving a portrait in greater depth of the German officer outsmarted. Rest of cast: *Anna Magnani, Virna Lisi, Sergio Franchi, Renato Rascel, Giancarlo Giannini, Patrizia Valturri, Valentina Cortese, Eduardo Ciannelli, Leopoldo Trieste, Gigi Ballista, Quinto Parmeggiani, Carlo Caprioli, Francesco Mule, Wolfgang Jansen, Aldo De Carellis, Marco Tulli, Chris Anders, Peter Kuiper, Dieter Wilken, Karlo Otto Alberty, Gigi Bonos, Clelia Matania, Pippo Lauricella, Carlo Capannelle, Renato Chiantoni, Pino Ferrara, Curt Lowens, Tim Donnelly.* Dir & Pro: Stanley Kramer. Screenplay: William Rose & Ben Maddow. (UA.) Rel: Aug. 2. (Pan & T.) 140 mins. Cert. A.

Serafino
Voluble, lively, loud and typically Italian comedy with satirical undertones about a young shepherd of the hills, a thick young man whose hobby is seduction. An amusing picture of the remote, still primitive life of most rural Italy. Cast: *Adriano Celentano, Ottavia Piccolo, Saro Urzi, Francesca Romana Coluzzi, Benjamin Lev, Nazareno Natale, Giosuè Ippolito, Ermelinda de Felice, Nerina Montagnani, Luciana Turina, Oreste Palella, Piero Gerlini, Goffredo Canzano, Gino Santercole, Nestore Garay, Amedeo Trilli, Orlando D'Ubaldo, Gustavo D'Arpe, Vittorio Fanfoni, Mara Oscuro, Gianni Pulone, Clara Colosimo, Nazzareno D'Aquilio, Lidia Mancani.* Dir & Pro: Pietro Germi. Screenplay: Leo Benvenuti, Piero de Bernardi, Tullio Pinelli & Pietro Germi. (Columbia.) Rel: Floating. (Colour.) 96 mins. Cert. X.

A Severed Head
A disillusioned but amusing look at love relationships in a story which revolves in La Ronde manner around three men and three women who switch partners in entirely superficial and selfish manner as they seek to satisfy their own pleasure. Dryly amusing, thanks to smooth direction and first-class performances; notably by *Ian Holm* as the cowardly heart of the matter and *Lee Remick,* the grasping, greedy female. Rest of cast: *Richard Attenborough, Claire Bloom, Jennie Linden, Clive Revill, Ann Firbank, Rosamund Greenwood, Constance Lorne, Robert Gillespie, Katherine Parr, Ann Jameson, Yvette Rees.* Dir: Dick Clement. Pro: Alan Ladd Jr. Screenplay: Frederick Raphael. (Jerry Gershwin/Elliott Kastner–Columbia.) Rel: May 9. (Colour.) 98 mins. Cert. X.

The Sextrovert
A story of the many efforts of the jealous Nicole to split up the affair between her girl-friend Desirella and the young man she falls in love with. Cast: *Jean-Claude Bouillon, Sabine Sun, Philippe Nicaud, Dominique Delpierre, Catherine Wagener, Roger Lumont, Jacques Bezard, René Chapotot, Jean Ride, Elisabeth Larivière, Elisabeth Ridel.* Dir (& Written): Jean-Claude Dague. Pro: H. A. Legrand. (S.F. Film Distributors.) Rel: Floating: first shown at Cinephone, March, 1971. 63 mins. Cert. X.

She Died With Her Boots On
Not, as you might think, a Western, but a Danish production about a nasty photographer, who lives with an even nastier aunt, and their assault on the pretty victim they lure as a photographer's model. Cast includes *Karl Lanchbury, Vivian Neves, Pia Anderson.* (E. J. Fancey.) Rel: Floating. (E.) 70 mins. Cert. X.

Shock Corridor
Sensational Samuel Fuller film (for five years banned in GB), based apparently on a true story, about a reporter who to investigate the killing in a lunatic asylum, has himself certified. Inside he does pin the crime on the murderer, but by this time he is himself off his trolley. Cast: *Peter Breck, Constance Towers, Gene Evans, James Best, Hari Rhodes, Larry Tucker, William Zuckert, Philip Ahn.* Dir: S. Fuller. (Amanda.) Rel: Floating. 101 mins. Cert. X (London).

The Sicilian Clan
French gangster piece: about a family gang from the island living in Paris and making a nice nefarious living behind the façade of a legitimate business, led by pappa *Jean Gabin,* who "springs" young thug *Alain Delon* from jail and with him embarks on a plot to rob a jewellery exhibition in Rome. It all goes well, but unfortunately *Delon* casts his avid eye – and more – on pappa's daughter-in-law *Irina Demick* and Sicilian honour demands that this shall bring a bloody end on their heads – and it does! Rest of cast: *Lino Ventura, Amedeo Nazzari, Sydney Chaplin, Elise Cegani, Karen Blanguernon, Marc Porel, Yves Lefebvre, Philippe Baronnet, Leopoldo Trieste, César Chauveau, Danielle Volle, Ed Meeks, Jacques Duby.* Dir: Henri Verneuil. Pro: Jacques E. Strauss. Screenplay: H. Verneuil, José Giovanni, Pierre Pelegri. (Fox.) Rel: Oct. 4. (Pan & D.) 117 mins. Cert. A.

Simon, Simon
Half-hour comedy film in mime about a couple of Council workmen whose disgrace after wrecking their platform-lorry becomes triumph when, with their new truck, they perform constant public services and end up by catching a hit-and-run thief. Cast: *Graham Stark, Julia Foster, Norman Rossington, John Junkin, Kenneth Earl, Paul Whitsun-Jones, Audrey Nicholson.* Dir & Written: Graham Stark. Pro: Peter Shillingford. (Hemdale–Shillingford.) Rel: Sept. 6. 30 mins. Cert. U.

Simon the Swiss (**Le Voyou**)
Beautifully engineered if intricately edited (and therefore a little confusing with its unobvious flash-backs) Claude Lelouch crime story: about a lawyer turned crook who carries out a daring and finely planned abduction of a small boy whom he then successfully holds for ransom – and only finally is he just a little too clever . . .! Cast: *Jean-Louis Trintignant, Christine Lelouch, Charles Gérard, Danièle Delorme, Yves Robert, Amidou, Pierre Zimmer, Judith Magré, Charles Denner, Jacques Valcroze, Sacha Distel, Paul le Person, Gabriella Giorgilli, Luciano Pigozzi, Aldo Maccione, Mimmo Palmara, Gerard Sire.* Dir: Claude Lelouch. Pro: Alexandre Mnouchkine. Screenplay: C. Lelouch, Pierre Uytterhoeven & Claude Pinoteau.

(Les Films Ariane : Les Films 13 : Les Productions Artistes Associés P.E.A., Rome–UA.) Rel : Floating : first shown at Classic, Baker Street, March, 1970. (E.) 120 mins. Cert. A.

Smoke
Disney film about a boy and a dog: the boy, resenting his stepfather's authority, finds a wounded Alsatian dog and through the affection which grows up between them learns to understand his elders. Cast: *Earl Holliman, Ronny Howard, Jacqueline Scott, Shug Fisher, Andy Devine, Pamelyn Ferdin, Kelly Thordsen, Custer* (the dog). Dir : Vincent McEveety. Pro: Ron Miller. Screenplay : John Furia, Jnr. (Disney.) Rel : Aug. 23. (T.) 84 mins. Cert. U.

Soldier Blue
Good, but horrifying, bloody and brutal Western which tells the story of two fugitives from an Indian ambush – the girl understanding and respecting the Cheyennes, the soldier seeing them only as animals – and their involvement in the terrible Sand Creek Massacre of 1864. Cast: *Candice Bergen, Peter Strauss, Donald Pleasence, Bob Carraway, Mort Mills, Jorge Rivero, Dana Elcar, John Anderson, Martin West, Jorge Russek, Marco Antonio Arzate.* Dir: Ralph Nelson. Pro: Gabriel Katzka & Harold Loeb. Screenplay : John Gay. (Joseph E. Levine–Avco-Embassy.) Rel : June 6. (T & Pan.) 114 mins. Cert. X.

Some Will, Some Won't
The final practical joke of a great old practical joker who becomes the victim of one of his own fun-fests. He leaves four people £150,000 each providing they prove they can step out of their present lives and become "human beings". And even when they achieve that their benefactor has a final laugh-ace up his sleeve. Cast: *Ronnie Corbett, Thora Hird, Michael Hordern, Barbara Murray, Leslie Phillips, Wilfrid Brambell, Dennis Price, James Robertson-Justice, Sheila Steafel, Eleanor Summerfield, Arthur Lowe, Noel Davis, Toni Gilpin, Harold Goodwin, Noel Howlett, Diana King, Stephen Lewis, Norman Mitchell, John Nettleton, Brian Oulton, Toni Palmer, Frank Thornton, David Lander, Claire Davenport, Robin Tolhurst, Vicki Woolf.* Dir : Duncan Wood. Pro: Giulio Zampi. Screenplay : Lee Schwarz from an original story – screenplay by Jack Davies & Michael Pertwee. (Transocean/Warner–Pathé.) Rel : Oct. 11. (T.) 90 mins. Cert. U.

Song of the Red Ruby
Continuation of the amorous, often erotic, sometimes amusing life story of the plump young man we first met in the very successful Danish film called "Seventeen". Older now, destined to be a concert pianist, he still finds the female irresistible and is soon faced with double-pregnancy! And lots of lovely dollies willing to drop their skirts at a twitch of the nose. Cast: *Ole Søltoft, Ghita Nørby, Lotte Horne, Annie Birgit Garde, Gertie Jung, Lizzi Varencke, Eva Weinreich, Lykke Nielsen, Elin Reimer, Paul Hagen, Per Pallesen, Claus Ryskjaer, Poul Bundgaard, Arthur Jensen, Poul Huttel.* Dir : Annelise Meineche.

Screenplay: A. Meineche & John Hilbard, based on Agnar Mykle's novel of the same title. (Palladium-Gala.) Rel : Floating. (E.) 106 mins. Cert. X.

Start the Revolution Without Me
Good – old-style – crazy comedy which owes something to Abbott and Costello and Wheeler and Woolsey and at the same time manages to stay original in the uproarious way it sends up Dumas, The Corsican Brothers, The Man in the Iron Mask and other famous literary and screen characters seen against a background of the French Revolution. Cast: *Gene Wilder, Donald Sutherland, Hugh Griffith, Jack MacGowran, Billie Whitelaw, Victor Spinetti, Orson Welles, Ewa Aulin.* Dir & Pro: Bud Yorkin. Screenplay: Fred Freeman & L. J. Cohen. (Warner–Seven Arts.) Rel : May 30. (T.) 90 mins. Cert. A.

The Statue
Near the . . . well . . . say knuckle comedy about a sculptress wife who models a vast nude statue of her husband, a complete likeness except for one part of his anatomy, and he gets the idea this part was modelled from someone else, an idea which sends him into a jealous search for the original model . . . Cast: *David Niven, Virna Lisi, Robert Vaughn, Anne Bell, John Cleese, Tim Brooke-Taylor, Hugh Burden, Eric Chitty, Derek Francis, Susan Travers, Desmond Walter-Ellis, David Allister, Maureen Lane, David Mills, Zöe Sallis, Mircha Carven, Christopher Cruize, Aldo de Carellis, Ann Ferguson, Pino Ferrara, John Frederick, Tony Gardner, Marco Gobbi, Hazel Hoskins, Marne Maitland, Bettine Milne, Gianni Musi, Troy Patterson, Bill Vanders, Granville Van Dusen.* Dir: Rod Amateau. Pro: Annis Nohra. Screenplay: Alec Coppel & Denis Norden, based on the former's stage play "Chip, Chip, Chip". (Josef Shaftel–CIRO.) Rel : May 23. 89 mins. Cert. X.

Street of Sin
German film about two brothers, one good, one bad, and their eventual confrontation: seen against a background of Hamburg's harbour district. Cast: *Curt Jürgens, Horst Naumann, Christiane Rücker, Heinz Reincke, Marianne Hoffman, Fritz Wepper.* Dir: Rolf Olsen. Screenplay: Rolf Olsen. (Terra Filmkunst.) Rel : Floating: first shown at Cinephone, Feb., 1971. 82 mins. Cert. X.

Subterfuge
Espionage thriller set against London backgrounds, where arrives dedicated, ruthless American secret agent *Gene Barry* apparently on holiday – but hardly that, it turns out, when after just four hours of landing at Heathrow he's been involved in a murder, is kidnapped, tortured and otherwise treated very much as if he were on duty! And all very complicated, confusing and intriguing it becomes. Rest of cast: *Joan Collins, Richard Todd, Tom Adams, Suzanna Leigh, Michael Rennie, Marius Goring, Scott Forbes, Colin Gordon, Guy Deghy, Dermot Kelly, Stuart Cooper, John Welsh, Clifford Earl, Ron Pember, Gary Clifford, Jane Blackburn, Harry Locke, Fred Peisley, Sidney Vivien, Robert Raglan, Graham Lines, Bill*

Nagy, John Clifford, Fred Dowie, Charles Lamb, Marian Diamond, Carmen Dean, Lyn Marshall, Donna Reading, Valerie Hudson, Sheila Sands. Dir: Peter Graham Scott. Pro: Trevor Wallace & Peter Snell. Screenplay & Story: David Whitaker. (Rank.) Rel : March 7. (E.) 86 mins. Cert. AA.

Sunday in the Park
Donovan Winter's documentary – which took five years to make ! – about the sort of people who each Sunday bring Hyde Park to lively life and the way that the mood of Speaker's Corner is changing, too. Dir, Pro & Edited: Donovan Winter. (Donwin–British Lion.) Rel : March 7. 52 mins. Cert. U.

Sunflower
Oddly old-fashioned-style woman's picture. Telling a sentimental, tear-flecked story of a North Italian soldier who weds a Neapolitan beauty and is, when caught trying to evade overseas service by feigning nuttiness, shipped to the Russian front. There he is rescued from a frozen death by a pretty little Slav, whom he weds. And then, after the war, his wife searches Russia for him and finds him. . . *Sophia Loren, Marcello Mastroianni* and *Ludmila Savelyeva* as an attractive trio. Rest of cast: *Galina Andreeva, Anna Carena, Germano Longo, Nadia Cerednichenko, Glauco Onorato, Silvano Tranquilli, Marisa Traversi, Gunar Zilinski, Carlo Ponti, Jnr.* Dir: Vittorio de Sica. Pro: Carlo Ponti & Arthur Cohn. Screenplay: Antonio Guerra & Cesare Zavattini. (Joseph Levine–Avco Embassy.) Rel : Floating. (Colour.) 107 mins. Cert. A.

Suppose They Gave a War and Nobody Came ?
Wild comedy along vaguely "M*A*S*H" lines with most of the noisy, boisterous fun revolving around the struggle between three army veterans in peacetime whose decision to improve the human relations between their base and the nearby town leads to a confrontation between them, and a tank, the wicked town's boss and his private army. Cast: *Tony Curtis, Brian Keith, Ernest Borgnine, Suzanne Pleshette, Tom Ewell, Bradford Dillman, Ivan Dixon, Arthur O'Connell, Don Ameche, John Fiedler, Bob Emhardt, Maxine Stuart, Christopher Mitchum, Pamela Britton, Grady Sutton, Clifford Norton, Jeanne Bates, Eddie Firestone, William Bramley, Sam G. Edwards, Buck Young, Paul E. Sorensen, David Cass, John Lasell, Dorothy Green, Pamela Branch, Janet E. Clark, Jean Argyle, Monty Margetts, Paula Stewart, Carolyn Williamson, John James Bannon, Vincent Howard, Stanley W. Barrett.* Dir: Hy Averback. Pro: Fred Engel. Screenplay: Don McGuire & Hal Captain, from the latter's story. (CIRO.) Rel : December 13. (Colour.) 100 mins. Cert. AA.

Swedish Love Play
Torrid passions in a Swedish film about a girl, an older woman who becomes possessive about her, the men who have affairs with her – all culminating in a literal flare-up. Cast: *Monica Nordquist, Birger Malmsten, Öllegård Wellton, Lissi Alandh.* Dir: Claes Fellbom. (Omega Film A.B. Production–Crispin Films.) Rel : Floating. 90 mins. Cert. X.

236

Take a Girl Like You

Slim little with-it sex comedy about a virginal little Northern miss (*Hayley Mills*) who comes South to teach and is immediately besieged by a number of sex-seeking males, among whom are a glowering *Oliver Reed* (with a heart of hidden gold, maybe), smoothly sophisticated seducer *Noel Harrison*, and drunken Labour Councillor *John Bird*. And it all ends on a possibly romantic note: based on the Kingsley Amis book. Rest of cast: *Sheila Hancock, Aimi Macdonald, Ronald Lacey, Geraldine Sherman*. Dir: Jonathan Miller. Pro: Hal E. Chester. Screenplay: George Melly. (Chester–Columbia.) Rel: Jan. 31. (Colour.) 98 mins. Cert. X.

Take Me, Love Me . . .

Anna Gaël as the courtesan Nana in a story that covers many of her complicated and intricate affairs. Rest of cast: *Gillian Hills, Lars Lunoe, Keve Hjelm, Gerard Berner, Rikki Septimus, Hans Ernback, Peter Bonke, Keith Bradfield, Poul Glagaard, Fritz Ruzicka, Erik Holme, Simon Rosenbaum, Willy Peters, Elsa Jackson, Yvonne Ekman, Helli Louise, Bonnie Evans*. Dir & Screenplay: Mac Ahlberg. Pro: Tore Sjöberg. (Miracle.) Rel: Floating: first shown at Jacey, Leicester Square, Feb., 1971.

Take the Money and Run

Very much the personal creation of American comedian *Woody Allen* (star, director and co-scripter): a quietly amusing, gently satirical biographical piece about a simple nincompoop whose ambition is to become one of America's most wanted men; but ends up, several bungled crimes later, with a 600-year jail sentence. *Janet Margolin* as his silly, but pretty little wife. Rest of cast: *Marcel Hillaire, Jacquelyn Hyde, Lonny Chapman, Jan Merlin, James Anderson, Howard Storm, Mark Gordon, Micil Murphy, Minnow Moskowitz, Nate Jacobson, Grace Bauer, Ethel Sokolow, Henry Leff, Don Frazier, Mike O'Dowd, Jackson Beck*. Dir: Woody Allen. Pro: Chas. H. Joffe. Screenplay: Woody Allen & Mickey Rose. (Palomar–Cinerama.) Rel: Dec. 13. 85 mins. Cert. A.

Tar Babies

Mexican film about the search for the last remaining city on earth, that of Tar, by a couple who set out after the – future – holocaust; he impotent, she paralytic, an impossible journey towards impossible happiness. A collector's piece: dipped in surrealism and shock. Cast: *Sergio Klainer, Diana Mariscal, Maria Teresa Rivas, Tamara Garina, Juan Jose Arreola, Rene Rebetez*. Dir: Alexandro Jodorowsky. Pro: Roberto Viskin, Juan Lopez Moctezuma. Screenplay: Fernando Arrabal, Alexandro Jodorowsky, based on the former's play. (Panic–New Cinema Presentations.) Rel: Floating: first shown at Jacey, Piccadilly, Jan., 1971. 98 mins. Cert. X.

Taste of Excitement

The mystery of the murder on the cross-channel ferry and the subsequent campaign to frighten, or divert, or kill the pretty young girl who crossed on it and is making her increasingly nervous way to her holiday at Cap Ferrat – where after some more murders the mystery is solved. Cast: *Eva Renzi, David Buck, Peter Vaughan, Paul Hubschmid, Sophie Hardy, Kay Walsh, Francis Matthews, Peter Bowles, George Pravda, Alan Barry, Alan Rowe, Tom Kempinski*. Dir: Don Sharp. Pro: George Willoughby, Brian Carton & Don Sharp. (Monarch.) Rel: May 16: first shown Jacey, Leicester Square, Jan., 1971. (E & Widescreen.) 99 mins. Cert. X.

10 Rillington Place

Careful, chillingly realistic reconstruction – made largely on location in the depressing Notting Hill cul-de-sac of the title – of the Christie murder case: with *Richard Attenborough* as the psychiatric sex killer who admitted to seven murders (when he left No. 10 the new tenant found some of the bodies behind a concealed door) after another occupant of the house, the unfortunate, simple, illiterate Timothy Evans had been hanged for the murder of two of them, his wife and baby. Based on the Ludovic Kennedy book. Brilliantly acted – exceptionally so by *John Hurt* as Evans – well and non-flashily directed. Rest of cast: *Judy Geeson, Pat Heywood, Isobel Black, Phyllis MacMahon, Geoffrey Chater, Robert Hardy, André Morell, Bernard Lee, Robert Keegan, Basil Dignam, Norman Henry, Edward Burnham, Edward Evans, Tenniel Evans, David Jackson, Jack Carr, George Lee, Richard Coleman, Edwin Brown, Norma Shebbeare, Sam Kydd, Rudolph Walker, Tommy Ansah, Reg Lye*. Dir: Richard Fleischer. Pro: Martin Ransohoff & Leslie Linder. Screenplay: Clive Exton. (Columbia.) Rel: March 21. (Colour.) 111 mins. Cert. X.

The 1,000 Plane Raid

World War Two story – up in the air! How the man they thought in the US Air Force was a coward turns out to be a right hero! And the mental strains for the men who lead the four-figure fleet of bombers. Cast: *Christopher George, Laraine Stephens, J. D. Cannon, Gary Marshall, Michael Evans, Ben Murphy, James Gammon, Gavin MacLeod*. Dir: Boris Sagal. Pro: L. J. Rachmil. Screenplay: Donald S. Sanford. (Oakmont–UA.) Rel: July 26. (D.) 92 mins. Cert. U.

There's a Girl in My Soup

Terence Frisby's screen adaptation of his own stage play success: a brilliant example of playing for three acts on one note and making it appear to be five! The story of an American teenager picked up by a middle-aged TV good food expert roué who is quickly deflated to size by her acid comments and cynical actions. With a superbly timed performance by *Goldie Hawn* as the girl: *Peter Sellers* is the man. Rest of cast: *Tony Britton, Nicky Henson, John Comer, Diana Dors, Gabrielle Drake, Geraldine Sherman, Judy Campbell, Nicola Pagett, Christopher Cazenove, Robin Parkinson, Roy Skelton, Caroline Seymour, Raf de la Torre, Constantin de Goguel, Thorley Walters, Georges Lambert, Andre Charisse, John Serret, Avril Angers, Ruth Trouncer*. Dir: Roy Boulting. Pro: M. J. Frankovich & J. Boulting. Screenplay: Terence Frisby. (Frankovich/Boultings–Columbia.) Rel: Feb. 14. (Colour.) 96 mins. Cert. X.

There Was a Crooked Man

Joseph L. Mankiewicz's highly enjoyable, literate and subtle version of the old prison break story: the story of the smiling, dimpled but ruthless Paris Pitman Junior, whose sojourn in the Arizona State Prison in the 1880's, his elaborate plans for escape (in which he coldly sacrifices all his fellow plotters), his strange relationship with the reforming governor, who after the riot launched by Paris rides after him determined to kill him, and the final, ironic climax, add up to a drily amusing if often horrifying commentary on human nature. Superbly acted by *Kirk Douglas* as the criminal, *Henry Fonda* as the reformer finally tempted too greatly. Rest of cast: *Hume Cronyn, Warren Oates, Burgess Meredith, Arthur O'Connell, Martin Gabel, John Randolph, Michael Blodgett, Claudia McNeil, Alan Hale, Victor French, Lee Grant, Jeanne Cooper, C. K. Yang, Bert Freed, Gene Evans, Pamela Hensley, Barbara Rhoades*. Dir & Pro: Joseph L. Mankiewicz. Screenplay: David Newman & Robert Benton. (Warner.) Rel: Floating. (Pan & Colour.) 126 mins. Cert. AA.

They Call ME MISTER Tibbs!

The return of the coloured 'tec we first met in "In the Heat of the Night", in a smooth, slick, unimportant San Francisco murder whodunnit! who murdered joy-girl Joy? And why? And inter-leaved with the search for clues, sorting of suspects and playing on hunches which leads MISTER Tibbs to his quarry, there are some quite charming domestic interludes. Cast: *Sidney Poitier, Martin Landau, Barbara McNair, Anthony Zerbe, Jeff Corey, David Sheiner, Juano Hernandez, Norma Crane, Edward Asner, Ted Gehring, Beverly Todd, Linda Towne, George Spell, Wanda Spell*. Dir: Gordon Douglas. Pro: Herbert Hirschman. Screenplay: A. R. Trustman & J. R. Webb from the former's story – based on the John Ball character. (Mirisch–UA.) Rel: Feb. 7. (D.) 108 mins. Cert. AA.

They Shoot Horses, Don't They?

Brilliant, brutal and superbly detailed re-creation of a time and place and an event: the record of a Hollywood dance marathon in the hungry thirties, the Great Depression days when people were willing to go to the edge, and over, of human endurance for some food and a chance of a monetary prize. Superbly acted by *Gig Young* (he won an Oscar for his role as organiser and MC), *Jane Fonda* (as the cryptic, born loser), *Red Buttons* (as Sailor), *Michael Sarrazin* and *Susannah York*. Rest of cast: *Bonnie Bedelia, Michael Conrad, Bruce Dern, Al Lewis, Robert Fields, Severn Darden, Allyn Ann McLerie, Jacquelyn Hyde, Felice Orlandi, Art Metrano, Gail Billings, Maxine Greene, Mary Gregory, Robert Dunlap, Paul Mantee, Tim Herbert, Tom McFadden, Noble "Kid" Chissell*. Dir: Sydney Pollack. Pro: Irwin Winkler & Robt. Chartoff. Screenplay: James Poe & Robert E. Thompson, based on the story by Horace McCoy. (Palomar/ABC–CIRO.) Rel: Oct. 11. (Pan & E.) 120 mins. Cert. AA.

Three Sisters

Alan Clore's film record of the superb Laurence Olivier directed production of Chekhov's classic play: beautifully acted and altogether one of the greatest and most understanding of the many productions of this subtle and deep play. Cast: *Jeanne Watts, Joan Plowright, Louise Purnell, Derek Jacobi, Sheila Reid, Kenneth Mackintosh, Daphne Heard, Harry Lomax, Judy Wilson, Mary Griffiths, Ronald Pickup, Laurence Olivier, Frank Wylie, Alan Bates, Richard Kay, David Belcher, George Selway, David Munro, Alan Adams, Robert Walker.* Dir: Laurence Olivier, with John Sichel as co-director. Pro: John Goldstone. (British Lion.) Rel: Floating. (E.) 165 mins. Cert. U.

...tick...tick...tick...

About a coloured sheriff in the deep American south and the problems of law and colour that he faces as he tries to do his job with justice and without prejudice. Cast: *Jim Brown, George Kennedy, Fredric March, Lynn Carlin, Don Stroud, Janet MacLachlan, Richard Elkins, Clifton James, Bob Random, Mills Watson.* Dir: Ralph Nelson. Pro: Ralph Nelson & James Lee Barrett (who also wrote the screenplay). (MGM.) Rel: Oct. 18. (Colour & Pan.) 98 mins. Cert. A.

Time Out for Sardinia

Half-hour (all but 2 mins.) interest film in which *Pete Myers* takes the audience on a comprehensive tour of the island of the title. Dir & Pro: Harold Baim. (Anglo–EMI/Warner–Pathé.) Rel: Aug. 30. (E.) 28 mins. Cert. U.

To Commit a Murder

An intricate web of deceit and revelation as a group of spies and counter spies revolve around a plot to get a talented young nuclear scientist out of France and into the hands of Mao. It's a sad first success for writer-playboy hero *Louis Jourdan*, who wins it at the cost of losing the woman he has come to love during the assignment. Rest of cast: *Senta Berger, Edmond O'Brien, Bernard Blier, Fabrizio Capucci, Giuseppe Adobatti, Maurice Garrel, Gamil Ratib, Patricia Scott.* Dir: Edouard Molinaro. Pro: Alain Poiré. Screenplay: E. Molinaro & Jacques Robert, based on the novel "Peau d'Espion" by the latter. (Gaumont International–CIRO.) Rel: Feb. 21. 91 mins. Cert. AA.

Too Late the Hero

Pretty consistently tense and exciting, if familiar story about a group of British soldiers and an American officer and their suicidal mission from one end of a Pacific Island to the Jap-occupied other, in order to smash a radio station. A sort of ten little niggers business which ends with a drawn-out but otherwise thrilling climax. Excellently acted. Cast: *Michael Caine, Cliff Robertson, Ian Bannen, Harry Andrews, Denholm Elliott, Ronald Fraser, Lance Percival, Percy Herbert, Patrick Jordan, Sam Kydd, William Beckley, Martin Horsey, Harvey Jason, Don Knight, Roger Newman, Michael Parsons, Sean MacDuff, Frank Webb, Henry Fonda, Ken Takakura.* Dir & Pro and, with Lukas Heller, written: Robert Aldrich. (CIRO.) Rel: Oct. 18. (Metrocolor.) 144 mins. Cert. X.

Toomorrow

Quite cheery little musical about a quartet of students from the London College of Art who form a Group and so impress an Alphoid Space Spy (here disguised as a human being!) that he decides to recruit them as agents to combat the sterility of sound in space! Cast: *Olivia Newton-John, Benny Thomas, Vic Cooper, Karl Chambers, Roy Dotrice, Imogen Hassall, Louis Cabot, Tracey Crisp, Maria O'Brien, Lynda Westover, Diane Keen, Lucy Fenwick, Patrick Tull, Joanna Henderson, Margaret Nolan, Allan Warren, Carl Rigg, John Dommett, Rohan McCullough, Richard Woo, Kubi Chaza, Lynn Lewis, Roy Marsden.* Dir & Written: Val Guest. Pro: Harry Saltzman & Don Kirshner. (Rank.) Rel: Sept. 13. (T & Pan.) 95 mins. Cert. A.

A Town Called Bastard

Doom-laden story of a small Mexican town after the defeat of the 1905 rebellion and dictator Diaz's search for its leader: and the equally insistent, equally deadly search of a mysterious widow for the man who killed her husband – with the idea of killing him. Cast: *Robert Shaw, Stella Stevens, Martin Landau, Telly Savalas, Fernando Rey, Dudley Sutton, Al Lettieri, La Paloma, Aldo Sambrell, Maribel Hidalgo, Cass Martin, Antonio Mayans, Tito Garcia, Tony Cyrus, Adolfo Thous, Elizabeth Sands, Felipe Solano, Luis Rivera, Howard Hagan, John Clark, Bruce Fischer, Nilda Alvarez, Charlie Bravo, Chris Huertas, George Rigaud, Stefano Charelli, Michael Craig.* Dir: Robert Parrish. Pro: S. Benjamin Fisz. Screenplay: Richard Aubrey. (Benmar/Zurbano–Scotia Barber.) Rel: June 27. (Colour.) 97 mins. Cert. X.

The Travelling Executioner

Broad, coarse black comedy set in America's deep South in the year 1918 and concerning the antics of a travelling executioner who for a fee will happily electrocute any condemned prisoner. But one of his intended victims, a pretty killer, spoils it all for him and leads to his eventual explosive demise, as a condemned murderer in his own chair! Cast: *Stacy Keach, Mariana Hill, Bud Cort, Graham Jarvis, James J. Sloyan, M. Emmet Walsh, John Bottoms, Ford Rainey, James Greene, Sammy Reese, Stefan Gierasch, Logan Ramsey, Charles Tyner, William Mims, Val Avery, Walter Barnes, Charlie Briggs, Paul Gaunt.* Dir & Pro: Jack Smight. Screenplay: Garrie Bateson. (MGM–EMI.) Rel: Feb. 7. (Pan & Metrocolor.) 94 mins. Cert. X.

La Trêve – The Truce

Rather charming little French comedy about two professional gamblers on the way to some wealthy players who are followed by three very pretty little crooks who also have their eyes on the loot. Cast: *Daniel Gélin, Charles Denner, Caroline Car, Virginie Vignon, Marc Lamole, Jean Mondain, Eric Husberg.* Dir & Screenplay: Claude Guillemot. (Amanda.) First shown at Everyman, July, 1970. 90 mins. Cert. U.

Tropic of Cancer

Henry Miller's notorious, bawdy book brought to the screen by the maker of "Ulysses", – Joseph Strick who cheerfully packs the screen with frontal nudity and four-letter words as he retells Miller's persistently wordy incidents about a footloose writer in Paris, shedding wife and mistresses and ending up in Dijon teaching at a boys' school there. Cast: *Rip Torn* (as Miller), *James Callahan, Ellen Burstyn, David Bauer, Laurence Lignères, Phil Brown, Dominique Delpierre, Stuart de Silva, Raymond Gérome, Gisèle Grimm, Ginette Leclerc, Françoise Lugagne, Magali Noel, Sheila Steafel, Elliot Sullivan, Sabine Sun, George Birt, Steve Eckardt, Philippe Gasté, Eleonore Hirt, Ed Marcus, Henry Miller, Christine Oscar, Gladys Berry, Jo Lefevre, Roger Lumont, Guy Marly, Loryanne, Catherine d'Hugues, Nada Vasil, Liane Saunier, Bernard Taine, Yves Rannon, Lionel Bejean.* Dir, Pro & Screenplay: Joseph Strick. (Tropic–Paramount.) Rel: Floating. (E.) 88 mins. Cert X

Two Or Three Things I Know About Her

Actually made in 1966, this typical Jean-Luc Godard film hangs on the peg of the story of a Paris suburban housewife who goes in for spare-time prostitution in order to buy the more simple luxuries of life – such as a car or a TV – his routine criticism of Society, the Establishment and various other highly disapproved-of facets of current life, suggesting, it finally appears, that prostitution is the result of the Capitalist Society! Cast: *Marina Vlady, Anny Duperey, Roger Montsoret, Raoul Lévy.* Dir & Screenplay: Jean-Luc Godard. Rel: Floating. (Contemporary.) (E & Techniscope.) 87 mins. Cert. X.

Under the Table You Must Go

All-but-one-hour interest film about the varied entertainment now offered in the pubs – in addition, of course, to good drinking and lots of cheerful atmosphere. (Butcher's.) Rel: Aug. 30. (E.) 52 mins. Cert. U.

Underground

The self-imposed mission of an escapee from a British mental asylum to complete his failed task of kidnapping a German General and spirit him back to England. Cast: *Robert Goulet, Danièle Gaubert, Lawrence Dobkin, Carl Duering, Joachim Hansen, Roger Delgado, Alexander Peleg, George Pravda, Leon Lissek, Harry Brooks, Jnr., Sebastian Breaks, Nicole Croisille.* Dir: Arthur H. Nadel. Pro: Jules Levy, Arthur Gardner & Arnold Laven. Screenplay: Ron Bishop & Andy Lewis. (Levy, Gardner & Laven–UA.) Rel: Jan. 17. (D.) 95 mins. Cert. A.

Up Pompeii

Largely successful transition of the small-screen comedy series to the large screen, with *Frankie Howerd* giving a broadly comic, typical performance as the resourceful slave surrounded by orgies! A film which plays on one comic note, and that a deep blue one, for most of the way but in spite of that is likeable and funny, and obviously marks the debut of a new "up" series in the "Carry On" traditions. Rest of cast: *Patrick Cargill, Michael Hordern, Barbara Murray, Lance Percival, Bill Fraser, Adrienne Posta, Julie Ege,*

238 Bernard Bresslaw, Royce Mills, Madeline Smith, Rita Webb, Ian Trigger, Aubrey Woods, Hugh Paddick, Laraine Humphreys, Roy Hudd, George Woodbridge, Andrea Lloyd, Derek Griffiths. Dir: Bob Kellett. Pro: Ned Sherrin. Screenplay: Sid Colin. (Anglo–MGM–EMI.) Rel: April 11. (E.) 90 mins. Cert. AA.

Uptight
Jules Dassin's variation on O'Flaherty's "The Informer"; switching the scene and the skin colours and the time: from Ireland to America, from an Irish brute to an out-of-work Negro steelworker and from way back to the death of Martin Luther King: but retaining the bones, the story of a man who sells his pals for money but finds it buys him only misery, fear and finally a traitor's death. Cast: Raymond St. Jacques, Ruby Dee, Frank Silvera, Julian Mayfield, Roscoe Lee Browne, Janet MacLachlan, Max Julien, Juanita Moore, Michael Baseleon, Robert DoQui, Ketty Lester, Dick Williams, John Wesley Rogers, Ji-Tu Cumbuka, L. Errol Jaye, Richard Williams. Dir & Pro (& co-written with Ruby Dee, Julian Mayfield): Jules Dassin. (Dassin–Paramount.) Rel: Floating. (T.) 94 mins. Cert. X.

The Vampire Lovers
Grisly little vampire chapter, another adaptation of the Sheridan le Fanu story "Carmilla", about lovely bloodsuckers, with all its lesbian implications. Cast: Ingrid Pitt, Pippa Steele, Madeline Smith, Peter Cushing, George Cole, Dawn Addams, Kate O'Mara, Douglas Wilmer, Jon Finch, Kirsten Betts, John Forbes Robertson, Harvey Hall. Dir: Roy Ward Baker. Pro: Harry Fine & Michael Style. Screenplay: Tudor Gates. (Hammer/MGM–EMI.) Rel: Oct. 4. (T.) 91 mins. Cert. X.

The Virgin and the Gypsy
A superbly right creation of a time and a place by director Christopher Miles in his film of the last of D. H. Lawrence's stories to be published: a typical piece about a frustrated young Miss living in a tension-filled parsonage who is physically attracted by a gypsy who, during the night of the flood, when they are marooned in an upstairs bedroom, fulfils her needs: to be gone in the morning, leaving her more able to face the future. Stylish, wonderfully visual, poetic. Cast: Joanna Shimkus, Franco Nero, Honor Blackman, Mark Burns, Maurice Denham, Fay Compton, Kay Walsh, Harriett Harper, Norman Bird, Imogen Hassall, Jeremy Bulloch, Roy Holder, Margo Andrew, Janet Chappell, Helen Booth, Laurie Dale, Lulu Davies. Dir: Christopher Miles. Pro: Kenneth Harper. Screenplay: Alan Plater. (London Screenplays.) Rel: Floating. (Colour.) 95 mins. Cert. AA.

Vixen
Three-quarter-hour film about a sexually involved holiday high in the Canadian Rockies, where fights and frustration and folly pass the time! Cast: Erica Gavin, Harrison Page, Garth Pillsbury, Jon Evans, Vincene Wallace, Robert Aiken, Michael Donovan O'Donnell, Peter Carpenter, John Furlong, Jackie Illman. Dir: Russ Meyer. Screenplay: Robert Rudelson. (Cinecenta.) Rel: Floating: first shown at Cinecenta, March, 1971. (Colour.) 47 mins. Cert. X.

A Walk in the Spring Rain
Rather charming, old-fashioned, middle-aged romance about a professor's wife who accompanies him to the Great Smoky Mountains so that he can get on with writing his book, and there meets a down-to-earth character who has a way with animals, and a knowledge of nature which impresses her into falling gently in love with him – until the book is given up, the couple go back to town and routine once more takes over their lives. Beautifully acted, especially by Ingrid Bergman. Rest of cast: Anthony Quinn, Fritz Weaver, Katherine Crawford, Tom Fielding, Virginia Gregg, Mitchell Silberman. Dir: Guy Green. Pro & Screenplay: Stirling Silliphant. (Columbia.) Rel: Nov. 1. (Pan. & Colour.) 98 mins. Cert. A.

The Walking Stick
Rather sad little tale of a crippled girl who falls in love with an artist, accepts living with him, and then finds he's a crook who is planning to rob the antique shop at which she works. A Chabrol-reminiscent menace-mood film, made on location in London. Cast: David Hemmings, Samantha Eggar, Emlyn Williams, Phyllis Calvert, Ferdy Mayne, Francesca Annis, Bridget Turner, Dudley Sutton, John Woodvine, David Savile, Derek Cox, Harvey Sambrook, Gwen Cherrell, Walter Horsburgh, Basil Henson, Anthony Nicholls, Nan Munro, Donald Sumpter, David Griffin, Susan Payne. Dir: Eric Till. Pro: Alan Ladd, Jnr. & Elliott Kastner. Screenplay: George Bluestone. (Winkast–MGM.) Rel: Oct. 18. (Pan. & Colour.) 101 mins. Cert. A.

Wanda
Brilliant solo screen début – as writer-director-star – of Barbara Loden (Mrs. Elia Kazan) in a story (reminiscent in vague outline of "Bonnie and Clyde" but sharper in impact, more realistic) about an ill-equipped, born loser: a girl who funks out of marriage, drifts into crime and ends up hopelessly enmeshed in her own sense of futility as she drifts from man to man towards an inevitably sad end. But the film is not all depressing: there is humour and richness and life in it: and it is imaginatively made. Rest of cast: Michael Higgins. Dir & Screenplay: B. Loden. (Filmakers–Academy.) Rel: Floating: first shown at the Academy, Jan., 1970. (Colour.) 110 mins. Cert. AA.

The Wanderer
French fantasy film, from the Alain-Fournier classic for young people: a great love story set in the strange mystic landscape of Sologne, where the boy finds, loses and then seeks happiness. Cast: Brigitte Fossey, Jean Blaise, Alain Libolt, Alain Noury, Juliette Villard, Christian de Tillière, Marcel Cuvelier, Serge Spira, Bruno Castan. Dir: Jean-Gabriel Albicocco. Pro: Gilbert de Goldschmidt. Screenplay: J.-G. Albicocco & Isabelle Rivière; from the novel by Alain-Fournier. (Fair Enterprises.) Rel: Floating: first shown at Paris-Pullman, March, 1971. 110 mins. Cert. A.

Watermelon Man
Thoroughly amusing one-off comedy which by its humour and general good nature illuminates with impact the harsh facts of being an American Negro by telling a story of a hearty-type, unloved white insurance agent who turns black overnight and finds in the morning what a different place the world has become. Cast: Godfrey Cambridge, Estelle Parsons, Howard Caine, D'Urville Martin, Mantan Moreland, Kay Kimberley, Kay E. Kuter, Scott Garrett, Erin Moran, Irving Selbst, Emil Sitka, Lawrence Parke, Karl Lukas, Ray Ballard, Robert Dagny, Paul H. Williams, Ralph Montgomery, Charles Lampkin, Vivian Rhodes, Erik Nelson, Matthias Uitz, Rhodie Cogan, Donna Dubrow, Frank Farmer, Hazel Medina. Dir: Melvin Van Peebles. Pro: J. B. Bennett. Screenplay: Herman Raucher. (Bennett–Mirell/Van Peebles/Columbia.) Rel: Floating. (T.) 100 mins. Cert. X.

Well of Time
Short interest film about legendary Siam.

What Do You Say to a Naked Lady?
A collection of somewhat untidy candid camera sequences and overheard discussions centred on the title question: showing the reactions of a number of males when faced and sometimes stopped in office corridor or country lane by a pretty nude girl: or their reactions when halted in the street by a pretty girl's request that they kiss her. Cast: Joie Addison, Laura Huston, Martin Meyers, Karil Daniels, Donna Whitfield, Richard Roundtree, Susannah Glemm, Norman Manzon, Joan Bell. Dir & Pro: Allen Funt. (UA.) Rel: Floating. (D.) 74 mins. Cert. X.

When Dinosaurs Ruled the Earth
The unfortunate – and, of course, thrilling – adventures of dawn-of-history glamour girl Victoria Vetri as she escapes being a sacrifice of two tribes, only in turn to fall into a dinosaur's nest – where she is accepted by the beast as one of its more attractive progeny! Jolly little Hammer thriller-spectacle. Rest of cast: Robin Hawdon, Patrick Allen, Drewe Henley, Sean Caffrey, Magda Konopka, Imogen Hassall, Patrick Holt, Jan Rossini, Carol-Anne Hawkins, Maria O'Brien, Connie Tilton, Maggie Lynton, Jimmy Lodge, Billy Cornelius, Ray Ford. Dir & Written: Val Guest. Pro: Aida Young. (Hammer–Warner.) Rel: Oct. 25. (T.) 100 mins. Cert. A.

When Eight Bells Toll
Anthony Hopkins as a Naval Secret Service agent assigned to the uncovering and smashing of a nice little racket in stolen and smuggled gold bullion: a task finally achieved by some well-aimed bullets, some hand grenades and a neatly handled harpoon! Routine, fast, exciting thriller by Alistair Maclean moving against refreshingly new backgrounds of the Highlands and Islands of Scotland. Rest of cast: Robert Morley, Nathalie Delon, Jack Hawkins, Corin Redgrave, Derek Bond, Ferdy Mayne, Maurice Roeves, Leon Collins, Wendy Allnutt, Peter Arne, Oliver MacGreevy, Jon Croft, Tom Chatto, Charlie Stewart, Edward Burnham, Del Henney. Dir: Etienne Périer. Pro: Elliott Kastner. Screenplay: Alistair Maclean. (Gershwin/Kastner–Rank.) Rel: April 25. (Pan & Colour.) 94 mins. Cert. A.

The Wife Swappers
A mixture of documentary and dramatised interludes about the new Permissive Period sex game, and where it leads; with plenty to please the voyeur, and some laughs too. Dir: Derek Ford. Pro: Stanley Long. Screenplay: D. Ford & S. Long. (Salon–Eagle.) Rel: Floating. 86 mins. Cert. X.

The Wild Country
Walt Disney Western about the struggle of the pioneering Tanners, Mom, Dad and two boys, who in the 1880's leave Pittsburgh for Jackson Hole, Wyoming, where they intend to farm, and where they find so many arrows of outrageous fortune – including fighting for water rights, stampeding cattle, arsonical neighbours, cyclone and gunning bullies – that at one point they consider giving up . . . but . . . Cast: *Steve Forrest, Vera Miles, Jack Elam, Ronny Howard, Frank de Kova, Morgan Woodward, Clint Howard, Dub Taylor, Woodrow Chambliss, Karl Swenson, Mills Watson.* Dir: Robert Totten. Pro: Ron Miller. Screenplay: Calvin Clements Junr. & Paul Savage, based on the Ralph Moody book "Little Britches". (Disney.) Rel: April 11. (T.) 100 mins. Cert. U.

Wild, Willing and Sexy
German sex comedy about four girls who take up residence on the farm inherited by a fifth and set up a unique labour scheme by inviting their gentlemen friends to pay for favours in kind, the kind being a little ploughing, or seeding or whatever! Cast: *Terry Torday, Ivan Nesbitt, Paul Loewinger, Andrea Rau, Heidy Bohlen, Uschi Mood, Honsi Linder, Ralf Wolter.* Dir: Franz Antel. (Delta–S.F. Film Distributors.) Rel: Floating; first shown at Cameo Moulin, Feb., 1971. (Colour.) 74 mins. Cert. X.

With Love in Mind
The long and very chequered (flag!) romance of English rose Carolyn and the fashion photographer she meets in Mexico: their parting and final coming together, seen largely against a background of the car racing circuits in Mexico. Cast: *Keith Baxter, Shirley Ann Field, Carl Schnell, Eva Wishaw.* Dir: Robin Cecil-Wright. Pro: Michael A. O. Topping. Screenplay: N. J. Crisp. (Anglo/EMI.) Rel: Aug. 2. (Technicope & T.) 49 mins. Cert. U.

Without a Stitch
A new kind of Pilgrim's Progress: that made across Europe by Danish *Anne Grete*, sent in search of complete sexual satisfaction by an understanding young doctor who prescribes it when she complains to him that her boy-friend can't really stand up to the test! Rest of cast: *Ib Mossin, Niels Borksand, Ki-Jo Feza, Niels Dybeck, Ake Engfeldt, Leif Fich, John Martinus, Søren Carlsbaek, Joan Gamst, Søren Strømberg, Dieter Eppler, Dale Robinson, Preben Ottesen, Jean Kress.* Dir: Annelise Meineche. Pro: Tenga Nielsen. Screenplay: A. Meineche, J. Hilbard. (Palladium–Gala.) Rel: Floating: first shown at Continentale, Jan., 1971. (E.) 78 mins. Cert. X (London).

Woodstock
Lavish and generally lively coverage, in depth and at length, of the American Pop Festival of the title: with its commentary during its three days when thousands of young people lived happily and peacefully together, on at least one aspect of modern American youth. Dir: Mike Wadleigh. Pro: Bob Maurice. (Warner–Pathé.) Rel: Floating. (T.) 184 mins. Cert. X.

The World at Their Feet
Documentary feature about the World Soccer Cup matches played in Mexico in 1970 with many of the great moments of the various games. Dir: Alberto Isaac. Pro: Morton M. Lewis. Script: Derek & Donald Ford. (Rank.) Rel: Floating. 95 mins. Cert. U.

Yojimbo
Somewhat bloodthirsty tale of Japan in the mid-19th century, when a wandering soldier of fortune comes into the town of Edo and, finding it seething with gamblers, racketeers and sundry other adventurers lured there by the wealth of the district, by the strength of his wit and sword brings justice and peace to the place. Cast: *Toshiro Mifune, Eijiro Tono, Seizaburo Kawazu, Isuzu Yamada, Hiroshi Tachikawa, Kamatari Fujiwara, Yoshio Tsuchiya, Yoko Tsukasa, Kyu Sazanka, Daisuke Kato, Tatsuya Nakadai, Takashi Shimura.* Dir: Akira Kurosawa (sharing screenplay credit with Ryuzo Kikyshima). (Contemporary.) First shown at Paris Pullman, June, 1970. 110 mins. Cert. A.

You Can't Win 'em All
A quite satisfying slice of good old Hollywood hokum: done in a spectacular and amusing way. *Tony Curtis* as the American adventurer going to Turkey to recover one of his family's ships, given to that country by the German, who captured it during the war, and becoming immediately involved with fellow adventurer *Charles Bronson* and his band of mercenaries in escorting a convoy of girls and gems through the disintegrating, seething Ottoman Empire of the year 1922. Rest of cast: *Michèle Mercier, Gregoire Aslan, Fikret Hakan, Salih Guney, Tony Bonner, John Acheson, John Alderson, Horst Jansen, Leo Gordon, Reed de Ruen, Paul Stassino, Suna Keskin, Yuksel Gozen, Jenia Halil, Patrick Magee.* Dir: Peter Collinson. Pro: Gene Corman. Screenplay: Leo V. Gordon. (Corman–Columbia.) Rel: May 9. (Pan & Colour.) 99 mins. Cert. A.

Zeppelin.
Michael York as the young Anglo-German in World War One who has the agonising experience of being selected as the perfect man for the job – of going into his home town in his family's Germany in order to steal the plans of the Zeppelin airships which in 1915 were increasingly worrying the British with their raids, initially on the coast, later inland and on London. Rest of cast: *Elke Somner, Peter Carsten, Marius Goring, Anton Diffring, Andrew Keir, Rupert Davies, Alexandra Stewart, William Marlowe, Richard Hurndall, Michael Robbins, George Mikell, Clive Morton.* Dir: Etienne Périer. Pro: Owen Crump. Screenplay: Arthur Rowe & Donald Churchill. (Warner.) Rel: May 3. (Pan & T.) 97 mins. Cert. U.

INDEX
Numerals in italic represent pictorial mentions

The Adding Machine *63*, 215
Adios Sabata *203*
Adventures in Perception 38
Adventures of Gerard *122*, 215
Again 215
Airport *83*, *192*, *194*, 215
AKA Cassius Clay 215
All About Women *126*, 215
All Coppers Are . . . *213*
All the Way Up *117*, 215
Alyse and Chloe 215
The Ambler's Race 79
The American Soldier 81
Amsterdam 37
Anada 79
An Echo of Evil 82
Anatomie des Liebesacken 216
Anatomy of Love 216
And Soon the Darkness *105*, 216
The Anderson Tapes *209*
Andy Warhol and his Clan 216
Angel's Face 82
The Angel Levine *203*
Angels from Hell 216
Ann and Eve 78
Anna Karenina 77
Anne of the Thousand Days 8, 9, *197*
Anthony and Cleopatra 41
Antonio des Mortes 216
Anybody's *177*, 216
The April Fools *64*, 216
Aqua di Roma 37
The Aristocats *99*, 216
The Arrangement *85*, 216
As You Like It 41, 42, 44
Assault *129*, 216
Asterix the Gaul *186*, 216
The Atlantic Wall 75
The Awful Story of the Nun of Monza *173*, 217

The Baby Maker *156*, 217
Baltic Tragedy 78, *193*
Bananas *204*
The Barefoot Executive *147*, 217
Battle of Algiers 217
Battle of Britain 9, *93*, 217
Bats in the Belfry 81
Bednobs and Broomsticks *205*
Bedroom Mazurka *181*, 217
The Bed-Sitting Room *121*, 217
The Beguiled *212*
The Bespectacled 81
Between Us 78
Beyond the Line of Duty 78

Beyond the Valley of the Dolls *124*, 217
Big Jake *211*
Big Reward for Butch Cassidy 77
The Birchwood *82*, 82
Birds, Orphans, Fools 79
Black Angels *195*
Black Beauty *146*, 217
Black Mountain 78
Blanche 76
Blind Terror *209*
The Blonde and the Black Pussycat *175*, 217
Blood Feud 81
Blood On Your Lips 80
Bloody Mama *157*, 217
A Bloody Tale 81, *195*
Bluebird 79
Blushing Charlie 78, *189*, 218
The Boat 76
The Boatniks *101*, 218
Bob and Carol and Ted and Alice *84*, 218
The Body *141*, 218
Boleslaus the Bold 82
The Bookseller Who Gave Up Bashing 78
Bordello *63*, *64*, 75
Borsalino *63*, *64*, 75, 218
Boulevard du Rhum 74
Bourvard and Pecuchet 78
The Bow of Queen Dorothy 80
The Boy—Shonen 218
The Boys in the Band *108*, 218
The Bride 80
The Bride of the Andes 218
Bronco Bullfrog *146*, *193*, 218
Brother Carl 78
Brother Sun, Sister Moon 78
Bubu Montparnasse 78
Burn, Boy, Burn *171*, 218
The Buttercup Chain *97*, 218
By the Lake 78, *195*

CC And Co. *158*, 219
The Cactus Flower *115*, 218
Calm Flat 82
The Cannibals 76
Carry On At Your Convenience *212*
Carry On Loving 218
Carry On Up the Jungle *117*, 219
Casanova's Childhood and First Adventures 77
Castle Keep *64*, 218
Catherine and Her Children 80

Celebrations at Big Sur *210*
A Challenge 82
Change of Mind *123*, 219
Chariots of the Gods 219
Charlie the Lonesome Cougar *100*, 219
The Chase 76
The Cheyenne Social Club *98*, 217
Chimes at Midnight 46
Chisum *90*, 219
The Christine Jorgensen Story *150*, 219
Ciao, Federico *12*, *158*, 219
The Circus *121*, 219
Claire's Knee 75
The Clowns 77, *195*
Colonel Wolodyjowski *185*, 220
Come Back Peter *127*, 220
Comin' Thro' the Rye *21*
The Competitors 220
Comptes à Recours 76
Comrades 77
The Confession—L'Aveu 216
Confessions of Sweet Seventeen 80
The Conformist 77
Cool It, Carol 220
Cotten Comes to Harlem *156*, 220
Count Yorga, Vampire *109*, 220
Countess Dracula *129*, 220
Creatures the World Forgot *150*, 220
Cromwell *192*, *197*
The Crows *82*, 81
The Cry 78
The Cry of the Banshee *109*, 220
A Cure for Love 82
The Cyclists 81, *193*

Dad's Army *144*, 220
Darker Than Amber *156*, 220
Darling Lili *197*
Day of Rest 220
The Day They . . . *193*
Deadline 78
Death By Hanging *184*, 220
Death in Venice *193*
The Decoy 79
Deep End *145*, 220
The Derby *206*
The Devil's Honeymoon 80
The Devils *207*
Die of love 75
Dirty Dingus Magee *92*, 221
Do You Believe in Swedish Sin? 78
Doctor in Trouble *118*, 221
Dodeska-den *77*, 79
Dog Days 78

Dogs and People 79
Domicile Conjugal *74*, 75
Donkey Skin 75
Don't Just Stand There *115*, 220
Don't Look Back 221
Dorian Gray 77
Doucement les Basses 76
Downhill Racer *192*
Dreams of Love 82
A Dream of History *193*
Drifters 37
Duck You Suckers *204*
The Duel of the Vultures 80
Dulcima *202*
The Dunwich Horror *111*, 221

The Ear 79
Easy Rider 8, *73*
El Condor *89*, 221
Elbow Play *175*, 221
Eloquent Peasant *195*
The Engagement *118*, 221
Erotissimo *165*, 221
Erste Liebe *195*
Escape from the Planet of the Apes *210*
The Executioner *104*, 221
Explosion *108*, 222
The Extraordinary Seaman *102*, 222
Eyewitness 9, *103*, 222

The Face 81
The Falcons *193*
The Family Life 82
The Farö Document 76
The Father *214*
The Fault of Abbé Mouret 75
Fear Has 1,000 Eyes 78
Fellini-Satyricon *197*
Female Sexuality *174*, 222
Fiddler on the Roof *73*, *205*
Figures in a Landscape *156*, 222
A Film About Love 82
The First Circle 75
The First Love 81, *195*
The First Stone 78
Five Candles 38
Flight of the Doves *208*
Fools Parade *210*
For a Few Bullets More *92*, 222
Four Murders are Not Enough, Dear 80
Fragment of Fear *103*, 222
Fraulein Doktor *187*, 222
Fright *208*

241

242

The Fruit of Paradise 193
Funeral Rites 79
Fyodor Chaliapin 78

The Gallery Murders 188, 222
The Games 94, 222
Games That Lovers Play 125, 222
Garden of Delights 81
The Garden of Finzi Cantinas 77
The Gay Deceivers 149, 222
A Gentle Creature 163, 223
Get Carter 148, 223
Getting Straight 158, 195, 223
Girls for Pleasure 223
Glass 37
The Go-Between 193, 201
Goodbye Gemini 95, 223
Gott Mit Uns 195
Grandmother 80
Granzie Zia 169, 223
The Great Bank Robbery 91, 223
The Great Unknown 80
The Great White Hope 151, 223
The Great White Road 80
The Green Wall 193, 195
Greetings 223
The Grisson Gang 206
Groupie Girl 96, 223
Guess Who's Coming for Breakfast 176, 223
Guess Who's Sleeping With Us Tonight? 176, 224
Guess What We Learned in School Today? 223

Hamlet 41, 42, 45, 48, 50
Hands Off Gretel 188, 224
The Hands of the Ripper 213
Hang Your Hat in the Wind 100, 224
Harry Munter 214
Havoc 81
He Who Sings Means No Evil 81
Hell Boats 224
Hello Abysynnia 77
Hello, Dolly! 73, 135, 224
Hello-Goodbye! 97, 224
Hell's Belles 136, 224
Henry V 45
Henry Nine Till Five 193
Heterosexual 224
Heroic Purgatory 79
Highway Pickup 166, 224
Hoffman 95, 224
A Hole Lot of Trouble 224
The Holy Sinner 81

Home Sweet Home 35
Hook, Line and Sinker 133, 224
Hornet's Nest 137, 224
The Horror of Frankenstein 109, 224
The Horsemen 209
Hospital 195
House of Dark Shadows 128, 225
House of Pleasure 186, 225
The House That Dripped Blood 128, 225
The House Under the Trees 75
How Do I Love Thee? 225
How I Unleashed the Second World War 82
Hugo Fogo Homolka 80
The Hunting Party 203

I Don't Like Mondays 82
I, Francis Skorina 78
I Had My Brother's Wife 185, 225
I Love My Wife 212
I Start Counting 102, 225
I Walk the Line 154, 225
If It's Tuesday It Must Be Belgium 119, 225
Image, Flesh, Voice 195
I'm An Elephant, Madame 187, 225
In Search of Gregory 225
In the Name of the Father 228
Interview with My Lai Veterans 195, 225
Investigation of a Citizen Above Suspicion 76, 192
Is It Always Right to be Right? 192
It All Goes to Show 225
It's the Only Way to Go 225
It's Tough to be a Bird 100, 225

Jane Eyre 151, 225
Jazz All Around 82
Jealousy, Italian Style 208
Jemina and Johnny 226
Joan 226
Joaquin Murieta 89, 226
Joe 8 75, 150
Joe Egg 209
Joe Hill 193
Johnny Got His Gun 193
Jonathan 80
Judgement 82
Julius Caesar 41, 42, 45, 47, 48, 65, 226

Kes 106, 192, 193, 195, 226
King John 41

King Lear 42, 47, 48, 50, 209
Knockout 81
Kotch 206
The Kremlin Chimes 78, 226
The Kremlin Letter 104

L'Amour de la Vie 227
L'Aveu 161, 216
L'Écriture Bleue 76
L'Enfant Sauvage 75, 221, 161
L'Homme Orchestre 75
L'Homme au Cerveau Grêffe 76
L'Ours et la Poupée 76
La Faute de L'Abbé Mouret 73
La Fin des Pyrenées 195
La Folie des Grandeurs 75
La Maison des Bonnes 75, 195
La Nuit des Temps 75
La Trève—The Truce 237
Le Boucher 195
Le Cercle Rouge 73
Le Chat 74
Le Chinoise 219
Le Force et la Droit 76
Le Gendarme en Balade 75
Le Grand Amour 164, 223
Le Mans 210
Le Rendezvous à Braye 76
Le Visiteur de la nuit 76
Les Affinités Électives 76
Les Choses de la Vie—The Things of Life 167, 219
Les Maries de L'An 11, 76
Les Novices 76
The Landlord 148, 226
Landscape After the Battle 82
Landscape With a Hero 82
The Language of Love 78, 111, 180, 226
Larks on a String 79
The Last Adventure 226
The Last Run 202
The Last Warrior 147, 226
Lawman 152, 226
Leo the Last 65, 226
Leonardo 77
Let's Go to Kill 76
Let's Stake Our Lives 79
Liberation 78
The Liberation of L. B. Jones 85, 227
Lieut. Basil 78
Light 38
Lilika 81
Little Faus and Big Halsy 205
Little Murders 211

Lokis 82
Loot 137, 227
The Losers 227
Love 82, 193
Love and Anger 227
The Love Circle 227
Love Me, Baby, Love Me 188, 227
Love of Life—Artur Rubenstein—L'Amour de la Vie 227
The Love of Three Oranges 78
Love Story 8, 73, 192
Love Variations 227
Lovely Hungarian Country 81
Lovers and Other Strangers 147
Loving 86, 227
Lust for a Vampire 127, 227
Lysenter 42

Macbeth 16, 41, 42, 45, 46, 49, 49, 75
Machine Gun McCain 172, 227
The McKenzie Break 147, 229
The McMasters 154, 229
Macho Callahan 155, 228
The Madwoman of Chaillot 65, 228
Mad Dogs and Englishmen 203
The Mafia Mob 171, 228
The Magus 67, 228
Malvolio 42
A Man Called Horse 88, 228
A Man Called Sledge 88, 228
A Man for Emmannuelle 170, 228
Man of Violence 228
Man on a Staircase 228
The Man Who Came for Coffee 78
The Man Who Had Power Over Women 97, 228
The Man Who Haunted Himself 104, 228
The Marquis de Sade 76
A Married Couple 141, 228
The Married Priest 76
Marry Me! Marry Me! 164, 228
Massacre Harbour 229
Master of the Islands 229
The Master Did Not Ask for Anything 80
May I Introduce Myself? 78
The Meeting 28, 29
Men and War 79
The Mephisto Waltz 211
The Merchant of Venice 41, 42
Mi-temps 76
The Midsummer Dance 78
A Midsummer Night's Dream 42, 43, 44, 50

The Militants 79
The Million Dollar Duck 205
The Mind of Mr. Soames 112, 229
The Minister 78
Mira 38
Mirror of Holland 37
Mississippi Summer 193
Mister Jerico 229
Mr. Kinky 229
Mondo Sex 229
Monte Walsh 139, 229
Monterey Pop 229
The Moonshine War 87, 229
Moonlighting Wives 229
More About the Language of Love 78
Moribund Spring 81
Mortadella 77
Mosquito Squadron 230
Mourir D'Aimer 74
The Movement 195
Mumsy, Nanny, Sonny and Girly 105, 230
Murder of Mr. Devil 79
Music 230
My Bed is Not for Sleeping 230
My Lover, My Son 96, 230
My Side of the Mountain 146, 230
My Swedish Meatball 190, 230
Myra Breckinridge 124, 230

Naked England 230
The Naked Kiss 230
The Navy is a Ship 230
Ned Kelly 107, 230
Negatives 123, 230
Nicholas and Alexandra 214
Nicolaus Copernicus 82
Night After Night After Night 103, 231
The Night Visitors 76
The Nourishee 81
The Nude Countess 80

The Oblong Box 111, 231
Obsessions 231
Odour, Gold and Incense 81
Olney a Sao Paulo 195
Omnia a Vincit Amor 195
On a Clear Day You Can See Forever 205
On the Comet 81
On the Way to Lenin 195
Ondata di Calore 195
One Brief Summer 142, 231
One Fine Day 173, 231

·One Hundred Years of Right 195
One More Time 119, 231
One on Top of the Other 231
Once Upon a Time in America 76
Othello 41, 42, 43, 45, 46, 50
The Out of Towners 8, 67, 231

Panic in Needle Park 193
Panta Rhei 37
A Passion 179, 231
Patton, Lust for Glory 141, 192, 194, 231
Peace and Resistance 193
Peau D'Ane 74
The People Next Door 155, 231
Percy 134, 232
Perfect Friday 149, 232
Performance 146, 232
Picture Mommy Dead 232
A Pink Spot 78
Pippa Langstrump on the 7 Seas 78
Plaza Suite 205
The Ponies of Karlový Vary 80
Pookie 63, 67, 232
Portraits of Women 190, 232
Post-war History in Japan 79
Pourquoi? 79
The President of the Borgorisso Football Club 77
The Priest's Wife 76
The Private Life of Sherlock Holmes 130, 232
A Prostitute Serving the Community Within the Law 76
Purgatory 80
Putney Swope 108, 232
Puzzle of a Downfall Child 212

Queimada 77
A Question of Honour—Una Questione d'Onore 232

R.P.M. 209
The Raging Moon 145, 232
The Railway Children 10, 99, 233
Raphael ou le débauché 76
Ravaged 112, 233
Reggae 233
The Red Circle 75
Red Crop 81
The Reivers 86, 233
Reinlich Keitseriehung 195
Rembrandt 37
Remembrance of Things Past 77
Requiem in the Hungarian Manner 81

Resurrection of Broncho Billy 192
The Return 82
Richard III 41, 42, 46
Rider on the Rain 75, 186, 233
Right On 195
Rio Lobo 139, 233
The Rite 191, 233
Riverrun 107, 233
The Rise and Fall of the Great Lakes 193
The Role of My Family in World Revolution 81
The Romantics 82
Rome 77
Romeo and Juliet 41, 42, 44, 45, 46
Rosalind 42
Run, Virgin, Run 174, 233
Ryan's Daughter 192, 194, 198, 198

Sabata 153, 233
Sacco and Vanzietti 193
Sad Song of Yellow Skin 193
Salt of the Earth 223
Sailing 35, 37
The Samourai 159
San Domingo 81
Sanjuro 183, 233
The Satamists 172, 234
The Scars of Dracula 109, 234
The Scavengers 77
Scrooge 198, 199
A Season in Hell 78
Secret French Prostitution Report 165, 234
The Secret of Santa Vittorio 87, 234
September 75
Serafino 170, 234
The Seventh Day, the Eighth Night 79
A Severed Head 149, 234
Sex Power 195
The Sextroverts 187, 234
Shadow of Progress 193
She 78
She Died With Her Boots On 181, 234
Shinjuku Mod 79
Shinken Shobu 79
Shock Corridor 123, 234
Shonen—The Boy 218
The Sicilian Clan 162, 234
Simon Bolivar 77
Simon, Simon 234
Simon the Swiss 75, 186, 234
Sky Over Holland 37
Smoke 100, 235

So Long Italy 77
Socrates 77
The Soil Always Yields Bread 195
Soldier Blue 153, 235
Some Will, Some Won't 116, 235
The Son 195
Song of Norway 198, 199
The Song of the Red Ruby 178, 235
The Sound of Music 9
Speed is the Essence 73
The Spider's Stratagem 79, 195
Star of Bethlehem 195
Star of the Season 82
Start the Revolution Without Me 149, 235
The Statue 149, 235
The Story of the Young Man Who Left His Will on Film 79
The Straw Dogs 207
The Straw Hat 80
Street of Sin 235
The Stripping Nun 76
Strogoff 77
Subterfuge 235
Sunday, Bloody Sunday 204
Sunday in the Park 235
Sunday Sun 37
Sunflower 169, 235
Suppose They Gave a War and Nobody Came? 114, 235
Swedish Love Play 191, 235

Take a Girl Like You 135, 236
Take Me, Love Me 182, 236
Take the Money and Run 114, 236
Taking Off 81, 193
The Taming of the Shrew 41, 41, 42, 46, 50
Tar Babies 236
A Taste of Black Earth 82, 195
Taste of Excitement 126, 236
Tchaikovsky 195
Technically Sweet 77
Tell Them Willie Boy Was Here 192
Ten Rillington Place 131, 236
The Testament 195
There Was a Crooked Man 143, 236
There's a Girl in My Soup 133, 193, 236
They Call Me Mister Tibbs 133, 236
They Might be Giants 212
They Shoot Horses Don't They? 84, 192, 236

244

The Things of Life—Les Choses de la Vie 219, *166*
The 1,000 Plane Raid 236
The Three Sisters *151*, 237
Through the Garden 38
Throne of Blood 50
tick . . . tick . . . tick *86*, 237
Time Out for Sardinia 237
Times For 195
'Tis a Pity She's a Whore 78
To Commit a Murder *166*, 237
Tomorrow *96*, 237
Too Late the Hero *94*, 237
Tora! Tora! Tora! 8, 192, *198*, 199
The Toth Family 81
The Touch 78, *207*
A Town Called Bastard *155*, 237
Traffic 38
The Trap 82
The Travelling Executioner *139*, 237
The Trojan Women *208*
Tropic of Cancer *108*, 237
Twelfth Night 42
Twins of Evil *213*

Two or Three Things I Know About Her *163*, 237

Uncle Vanya *77*, 78
Under the Counter You Must Go 237
Underground 237
Une Journée bièn remplie 76
Up the Chastity Belt 11, 52
Up Pompeii *11*, *52*, *53*, *144*, 237
Uptight *152*, 238

The Vacation 78
Valerie and Her Week of Wonders 193
The Vampire Lovers *111*, 238
The Vicar 78
Villain *201*
The Virgin and the Gypsy *145*, 238
Vixen *155*, 238
Voice of the Water 37

A Walk in the Spring Rain *87*, 238
Walkabout *211*

The Walking Stick *45*, 238
Wanda *142*, 195, 238
The Wanderer *187*, 238
The Wanton of Spain *214*
Waterloo 68, 70, 72, 68–72, 192, 199
Watermelon Man *152*, 238
Way to Paradise 81
We'll Call Him Andrea 77
Well, Hello! 80
Well of Time 238
What Do You Say to a Naked Lady? *154*, 238
What Rights Had a Child 195
When Dinosaurs Ruled the Earth *101*, 238
When Eight Bells Toll *143*, 238
When Women Had Tails 76
Where Spring Came Late 79
Where There's a War, There's Hope 77
White, Red, Green 78
Who Killed the Sale 193
The Wife Swappers 239

Wild Angels 81
The Wild Country *153*, 239
The Wild Rovers *202*
Wild, Willing and Sexy *176*, 239
Wir Zevei 81
The Winter's Tale 48
With Love in Mind 239
Without a Stitch *182*, 239
Women in Love 192, *194*
Woodstock *152*, 192, 239
The World and the Fat 239
The Working Class Go to Heaven 78
The Wrestler 38
WR or The Mysteries of the Body 81
WUSA *206*

X, Y and Zee *210*

You Can't Win 'Em All *143*, 239
Yojimbo *183*, 239
You're Lying 78, 193

Zeppelin *143*, 239

FOUR NEW FILM BOOKS FROM W.H. ALLEN

Publishers of the best show–biz books

HOW TO MAKE A JEWISH MOVIE

BY

MELVILLE SHAVELSON

The producer's hilarious account of the making of *'Cast a Giant Shadow'*.

BOGIE

BY JOE HYAMS

The authorised biography of Humphrey Bogart by the journalist who knew him best. Introduction by Lauren Bacall.

THALBERG

BY BOB THOMAS

The life and legend of the great Hollywood producer.

ZANUCK

Don't Say Yes Until I Finish Talking

BY MEL GUSSOW

A candid, revealing biography of the last of the great movie moguls.

COLUMBIA PICTURES presents

ROBERT SHAW
as Lord Randolph Churchill

ANN BANCROFT
as Lady Jennie Churchill

and # SIMON WARD
as

YOUNG WINSTON

JACK HAWKINS · ANTHONY HOPKINS
PATRICK MAGEE · EDWARD WOODWARD
Written and Produced by **CARL FOREMAN**
Directed by **RICHARD ATTENBOROUGH**
PANAVISION® COLOUR

A CARL FOREMAN –
RICHARD ATTENBOROUGH film

COLUMBIA PICTURES Presents

ELIZABETH TAYLOR
MICHAEL CAINE
SUSANNAH YORK

A KASTNER–LADD–KANTER PICTURE

ZEE & CO

Original Screenplay by EDNA O'BRIEN · Executive Producer ELLIOTT KASTNER
Produced by JAY KANTER · and ALAN LADD, JR. · Directed by BRIAN G. HUTTON
COLOUR